A Road to Damascus

A Road to Damascus

Mainly diplomatic memoirs from the Middle East

Ivor Lucas

The Radcliffe Press
London • New York

Published in 1997 by
The Radcliffe Press
Victoria House
Bloomsbury Square
London
WC1B 4DZ

In the United States of America
and Canada, distributed by
St Martin's Press
175 Fifth Avenue
New York
NY 10010

A full CIP record of this book is available from
the British Library and the Library of Congress

ISBN 1 86064 152 0

Typeset and designed by Dexter Haven, London
Printed in Great Britain by WBC Ltd, Bridgend, Mid Glamorgan

For

Christine,

Mark, Crispin and George

who bore the brunt

And diff'ring judgements serve but to declare
That truth lies somewhere, if we knew but where.

William Cowper, *Hope*

Though syllogisms hang not on my tongue,
I am not surely always in the wrong!
'Tis hard if all is false that I advance –
A fool must now and then be right, by chance.

William Cowper, *Conversation*

Contents

Foreword

Sir James Craig

It is difficult (but I don't try very hard) not to feel sad that in the publishing world the wrapping of the parcel counts more than the contents. A book with a film star's name on the cover sells by the hundred thousand, even if he has not, thank Heaven, written a word of it. Ivor Lucas is not famous and his book will not, I suppose, reach best-seller status. But the world would be a better place if it did; and his readers may make up in quality for what they fail to reach in quantity.

George Brown said of Ivor, in an enviable tribute, that he would never use one word where half a word would do; and in the spectrum of self-expression, I have always thought him nearer the taciturn and diffident than to the prolix and cocky. So it is a surprise – a delightful one – that he has given us at some length an account not only of his life but also of his opinions.

His experiences have been quite similar to my own: we were both head of a Middle East department in the Foreign Office, and we both had the luck to work in that most fascinating of countries, Syria. In our opinions, we are not so consistently close. His scruples are tenderer than mine. He feels deeply, and he is not afraid to doubt.

What his book does, above all, is to dispel the irritating myth that British diplomatists are Woosterish flibbertigibbets, born with a silver spoon and a well-lined pocket, who spend an hour or so in the office and the rest of the day at cocktail parties, remote from the real world of the harassed and the humdrum. Here is a man, deeply conscientious, who thinks and worries about the world's problems and strives hard for fair and kindly answers; a member of the so-called mafia of Foreign Office Arabists who regretted the injustice done to the Palestinian Arabs, yet had a Jewish mother and felt anguish and compassion for the Jewish victims.

His book shews him to be a decent, responsible, honest and honourable man. He has earned all those adjectives by skilful and loyal service to his country. His country should be proud of him.

Preface

Nearly 100 years ago, Curzon coined the aphorism (later appropriated by Ronald Storrs) that 'The East is a university in which the scholar never takes his degree'[1].

The phrase has always seemed to me apposite. After 40 or more years devoted largely to the Middle East in various capacities, I agree that there is always something new to learn. For this, if for no other reason, this memoir does not purport to be a comprehensive treatise on the region. I have written of what particularly interested or amused me: a ready sense of humour was an essential part of a diplomat's equipment in that part of the world.

The latter half of the twentieth century has seen some remarkable changes in the Middle East and other parts of the Muslim world which were my main sphere of interest. I hope to have contributed something to the collective memory of what it was like to live and work in that area and that era. As will be evident, the views expressed are not necessarily those of Her Majesty's Government.

Most diplomatic memoirs are written from more exalted vantage points. They have often reinforced the popular and media image of the Diplomatic Service as a privileged group living it up abroad at the taxpayers' expense. My perspective is that of one who toiled in the vineyards (without, I trust, developing a taste for sour grapes), and may help to redress the balance.

Ivor Lucas

London, 1996

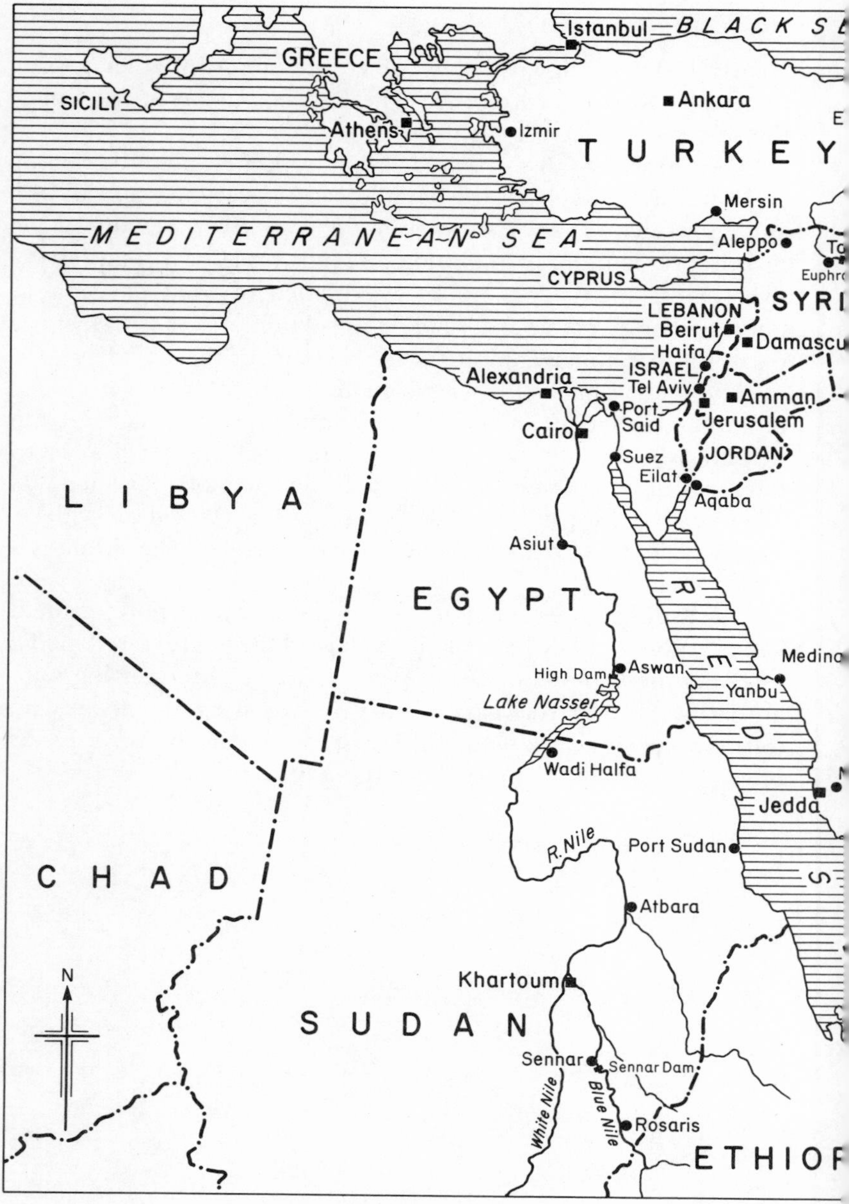

Istanbul
BLACK S
GREECE
SICILY
Ankara
Athens
Izmir
TURKEY
Mersin
MEDITERRANEAN SEA
Aleppo
Euphr
CYPRUS
SYRI
LEBANON
Beirut
Damascu
Haifa
ISRAEL
Alexandria
Tel Aviv
Amman
Port Said
Jerusalem
Cairo
Suez
JORDAN
Eilat
Aqaba
LIBYA
Asiut
EGYPT
RED SEA
Medina
High Dam
Aswan
Yanbu
Lake Nasser
Wadi Halfa
Jedda
R. Nile
Port Sudan
CHAD
Atbara
N
Khartoum
SUDAN
Sennar
Sennar Dam
White Nile
Blue Nile
Rosaris
ETHIOP

THE MIDDLE EAST TODAY
International boundary
KILOMETRES
0 200 400 600 800
0 100 200 300 400 500
MILES
CASPIAN SEA
an
Tabriz
Tehran
aghdad
Isfahan
Q
IRAN
Abadan
Basra
Shiraz
KUWAIT
Kuwait
Bushire
Jubail
PERSIAN GULF
Damman
Sharja
Dhahran
Dubai
GULF OF OMAN
QATAR
BAHRAIN
Abu Dhabi
Muscat
Riyadh
UNITED ARAB EMIRATES
AUDI ARABIA
OMAN
ARABIAN SEA
Salala
REPUBLIC OF YEMEN
anaa
da
Mukalla
ez
SOCOTRA ISLAND
Aden
INDIAN OCEAN
GULF OF ADEN
SOMALIA

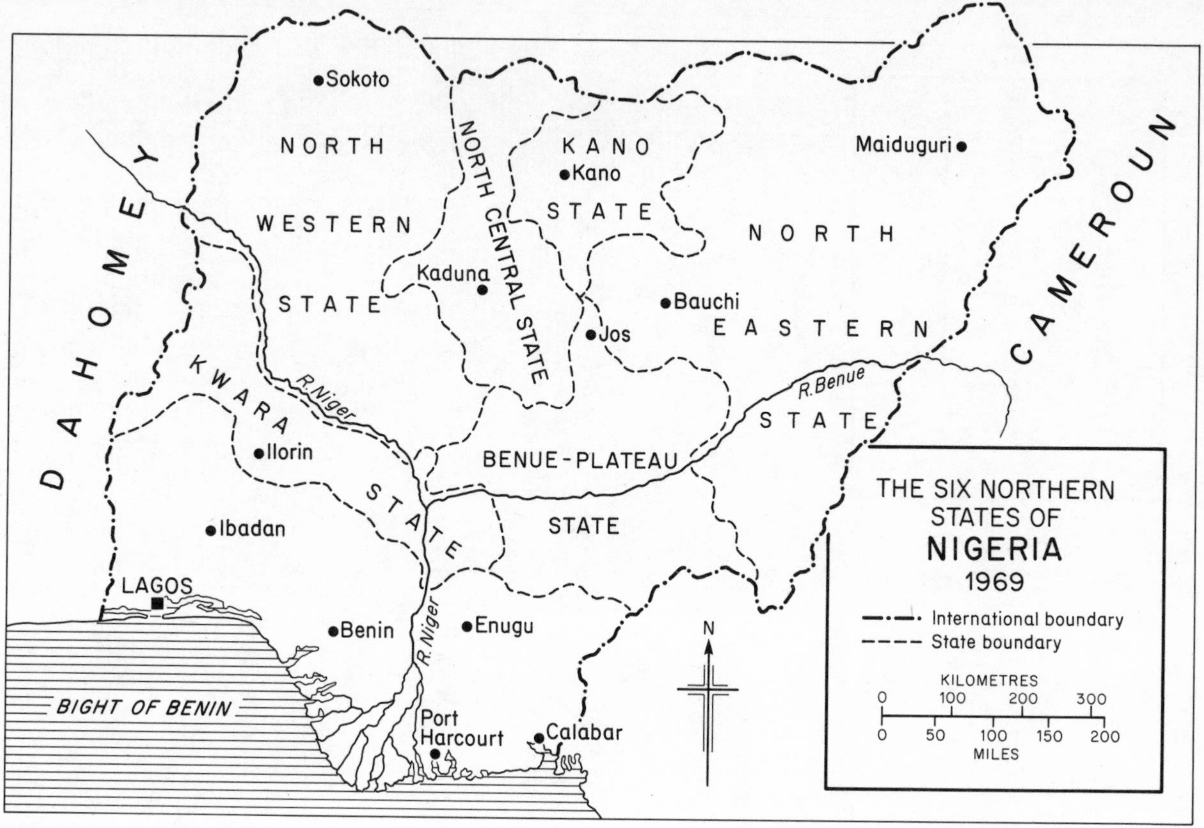
THE SIX NORTHERN STATES OF NIGERIA 1969
International boundary
State boundary
KILOMETRES
0
100
200
300
0
50
100
150
200
MILES
N
DAHOMEY
CAMEROUN
NORTH WESTERN STATE
NORTH CENTRAL STATE
KANO STATE
NORTH EASTERN STATE
BENUE-PLATEAU STATE
KWARA STATE
Sokoto
Kaduna
Kano
Maiduguri
Bauchi
Jos
Ilorin
Ibadan
LAGOS
Benin
Enugu
Port Harcourt
Calabar
R. Niger
R. Niger
R. Benue
BIGHT OF BENIN

A Road to Damascus

1
Early Days

One day in the summer of 1914 a dark-eyed, olive-skinned Latvian girl of 17 arrived in Norfolk to spend a holiday with her paternal uncle. Her name was Sonia Finkelstein. Her father Marcus was in the fisheries industry in Libau, and his brother ran the English end of the operation in Great Yarmouth. She had never known her mother, who had died giving birth to her. Marcus had subsequently remarried.

When the First World War broke out that August, Sonia was stranded. But not for long. She soon met a young man who was serving nearby in the Royal Naval Air Service. He was about a year her senior, the son of a clerk in the Bank of England. His education was limited to technical schools and he was a motor engineer by trade: before the War he had helped William Morris build the first Morris car in a small shed in Cowley. George Lucas – 'Luke' to his friends – seems to have fallen for Sonia at first sight. Her Jewish proxy family were evidently none too keen on the idea, and the match must indeed have appeared an odd one. Nevertheless, the couple married in 1917, and once the war was over settled in Southampton, where George set up as a motor vehicle retailer. The business prospered and the marriage flourished. It lasted for 50 years and produced four children, of whom I was the third.

Despite his lack of formal education, my father possessed innate intelligence, considerable charm and burning ambition. His ability came to be recognised well beyond the bounds of Southampton. In 1927 – the year of my birth – he became the youngest-ever President of the Motor Agents' Association. This task he performed with such distinction that he was recalled to it during the Second World War. He also served at that time on the National Joint Industrial Council and various other bodies concerned with harnessing the capacity of the motor industry to the needs of the war effort.

In recognition of these services – as well, no doubt, as the fact that the postwar Attlee Government was woefully under-represented in the House of Lords – my father was created in 1946 the first Baron Lucas of Chilworth (a small village near the northern outskirts of Southampton where we lived). Though in general sympathy with the aims of the Labour Party at that time, the new peer was certainly no socialist. He described himself rather as a 'radical liberal'. But his qualities of precise thinking and lucid expression soon made their mark in political circles. He was appointed by his good friend the worthy Tom Williams, a former Yorkshire miner who had become Minister of Agriculture, to chair an enquiry into agricultural marketing in Britain. The Lucas Report was a model of its kind but proved ahead of its time, and like many other documents of that nature was consigned to gather dust in some bureaucratic pigeon-hole. But it did its author's reputation no harm, and he was subsequently appointed a Lord-in-Waiting and then Parliamentary Under-Secretary in the Ministry of Transport under the less than redoubtable Alfred Barnes.

Churchill's return to office in 1951 proved to be the end of his ministerial career, though for the next 16 years Lord Lucas played a prominent role in the Lords, first in opposition and then from the cross-benches, until the only illness in his life laid him low and finally destroyed him in 1967 at the age of 71, in the year of his golden wedding.

My mother survived him by 12 years. She had revisited Latvia only once – in 1935 – and I recall grandfather Marcus coming to stay with us in Southampton the following year. He was a kindly and fine-looking man, but with an air of sadness about him: as well he might, for so far as my mother knew he and many of his family perished later in the holocaust. Her first language was Russian, and having been to school in Frankfurt-am-Main she also had a fluent command of German. To the end of her life she spoke both tongues well, and English with an increasingly noticeable accent the older she grew. Unfortunately, since my father spoke no foreign languages, English alone was used in the home; and I often wondered whether my subsequent career would have taken a different course if she had imparted some Russian and German to us children. As it was, she became almost totally absorbed in, if not subordinate to, my father's progress, and somewhat divorced from her own family background. This was perhaps not surprising in the circumstances, but it was a pity, because she would only with difficulty be persuaded to talk about her early life, and it was not until ten years or so after her death that we established contact with her cousins from the 'Norfolk branch' of the family.

When my brother, who was 15 months older than me, started at a day-school in Southampton, I apparently missed him so much that I was sent to join our elder sister at an institution which felicitously advertised itself on a huge hoarding facing the Avenue as 'The Convent High School for Girls, Preparatory for Boys'. My own preparation was largely confined to falling for my secular form mistress, a Miss Whit, who at my insistence had the rare distinction of being invited to tea at 'Nashdom' ('our home' in Russian).

We enjoyed a conventional and happy middle-class upbringing. My recollection is of long, hot summers untrammelled by the traumas of depression or by the gathering clouds on the international horizon. I spent many a drowsy hour watching Hampshire play cricket at the County Ground in Northlands Road and pestering players for their autographs. My greatest coup was to obtain the signatures of the entire Australian touring team of 1938: Don Bradman had the honour of a page to himself, protected by a sheet of tissue-paper. That same summer, my brother and I were taken to the Oval by our paternal grandfather to watch the test match in which Len Hutton scored his record-breaking 364. What we saw of his innings was in fact remarkably dull by comparison with that of his county colleague Maurice Leyland.

We spent weekends picnicking in bluebell-covered glades in the New Forest or on trips to sandy beaches on the Solent; and family holidays on the Isle of Wight and later at Gorleston on the Norfolk coast. One of my early exploits was to steer a boat into the rushes on the Broads. Our lives as children were largely supervised by a series of nannies, with some of whom we established closer relationships than with our parents: for most of the year we did not see a great deal of them apart from the privileged Sunday lunch, and my father was in any case what would nowadays be described as a 'workaholic'. He did not take a great deal of interest in us as children until we were old enough to answer back, and it was not often that we dared to do that. Consequently, he inspired respect rather than affection.

This relaxed existence came to an abrupt halt a year after the outbreak of war in September 1939. For the first few months of hostilities, nothing much happened. My mother helped to run a canteen down the road for troops on their way to embark for France, and occasionally some of us children dispensed 'char and wads' as our modest contribution to the war effort. Then when the tide of war began to change my father decided to pack my mother, my brother, my younger sister and myself off to the wilds of Exmoor, while he and my elder sister stayed in Southampton running the family business. We exiles spent an idyllic golden summer of 1940 in the remote village of Simonsbath. My abiding memories are of picking bilberries on the moors; competing with my brother for the affections of a girl older than both of us from a school evacuated nearby from the south coast; and hearing a Scotsman staying in the same hotel pronounce a gloomy verdict on the fall of France: 'the tairrms are seveere'.

Nevertheless, when the threatened invasion of Britain failed to materialise, we were summoned back to Southampton, just in time to experience the first onset of the 'blitz'. We lived far enough out of town to be comparatively safe from actual hits; but the terror of nights in the air-raid shelter with hell being let loose all around is something that still remains vividly in my mind.

As the third child and second son of the marriage, I seemed destined to be the 'lucky one' of the family. My brother had the misfortune to exhibit at an early age an ability with his hands which marked him out to follow father's footsteps into the motor industry, and equally to eschew the groves of academe. Although he did not enjoy the same professional success as my father, and was far less interested in politics than I was, he was later to emulate, as the second baron, the ministerial attainments of the first. Having moved from the cross-benches to the Conservative side of the house, he eventually became Parliamentary Under-Secretary in the Department of Trade and Industry in the second Thatcher administration but, like his father before him, was perhaps too much of a free spirit for higher party advancement.

As a boy of 13, I was taken one Saturday afternoon to a political meeting at the Southampton Guildhall. The principal speaker was a Conservative minister named R.S. Hudson. His performance, and the whole atmosphere of the gathering, made a deep impression on me. Thereafter I formed a personal 'Government' of my own, and every Saturday afternoon for some time I would repair to a private spot where one of my 'ministers' would be called upon to deliver an account of his 'department's' stewardship. The Foreign Secretary was responsible for the state of my relations with other people; the Chancellor of the Exchequer had the much simpler task of reviewing my finances; woe betide the Minister of Education, who bore the heavy responsibility for my progress – or otherwise – at school. The infantile weekly orations which resulted gave me some sort of practice in marshalling my thoughts and expressing them, if only to myself.

After I joined my brother at his day-school, we competed, with fluctuating fortunes, on the playing-field, though less so in the classroom, where the institution in question did not in any case enjoy a brilliant reputation. I was adjudged to have more of an academic bent and, despite my failure to win a scholarship to St Edward's Oxford, it was decided that I should go there nevertheless soon after my fourteenth birthday – at some sacrifice, I was led to understand, to the rest of the family. It was a relatively advanced age to be going away to boarding school for the first time. Moreover, St Edward's in wartime under the watchful eye of Warden Kendall was not exactly a paradise. We lived in an ivory tower, fed badly, involved ourselves in domestic chores as well as excruciatingly boring periods of 'making munitions' in the school workshop, attended farming camps at Ross-on-Wye during the summer holidays, and had our thoughts regularly turned to the growing lists of old boys who would never come back from the battlefields. Our particular heroes were Douglas Bader (who did return) and Guy Gibson (who did not). It was, in retrospect, a gloomy existence.

Many of my contemporaries certainly seemed to loathe it while they were there, only to claim subsequently that this was the best time of their lives. Perversely, I enjoyed the three-and-a-half years which were vouchsafed me and only later wondered how I had tolerated its less agreeable aspects. One of these, which had nothing to do with the war, was the relative importance attached to the playing-field as against the classroom. In my case, earlier sporting prowess proved to have owed more to enthusiasm than to ability, but on the academic front a number of inspired and inspiring mentors brought out what was best in their plodding pupil. In the process, the Rev. Leslie ('the Count') Styler instilled a positive joy in English, and Philip ('Guts') Whitrow in History. I recall in particular long summer evenings preparing an essay on Robert Peel as 'the only English statesman on whose death the poor have cried in the streets', which nearly gained me the school's major history prize. I was, predictably, pipped at the post twice running by a real intellectual named Brian Tovey. When 35 years later, as Director of GCHQ, he was awarded a KCMG at the same time as I received my CMG, I was able to write and congratulate him from my position as 'still *proxime accessit*'. I recall, too, my naivety in thinking, as my studies in English history approached the twentieth century, how little time there was left for the story to have the happy ending which I had simplistically assumed must be the case.

I also developed an interest – first imparted by my father – in 'serious' music. I was able to indulge this especially in the chapel choir, as successively a treble, an alto and a tenor. One advantage of being in the choir was that there was slightly more room in its stalls than in the crowded congregational pews. The experience also helped to turn me into what an army chaplain was later to disparage as a 'public school Christian', by which I took him to mean one whose faith was based more on convention than conviction.

1945 was a watershed in my life, as in so many others. In January, I was genuinely surprised to be awarded a history scholarship at Trinity Oxford. In my last term I was President of my house senior day room – the giddiest height I reached so far as school appointments were concerned. More rewarding was the editorship of the school chronicle. I contributed a staggeringly sanctimonious leader about the postwar world, with distinctly 'red' sentiments which even now make me blush. However, its purple prose did earn me a 'posthumous' literary prize. By the time it appeared I had joined up, on 1 May. Exactly one week later the Germans surrendered and the postwar world was upon us.

2

Once a Gunner

VE Day found me enduring the rigours of a primary training centre outside Lanark. For a few weeks this provided not only elementary military instruction but a much broader education than St Edward's. All sorts and conditions of young men – and some not so young – rubbed shoulders and had the stuffiness, if not the stuffing, knocked out of them. An early experience left its mark on me in more ways than one. Reclining on the grass outside my platoon's Nissen hut for a brief post-prandial nap, I was suddenly conscious of a rushing sound in my ears and a salty and gritty taste in my mouth. Then everything went blank. I woke up in hospital at Carluke with a stitched upper lip and without two front teeth, where one of my fellow trainees had inadvertently dropped a brick while playing 'catch' across me. Not long afterwards, I fell foul of my battery commander at the Royal Artillery Officer Cadet Training Unit for displaying less than the required enthusiasm for risking the wound being opened up in the boxing ring.

Meanwhile some pleasant summer months passed at another training establishment at Watchet in Somerset, learning the skills of a field-gunner. This enabled me to revisit some of the haunts we had frequented during our evacuation to Simonsbath. I also fell in with an eccentric character named Teddy Boston, whom I accompanied on several tramps round the local country churches, where he indulged a passion for brass-rubbing. In later life, as a parson, he discovered an equal affection for, and expertise in, old steam engines.

It was also from Watchet that I observed the political upheaval resulting in the election of the Labour Government under Attlee. I remember being surprised at the outcome, yet at the same time elated and excited. This was partly because of my father's influence but partly that of my environment. There was a distinct leaning to the left among the military fraternity, and it was encouraged by the Army Bureau of Current Affairs whose educational activities formed part of our curriculum. Nor were such views undermined by the selection process for officer trainees which I was shortly to undergo: undue priority appeared to be attached to where one had been to school and whether one had any relatives in the services.

Despite this, there was still a fair 'mix' of contenders during the period of the pre-OCTU and OCTU training lasting for nearly a year and involving postings to Wrotham, Aldershot and Deep Cut. To me the most interesting aspect was what the military authorities called 'methods of instruction', which gave practice in handling an audience – later to be supplemented by the more daunting experience of taking 'education classes' for soldiers under one's command.

Having been trained as a field-gunner on 25-pounders – the stock-in-trade of the Royal Artillery in its ground support role – I naturally found myself commissioned into a unit equipped with self-propelled M10 guns, mobile anti-tank weapons. The 20th Anti-tank Regiment RA was stationed in the Canal Zone in Egypt. So, at the age of 19, I went abroad for the first time, experiencing modestly en route the delights of the French Riviera, the tranquillity of a Mediterranean cruise and the sights, sounds and smells of Cairo. These were all too soon forgotten in the sandy wastes of El Ballah on the banks of the Suez Canal north of Ismailia. I arrived there six days before Christmas 1946. The kind of welcome which Sergeants' Messes reserved for green subalterns ensured that it was not the most memorable – or best remembered – Christmas I have ever spent. Thereafter it was down to earth with a vengeance as I grappled with the technical mysteries of the M10 and duties of a regimental officer.

Life was further complicated by the departure on demobilisation of my highly experienced troop commander, leaving me in charge. My battery commander left soon after. Bertie Tozer, the BC, was a luxuriantly mustachioed extrovert whose main requirement of his subordinate officers was that they should share his inordinate enthusiasm for motorcycle rallying, in which they were expected to participate. Fortunately in a way, within a month of my arrival all this was to change when the regiment was ordered to Palestine. Meanwhile, I was entrusted with the thankless task of commanding the rear party, which was left to hand over the camp to an incoming unit. One way and another, this was a traumatic experience which dented my confidence, and it was with a sense of relief that I finally led my little band across the Sinai to our new home at El Khassa camp close to the shore of the Mediterranean and not far from Gaza.

Immersion in the complexities of the local political situation provided therapy for a bruised ego. I obtained from GHQ an excellent brief on 'The Palestine Problem', supplementing this with a more independent account by Richard Crossman in his book *Palestine Mission*[2]. This recounted the story of the Anglo-American Committee which in the previous summer had been the latest in a long series of bodies despatched during the mandate period in successive but unsuccessful attempts to reconcile the irreconcilable. No wonder the wags complained that the British Government's record in Palestine had been one not of errors of omission but of commission after commission. The fact was that the various undertakings given to Arabs and Jews by the French and British during the First World War – making Palestine 'the twice-promised land' – had proved wholly incompatible, and the chickens were now coming home to roost.

My baptism of fire was conducted, appropriately enough, by the regimental chaplain, who led an expedition to Bethlehem and Jerusalem one day in March 1947. It happened to be the day on which the Goldsmith Officers' Club was blown up in the worst Jewish terrorist incident since the explosion at the King David Hotel eight months earlier.

A couple of weeks afterwards, the regiment was involved in the unpleasant task of intercepting a beach landing by illegal Jewish immigrants. 800 of them had been crammed into a tiny vessel named the *Susannah.* Our job was to round up those who had already got ashore, and to remove the minority who were still aboard. The first part was complicated by the fact that the immigrants had rapidly mingled with the large reception party from various nearby Jewish settlements which had assembled on the beach. On being interrogated by the Palestine CID, the newcomers claimed that they were legal residents of long standing. Many were naturally unable to remember, or to pronounce correctly, the name of their 'home village'. In the resulting confusion, a number of illegals certainly got through, while a few genuine residents may well have found themselves deported to Cyprus along with those who were caught.

The more distasteful part of the operation was forcibly removing the immigrants still aboard the *Susannah*. Many of them were women who had shirked jumping ship and swimming or wading ashore. On deck they were wallowing in piles of rubbish, scraps of food, bits of clothing and odds and ends of all sorts. Below, the scene and the stench were unforgettable: tier upon tier of densely-packed hammocks, and the same conglomeration of detritus. The frustration of being denied the Promised Land after undergoing such privations must have been shattering.

But we had a job to do, and did it with as much decency and compassion as possible. This was the more praiseworthy, perhaps, because the British soldiery was, to put it mildly, less than enamoured of the Jews at the time. What had at an earlier stage of the mandate been a triangular struggle between Arabs, Jews and British had now become a straight fight between the last two. Extreme Jewish elements were resorting to crude terrorist tactics designed to force British withdrawal – which was precisely what they were to achieve a little more than a year later. The episode which made the greatest impact, both on British troops on the spot and on public opinion at home, was the cold-blooded murder of two British sergeants as a reprisal for the execution of a convicted Jewish terrorist: not only were they hanged in an olive-grove, but one of the corpses had a booby-trap attached to it. The resulting security situation required us to move around armed and in pairs. This unfortunately made it impossible to see much of the other, more positive, side of the Jewish presence, though visits to one or two experimental farms provided impressive evidence of what was being done.

The men under my command were concerned less with what was going on around them than with the prospects of demobilisation.

Training programmes held little appeal for those who looked forward only to the day when the army would be only a bad memory. Meanwhile my efforts to create an informed opinion among my Troop fell understandably flat. After spending hours composing a lecture based on GHQ's brief, the only reaction I got was from my sergeant, patrolling the audience with his baton at the ready and the occasional remonstrance: 'Keep awake, you bastard, while the officer's talking'!

In accordance with the prevailing confusion, the 20th Anti-tank had hardly settled into its new surroundings when we were told that the regiment was to convert to a heavy anti-aircraft role, and to be transferred to Tripolitania. For me, this meant returning to yet another transit camp, this time at Kabrit, on the Little Bitter Lake in the Canal Zone. At least I was able to celebrate my brother's twenty first birthday with him at the Officers' Club in Fayyid, not far from where he was serving with the Royal Armoured Corps. Then back to Palestine for a most enjoyable six weeks attending a conversion course at the Middle East School of Artillery outside Acre; a second Mediterranean cruise, including on this occasion a few delightful days at a holiday centre at Ghain Tuffieha in Malta; and finally to Libya, where I was to spend my last seven months under arms.

On the way there, I confided to the diary which I had begun to keep the day I left England some thoughts on the Middle East, with all the authority of six months' experience. At this distance, they appear naive in the extreme. Yet some of the arguments are still relevant, even though I would give them a different balance 50 years on.

The Arabs' historical claim to Palestine seemed to me unassailable; and their complaint fully justified that they should not be called upon to pay the price of European persecution of the Jews. But left-wing leanings at the time led me to attach more importance to certain other considerations. The blatant disparities of wealth in Egypt; the fact that Arabs had not been averse to selling Palestinian land to Jews when it suited them; and the obvious divisions within the Arab ranks all contrasted so sharply with the single-minded and socialist motivation of the Jews that their image was dynamic and that of the Arabs static. I even went so far as to convince myself that the real opposition to Jewish settlement had come from prosperous Arabs who had exploited latent feelings of Arab nationalism in order to preserve their ill-gotten gains. Ordinary Jews and Arabs could live side by side in reasonable amity to their mutual benefit were it not for outside interests with their own axes to grind. This simplistic analysis may have contained some grains of truth, but it was to undergo some drastic revision when I became more familiar with the issues involved.

My first abode in Libya was in some abandoned Italian barracks at the hill town of Garian, reached by a spectacular pass through which climbed a road consisting of a series of dramatic hairpin bends from the point where it suddenly rose from the hot and dusty Azizia plain south of Tripoli. More interesting than Garian itself was the nearby village of Tigrinna, with its troglodyte dwellings. Then we moved down to the Mediterranean town of Zavia, some 25 miles to the west of the capital. I remember that one of the few amenities in the officers' mess was an old gramophone of the wind-up variety. The only records we had were a set of 78s of Beethoven's Pastoral Symphony. We played these over and over again. For years afterwards, whenever I heard this piece of music I involuntarily recalled the breaks where the discs needed to be turned over. Tripoli itself was a pleasant city, still in 1947 with the advantages of Italian artisans and restaurateurs. The coastal strip boasted among its tourist attractions the Roman ruins at Sabratha and Leptis Magna.

These were some of the compensations for the increasing frustration of military life in Tripolitania. We were trying to do several things at once. Our major role was internal security. Libya was still under the wartime British military administration, pending international decisions about the future of this former Italian colony. Superimposed on the politics of independence were the potential repercussions of the Palestinian imbroglio. These did not make themselves felt until after I had left, but once again it was necessary to maintain a reasonable state of alert and of interest in the local scene on the part of the soldiery. At the same time, we were supposed to be training the gunners in their new anti-aircraft role, which not unnaturally failed to enthuse the majority whose sights were set rather on imminent demobilisation.

Although the local political scene lacked the intrinsic fascination of that in Palestine, there were greater opportunities of getting out and about and seeing something of how Libyan Arabs lived, in town, village and desert. One particular such opportunity fired me with the desire to become more closely acquainted with this way of life. During a period of attachment to an outstation at Tarhuna, I was invited by the resident Civil Affairs Officer to join him in a desert trip to some of his Bedouin charges. This involved a long and difficult drive of some hours across barren steppe-land, ending in my first experience of a 'mutton-grab'. We sat cross-legged on carpets, around a whole roast sheep on top of a massive bed of rice and surrounded by an alarming-looking array of side dishes, mostly of a lukewarm and greasy nature, which one attacked Muslim-style with the right hand only. Gastronomically, it was nothing to write home about, but somehow the simple and friendly atmosphere of the Bedouin encampment in the middle of nowhere, the genuine warmth of the welcome we were given and the enviable ease with which Major Norman Hall was able to converse in Arabic with our hosts struck a chord in me.

After all the ups and downs of my three-and-a-half years' military service it came as an agreeable surprise when a somewhat austere commanding officer, cast in the Monty mould, promoted me to Captain for my last few months. I was almost tempted to stay on, but wiser counsels prevailed, and in February 1948 my 'age and service group' – 68C – finally came up for demobilisation.

My father, not long ennobled, was at Southampton to meet me when the troopship docked. When the ship's Captain was told 'The Lord's aboard,' he involuntarily responded, 'What! Is this the Second Coming?'

3

Second Class Return

With the prospect of three years at Oxford and the ambition to join the Foreign Service thereafter, I now had eight months in hand before taking up my scholarship at Trinity. I was lucky enough to spend four summer months as a temporary in the German Political Department of the Foreign Office. My own role in it was naturally a humble one: dealing with visitors to the British Zone, writing summaries of complex but minor subjects and occasionally standing in for absent colleagues. But it gave me a marvellous opportunity to see how 'the Office' functioned and whether I was likely to fit in. My mentors could hardly have been kinder, or better examples to follow. The Head of the Department was Pat Dean who, like most of the great men I was to encounter later, always had time for those less exalted; and the assistant was the bearded and ebullient Andrew Gilchrist. Among their juniors was Brooks Richards, who would be my Head of Chancery in Bahrain; and my colleagues in the 'third room' included the formidable duo of Gill Brown and Grace Rolleston, Donald Gordon – my 'principal instructor' – and Andrew Stark. Andrew joined the department on the same day as myself, though from the Board of Trade and on a permanent basis. Like most of the other luminaries, he was destined to reach ambassadorial rank, and had aged enviably little when I next met him, as his Head of Chancery in Copenhagen 24 years later.

The major issue during my spell in the department was the Berlin Airlift. Berlin had been left by the interim postwar settlement within the Russian Zone of occupied Germany. The city was itself split into Russian, American, French and British sectors. The Soviet Union was therefore well placed to throw down the gauntlet to the Western powers of closing the road and rail links between their zones and their sectors. This challenge represented the most serious move hitherto in the Cold War. To have acquiesced in it would have meant surrendering Western rights in Berlin, untold privation for its citizens and an even greater psychological blow. Presumably the Kremlin calculated that the West would not use force to keep the supply routes open. But the West neatly turned the tables on Moscow by mounting the most massive peace-time airlift in history. It was now the Russians who were faced with the option of using force or climbing down. The bold stroke paid off, and after some time and enormous expense they backed off.

As an observer of the operation from the London end, one had to admire the steadfast, common-sense approach of Ernest Bevin to this and other problems. Tales (which were to become legendary) of his bluff and blunt working methods percolated down to the third room. Perhaps my favourite was one about a senior official who had sought the Secretary of State's guidance on a point of policy, but had felt obliged to return shortly afterwards for further clarification.

'What's this?' Bevin expostulated, ''ardly is the ink dry on the words out of my mouth when 'ere you are, back again...'

Foreign Office officials who had so little in common with him soon recognised his grasp of essentials and powers of decision, and came to hold him in great respect and affection. With the possible exception of Palestine, which he unhappily staked his political future on solving, Bevin not only knew his own mind but was instinctively right about fundamentals. The decision about the Berlin blockade was to be followed within the next year or so by his even more momentous initiatives involving the establishment of NATO and the formulation of the Marshall Plan for European economic recovery.

So far as I know, the only occasion when a case with which I was dealing rose to the stratosphere inhabited by Bevin was also an object-lesson for me in the arts of diplomacy and bureaucracy. My work on visits to Germany consisted partly of helping to make the practical arrangements and secure the necessary clearances for such journeys. More often than not, these were fraternal visits by Labour politicians and intellectuals to the Social Democratic party. One day a mild little man came to see me on an errand of this kind. He had a passport bearing a military permit which had not been utilised because an earlier planned trip had been cancelled, and wished to confirm that there would be no problem about renewing his permission to travel. I had no reason to think there would be, but something told me that it would be prudent to hold on to the passport while I made sure. After he had left, one of the formidable duo asked the name of my caller. When I told her, she exclaimed, 'Oh, but he's a well-known Communist. We'll have to refer the matter higher up'. This was duly done. While the bureaucratic wheels were still turning, I received several telephone calls from my increasingly disgruntled red friend, who eventually adopted a rather threatening tone, on the basis of what he claimed were his connections in high places. Worse still, I actually came face to face with him in the underground one morning, when the continued stone-walling prompted him to burst out that we seemed to regard him as an 'undesirable person'. Bevin clearly did, and eventually the oracle pronounced, 'We must stop him'. He earned plaudits in the third room for his firmness in the face of party pressures, while I basked in the modest glory of my alleged tact in handling such a potentially dangerous character and my stroke of genius in purloining his passport!

To round off my German summer, I travelled as pillion passenger with a school friend on a motorcycle trip to Austria. The experience did little for my German and less for our friendship, but it had its moments. Most of these derived from the fact that my companion had German antecedents and had spent his early childhood around Munich and Berchtesgaden. En route to Salzburg, our somewhat disappointing main objective, we visited places and met people the family had known before they emigrated to England in 1938. We heard harrowing stories, like that of the professor we stayed with in an enchanting village called An. He was condemned to death by the Nazis, only to be rescued in the nick of time by the advancing Americans, to become the first postwar Mayor of Berchtesgaden. He and others who received us so hospitably were the 'good' Germans. But even so it came as something of a shock to hear them talk as though the Nazi era was a phenomenon of long ago for which they bore no responsibility and seemed to regard as a tragic experience suffered in common with ourselves.

And so to Oxford in October 1948. Trinity was not famed for its academic distinction, and the college's reputation for sporting prowess was also becoming a little tarnished at this time. I switched from history to philosophy, politics and economics in the mistaken belief that this would be more relevant to my chosen path to the Foreign Service: in fact it was the grade of one's degree that mattered more than its subject, and even those competitors who wallowed in topics like the classics and ancient history proved equally capable of turning their minds to current affairs. But at least the choice brought me some distinguished mentors, even if I was not among their most distinguished pupils. Anthony Crosland tried to teach me economics, until he went off to win Gloucestershire South for Labour in 1950 and was succeeded by Ian Little. Philip Williams, another left-winger who was an expert on French politics and was to die young, and Asa Briggs, the historian, were my tutors in politics. Patrick Nowell-Smith and Austin Farrer vied for my soul in philosophy. An atheist and logical positivist, Nowell-Smith taught general philosophy, while moral philosophy was the province of the Rev. Farrer. As the college chaplain, he tended to have the last word, since his lucid sermons in chapel did not permit of answering back. He was also to die young, having become Warden of Keble and the most brilliant Oxford theologian of his generation.

I supplemented this array of talent by attending a range of lectures, though it soon became apparent to my critical 'methods-of-instruction' mentality that first-class intellects and the ability to communicate did not always go together. One shining exception was the historian A.J.P. Taylor, who became my favourite lecturer. He would march into an invariably thronged hall in the examination schools, ascend the platform at one end and pointedly put aside the lectern on which lesser mortals placed their copious notes. Taylor would then stand with feet apart and hands thrust behind his academic robes, and launch into a fascinating non-stop discourse lasting for an hour, and beginning as likely as not with some such arresting introduction as 'The Concert of Europe was the period when, as Metternich was driving up to visit his mistress, Talleyrand would be driving away'.

Despite sitting at the feet of these great men for three years, I failed to achieve more than a 'good second'. This was not a grave disappointment, however, since by then I had managed to pass the Foreign Office examinations which required no more than that as a basic qualification. What did annoy me was that I could have reached that standard without working as hard as I had done, perhaps to the detriment of extra-curricular activities. Together with certain emotional distractions which afflicted me at the time, this made me feel that I had not made the best possible use of my Oxford years.

In particular, I should like to have made a name in the Union. The nearest I got was a forthright attack on vested interests during a debate on iron and steel nationalisation. This prompted the *Oxford Magazine* scribe to comment, 'We should hear Mr Lucas more often'. Unfortunately, Mr Lucas was by then heavily involved in the run-up to finals and this was his last contribution to the Union's deliberations.

A more rewarding experience was involvement in the University Labour Club. Oxford was, as usual, 'agin the Government' of the day; and Trinity was hardly a happy hunting ground for Labour, even in the heyday of the Attlee administration. Though never a member of the Party itself, I rashly took on the college secretaryship for the Labour Club in my second year. By dint of persistence rather than persuasion I managed to lift the number of Trinity subscribers to the club to record levels, and this eventually won me election to the committee. It was dominated at the time by some particularly able and admirable people, including Shirley Catlin (later Williams), Bill Rodgers, Dick Taverne and Oleg Kerensky. The first two were to be founder-members of the ill-fated Social Democratic Party; Taverne another Labour dissident; while Kerensky, the grandson of the Russian revolutionary, became a celebrated ballet critic who unfortunately also died prematurely.

Apart from the normal run of political club activities, we involved ourselves in electioneering on behalf of Lady Pakenham in Oxford (her daughter Antonia being one of the club's more decorative adornments) and Dr Edith Summerskill in Fulham East (she had both a son and a daughter among our office-holders). I also recall travelling to London on the eve of the general election in 1950 with a group of volunteers ready to do battle on behalf of the faithful. I was assigned to a meeting in a cold, cheerless and almost empty classroom somewhere in Putney. Having tried to explain why, as an aspiring diplomat, I supported Labour because of its more realistic appraisal of the world and Britain's position in it, the only interest I succeeded in arousing from the floor was in the Foreign Office recruitment system, about which the questioner clearly entertained the gravest doubts.

A more discouraging experience was said to have befallen one of our Tory opponents while canvassing in the Oxford area. A lady in a fur coat answered his knock on the front door. Confident from her dress and demeanour that she was 'one of us', great was his consternation when she told him firmly that she was voting Communist: 'After all, look at the aid this Marshal Stalin's giving us'!

In the summer vacation of 1950 I made another German trip. This time I enrolled for a 'ferienkurs' at Kiel University, hoping to improve my German sufficiently to impress the Foreign Office that I had at least the linguistic aptitude they required. It turned out to be more 'holiday' than 'course', but none the less enjoyable for that. A bonus for me was being invited to spend a further week in the home of a German student at Stadthagen, near Hanover. Here I found, once again, the same air of detachment from what had happened between the wars, as though it had nothing to do with my hosts.

For me, 1951 was a year of examinations. My boyhood ambition to join the Foreign Service had been confirmed by a youthful proficiency in languages (which, however, was not altogether sustained in later life), an abiding interest in history and the desire to travel. In pursuance of this goal I embarked on the triple obstacle course which the Civil Service Commissioners devised for candidates for the Higher Civil Service. Following a basic written qualifying examination, the main and the most daunting lap was the modified 'country house party' designed to discover candidates' personal and potential professional qualities by exposing them to a series of tests, interviews and simulated bureaucratic situations. These were conducted by a trio consisting of a retired civil servant, a psychiatrist and an independent chairman. While some of my competitors balked at writing accounts of themselves as seen by their best friend and their worst enemy, I found this an unusual and welcome chance of dilating on a favourite subject! The 'house party' was so called because it was originally carried out on a residential basis, supposedly giving the examiners an opportunity of assessing contenders' social behaviour, but it had by now been telescoped into two separate days' attendance at the Commission's offices at Chesham Place.

The day before undertaking this exercise I had to have an abscessed tooth extracted, so arrived in something of a devil-may-care frame of mind. Perhaps a 'relax and enjoy it' attitude was the best approach. At all events, I did enjoy it, and survived to face the Final Interview Board a few weeks later. This was a fairly rigorous inquisition by about a dozen distinguished figures drawn from the official, academic and commercial worlds. They seemed to appreciate the interviewees who had made the most of their opportunities, did not take themselves too seriously and managed to retain their sense of humour. The day after finishing my Oxford finals I learned that I was one of the 25 successful candidates for the Foreign Service.

4

Eastward Bound

September 1951 was not the most auspicious time to join the Foreign Service. A few months earlier, public opinion, never particularly well-disposed to those it regarded as 'elitists' living it up abroad at the taxpayers' expense, had a field-day following the defection of Burgess and Maclean. Their homosexual proclivities as much as their espionage activities provided friends with a suitable stock of ribaldry.

More importantly, a change of government was imminent: would Churchill's return to power herald 'setting the people free' abroad as well as at home? Withdrawal from India and Palestine may have reflected the popular mood against maintaining outdated and costly imperial commitments, yet there were many who found it difficult to accept that Great Britain was no longer in the front rank. My time in the Service for the next 33 years was to have as its backdrop just that process of adjustment to Britain's new place in a world dominated on the one side by the emergence of two super-powers and on the other by the forces of nationalism and independence. The Foreign Service naturally suffered its fair share of the pains involved.

For the moment, however, there were more mundane things to think about. One was how to respond to the pressures and the blandishments to which new entrants were subjected to learn a 'hard' language: visions of quick promotion and generous allowances seemed attractive, though were later to prove largely illusory. Choosing this path would mean *inter alia* devoting most of one's career to a single area, if not a single country, though not to the complete exclusion of others: the Service was trying to find a middle way between the expert who knew more and more about less and less, and the all-rounder who knew less and less about more and more. Still under the influence of the more positive memories of my military service in Palestine and Tripolitania, and thinking that it would be wiser to volunteer for something acceptable rather than being forced into something disagreeable, I opted for Arabic. This seemed in any case to be a better bet than most of the other options, as embracing a wider geographical range. My mother's background was apparently not seen as a bar, nor for the most part did it become one, though it afforded me some wry amusement from time to time.

Thus I embarked, with others, on ten weeks' basic Arabic at the School of Oriental and African Studies, followed by ten months of a more concentrated course at the Foreign Office's Middle East Centre for Arab Studies (MECAS for short) at Shemlan, a mountain village overlooking Beirut.

An American pastor who lived for many years in Iraq, and acquired a mastery of the language sufficient to enable him to write a text-book on the subject, was once asked how long it took to learn Arabic.

'I can't really say,' he replied. 'I've only been trying all my life'.

I know the feeling. Although Arabic does not deserve the mystique it is often accorded in the west, it does require the production of some extraordinary sounds (said to be how the Bedouin expelled the sand from their throats) and the acquisition of an enormously wide vocabulary to accommodate the richness and the nuances of the language. Moreover, I happen to be better at retaining pictures than picking up sounds, and the good linguist needs to be a good mimic.

So I struggled. Not entirely in vain, because apart from learning enough Arabic to 'get by', I found that MECAS had a great deal else to offer. I immersed myself in 'background studies' of the region, which were much more absorbing than the language itself, though the two were, of course, closely related.

The Arab and Muslim worlds seemed in 1952 to be suffering from a form of schizophrenia. They badly wanted the material advantages which the Christian West had gained from modern technology. But at a time when they were just beginning to throw off the shackles of Western politico-economic domination, they feared the more liberal aspects of Western society which technology might bring with it. Many saw an inevitable conflict between these two sets of desiderata. Some, particularly among the younger generation, were inclined to draw the conclusion that Islam had become a static religion which might have been applicable to the circumstances of the seventh century AD but was not appropriate to the dynamics of the twentieth. For them, if a choice had to be made between the all-embracing precepts of the Holy Qur'an and the requirements of the modern world, so much the worse for the scriptures. This was a pity, because throwing the book out of the window tended to leave a vacuum which alien ideologies were only too ready to fill. Meanwhile there was a perceptible loss of confidence in Islam. I shall describe in due course how (as it seemed to me) this attitude was to undergo a dramatic reversal twenty years later.

The Arab situation was further complicated by three other factors. First, with the attainment of political independence by an increasing number of Arab countries 'pan-Arabism' was in the air. The ideal was itself complicated by the difference in the levels at which Arab unity operated. At the emotional level the ties of history, language and religion, though not universally shared, exerted a powerful influence. And as Albert Hourani perceptively observed, 'It is unwise to ignore the historic (sic) imagination of peoples, even when its content is partly legend and only partly history.'[3]

At the practical level, there were often other, overriding considerations. Up to a point, the resulting contradiction was encapsulated by the Arab proverb 'My brothers and I against our cousins; we and our cousins against the stranger' – except that confrontation with the common enemy did not always produce unity.

The second source of confusion was the quest for social justice. The sweetness of independence would soon turn sour if foreign masters were simply to be replaced by indigenous tyrants who were recognised as corrupt and self-seeking. The third factor was the shame of Palestine, which was laid at the door of the same Arab leaders and which had to be wiped out.

Such traumas did not apply equally throughout the Arab world. In 1952 some of the Arab countries were still far from independence; others which had obtained it were – and would remain – a long way from abandoning their traditional forms of rule. Yet the potent mix of nationalism, social change and reversing the verdict of 1948 was beginning to have its effect throughout the region.

Lebanon itself provided a second source of intense interest. In 1952 it was still known as 'the Switzerland of the Middle East'. Its tourist attractions were summed up in the proud boast that this was the only country in the world where you could ski in the morning, lunch with a shaikh and swim in the afternoon. Beirut was rapidly becoming a sophisticated modern capital, with East and West – not always the most admirable aspects of each – cheek by jowl. The mountainous hinterland was dotted with attractive little towns and villages almost concealed in the orchards and olive-groves, but their red-tiled roofs peeping through the greenery. As a centre from which to explore the historical and archaeological wonders of Byblos and Ba'albek or, further afield, of Damascus and Palmyra, or Jerash and Jerusalem, Beirut offered excellent facilities, even if the taxi-drivers often endangered life and limb in the pursuit of these delights.

The legendary business acumen of the Lebanese was illustrated to every newcomer by the story of the small boy in class who is asked, 'What are two and two?' and immediately responds, 'Am I buying or am I selling?' On a more exalted plane, one was told how the United Nations had despatched a distinguished Belgian economist and ex-Prime Minister to report on the Lebanese economy and to make recommendations. M. van Zeeland made a lengthy study of the adverse trade balance and other depressing economic indicators. But his report was short and to the point. Whatever the official statistics might say, the economy was obviously booming. While he had been unable to discover exactly what the Lebanese were doing to deserve this, he recommended that they should go on doing it. Nowadays the jargon would have it that the visible deficit was outweighed by the invisible surplus derived from native expertise in banking, insurance and other more dubious activities, together with the flood of visitors.

The fact that most influential Lebanese were preoccupied with making money may have helped to take their minds off politics. At all events, little attention seemed to be paid to the growing demographic imbalance between Christians and Muslims which was potentially far more significant – and was eventually to prove infinitely more damaging – than any trade deficit. For while Lebanon appeared on the surface to be a model for all Arab states, with a lively parliament, a free press, a flourishing private sector and a pluralist society, the reality was that the country was run by a confessional clique representing barely a majority of the population, largely in the interests of the ruling group and the richer members of some others, and with hardly a vestige of social conscience or patriotic motivation. Thus were the seeds sown of the disaster which was to befall Lebanon once the demographic balance changed so much in favour of the Muslim population but the Christians refused to have this reflected in the constitutional arrangements which enshrined their own outdated dominance.

Such weighty thoughts did not take up all my time in the rarefied atmosphere of Shemlan. For the third source of my enjoyment of Lebanon was to become my wife. After ten months at MECAS, my Arabic aspired to nothing higher than the 'intermediate' standard, despite the often alarming endeavours of the formidable Danish pastor Alfred Nielsen, our chief mentor in the language. I did rather better in the background studies, thanks largely to the interest aroused by our principal instructor, Norman Lewis. But the main prize I won was the hand of Christine Coleman, who worked in the British Legation in Beirut, and to whom I became engaged at the end of the course.

One way and another, this proved no simple matter. In accordance with the custom of the time, I had written to my prospective father-in-law to seek his blessing. The laboriously composed missive got lost in the post, and no response had been received by the time we wanted to announce our engagement before I left Shemlan. We went ahead nevertheless, and I sent a further letter. By the time this reached home, the original version had turned up. I could only hope that they both told the same story.

Meanwhile, this *annus mirabilis* included two memorable journeys. One was an Easter pilgrimage to Jerusalem, via a circuitous route which took in Hama, Homs, Damascus and Amman. John Moberly, Alec Stirling and I formed a MECAS trio, with John at the wheel of his new Morris Minor. The weather was marvellous – we travelled with the roof down and got horribly sunburned – and we spent a highly instructive few days with the Anglican establishment at St George's, thanks mainly to Canon Edward Every, an expert guide and an eminent authority on the Eastern churches. Moreover, being able this time to 'aim off' for the commercialisation and other less attractive aspects of the Holy City, I found it much more rewarding than on my visit five years before.

A few months later, I embarked on a 'language break' tour of southern Iraq, as part of the MECAS routine. Thanks to the offer of accommodation from a friend of a friend, I chose Basra as my base for putting to the test such Arabic as I had acquired. John Moberly and I drove once again in his Morris as far as Baghdad, where he was to pursue his studies. I then proceeded, by a comfortable overnight train and in the agreeable company of the Assistant Director-General of the Iraqi Date Association, to Basra. The report I subsequently wrote about my experiences there on return to Shemlan was entitled 'Min Janna ila Jehannam', 'From Heaven to Hell'. The combination of heat and humidity in July and August was so appalling that one was driven to get out and about for fear of spending the entire time lying under a ceiling-fan.

My particular antidotes worth remembering were three. The first was a Muslim weekend spent in a charming village of reed huts built amidst a cluster of date-palms on the banks of a tributary of the Shatt al Arab north of Basra. I had an introduction to the local shaikh, who accommodated me in his reed hut 'madhif' or guest-house, though at night I slept on a special bed under stars, swaying palms and a mosquito-net. He and his friends conversed animatedly about politics and, more reticently, about religion. In Nasriyah, the principal town of the Muntafiq district north-west of Basra, where I next ventured, Iraqis were less inhibited about expressing their views on Islam. Indeed, I nearly precipitated a local version of the Thirty Years War when I initiated an after-dinner debate between an official and a merchant on the Qur'an's relevance to the contemporary world.

My Muntafiq journey was undertaken in the often exhilarating company of three Iraqis who operated the British Consulate's cinema van. The value of the exercise from HMG's point of view struck me as dubious. Our audiences in the small towns and rural areas we visited were less than receptive to the mixture of entertainment, information and propaganda we purveyed. But for me it was an excellent education. For ten days I spoke nothing but Arabic, lived comparatively rough and learned something of the Iraqi life-style and thought-processes.

My third foray was to the marshes. This was a fascinating and primitive area lying north of Basra between the Tigris and the Euphrates near the point where the great twin rivers join to form the Shatt al Arab waterway. It was about to be made better-known to the outside world through the writings of a number of intrepid British travellers, pre-eminent among them Wilfred Thesiger. I cannot claim to have emulated any of their exploits. Indeed, after four days my internal economy collapsed, and obliged me to return to the relative comforts of the city.

Once again, I had an introduction to a local shaikh. To reach him involved first of all a taxi ride to Qurna, the confluence of the two rivers 40 miles from Basra. There I hired a motor launch of ancient vintage which chugged along the Euphrates for two and a half hours until it brought me to Chubaish, the 'capital' of the marshes. It was a long, straggling village of reed huts with an imitation 'corniche'. My intended host proved to be out of town, but in no time at all I was being warmly welcomed by his nephew and comfortably installed in the family's reed house, with no questions asked.

From there, the nephew's 13-year-old-son, three boatmen and I set off on an eight-hour voyage by 'mashuf' – a kind of canoe – to Saiqal, in the very heart of the marshes. We punted and paddled up streams which wound their way through the reeds, barely giving room to pass in places, and across spacious, tranquil lakes. Buffaloes were everywhere, snorting through the water and sharing the huts with the inhabitants. Against the sun, my companions erected an ingenious canopy of reeds and rags, making me feel rather like Old Bones of the River. We fed on fish speared from the water and cooked, with skilful improvisation, by burning a long bundle of reeds. Bread was made on the spot in the same way. Eventually, through the gloom of dust and dusk, there appeared a large island of the now-familiar reed huts with an occasional madhif standing out like a cathedral.

As we drew nearer, the island proved to be several islets, each with its complement of men, women, children, buffaloes and cows. As the waters rose, so the occupants had to move to higher ground. Communication between the tiny floating colonies was by mashuf, so that the vast marsh area looked something like an unglorified cross between Venice and the Norfolk Broads. The main occupations were growing rice and breeding buffaloes. Illiteracy was as near 100% as makes no difference, and there were no medical or sanitary arrangements of any kind. One pathetic old man, no doubt accustomed to the tender ministrations of Thesiger, came up to ask whether I had any medicine for his son, who had been ill for a fortnight with malaria. He picked up an almost empty bottle labelled 'hydrogen peroxide', and enquired plaintively if that was any good.

Six years later, Iraq was convulsed by a violent coup, which began with the brutal murders of the young King Faisal, his uncle the Prince Regent, and Prime Minister Nuri Sa'id, Britain's best friend in the Middle East. It should have come as less of a surprise than it did. The report I wrote on return to Shemlan referred to glaring disparities of wealth, disappointed hopes born of the tardy exploitation of the country's natural resources, and a lively political consciousness. But I cannot say that it forecast revolution.

Forty years after my visit to the marshes, the oppressive regime of Saddam Hussain drained them, ostensibly for economic but actually for political reasons: the region was the centre of Shi'a opposition to Saddam. A traditional way of life was destroyed. But at the end of 1952 I was about to encounter another which, from entirely different causes, has also been transformed in the past half century.

5

Arabia Infelix

Shortly before Christmas 1952, John Moberly and I arrived in Bahrain to join the staff of Her Majesty's Political Resident in the Persian Gulf ('PRPG' for short). Five years earlier, when the Foreign Office had assumed responsibility from the Government of India for the manning of the Gulf posts, it had had no senior official with the necessary experience and qualifications to take charge in Bahrain itself and in Kuwait, Qatar, the Trucial States and Muscat and Oman. It was therefore to Lt Col Sir Rupert Hay, late of the Indian Political Service and the last of the old Indian hands to hold the appointment, that we reported.

Sir Rupert's portly and florid appearance, together with his military bearing, seemed to confirm what we had already heard of his reputation as something of a tiger. In fact, his roar was more often heard outside the office than in it, where, with six months to go before an honourable retirement, he seemed content to let his Foreign Office underlings get on with the job while he kept his nose clean.

Nevertheless he was one of the last real 'characters' in the Gulf. The stories told of him were legion. As the dinner guests were gathering one evening on the verandah outside the long single-storey building which served as the Residence, Lady Hay was doing the honours pending Sir Rupert's appearance. Suddenly a faint noise was heard coming from inside the house. Nobody took any notice. Then again, more urgently, what sounded like a strangulated 'Ah-li'. The guests began to feel a little uncomfortable. A moment later, the cry came a third time: 'Sybil, why the HELL don't you come when I call you?'

Amid acute embarrassment all round, Lady Hay rushed inside, protesting, 'I'm sorry, Rupert, I thought you were calling Ali'.

'No,' came the roar, 'I was calling DARLING, damn you'.

One of the PR's pet hates was being kept waiting for his dinner. The British expatriate community tended to go in for lengthy pre-prandials and late food. On one such occasion, by 10 o'clock and with still no sign of a meal, Sir Rupert's patience was exhausted. Crossing the room to where his wife was sitting, he declared loudly, 'Come on, Sybil, I think there's some cheese at home in the fridge' – and out they swept.

Among the extra-mural duties of the third secretaries was making up a four at tennis with Their Excellencies. It could be a delicate undertaking. Lady Hay was a base-line player, rarely summoning the effort to advance further into the court. Sir Rupert's favourite tactic was to lob the ball gently over the net, and to stand with arms akimbo, his great frame shaking with uncontrollable mirth at the wretched lady's forlorn attempts to return the shot. The problem for their younger partners was that to applaud such play would have been ungallant, while not to do so could impair one's prospects of promotion.

For all that, the Hay-days were a lot of fun. There were two tomboy daughters in the family who roped us in mercilessly for mixed hockey or Scottish dancing, and elaborate picnics in Bahrain's few beauty spots. I recall one in particular, when we had driven down to a desert area at the southern tip of the island. Sir Rupert was having a difficult time juggling with a gin and tonic while trying to balance an overladen plate on an ample knee. He suddenly exploded in frustration: 'Why the hell we have to come all this way to eat in such confounded discomfort is beyond me!'

Quoting Kipling out of context, Stanley Baldwin once referred to the press barons of Fleet Street as exercising 'power without responsibility, the prerogative of the harlot down the ages'. Our problem in the Gulf of the 1950s was the precise opposite: we had responsibility without power. As 'British-protected states', the shaikhdoms had yielded to Britain by treaty the authority to conduct their external relations and defence. But we had no formal standing in their internal affairs except for a degree of extraterritorial jurisdiction which was a hang-over from the Ottoman 'capitulations'.

The outside world understandably failed to grasp these fine distinctions. So far as it focussed at all on the Gulf, international opinion tended to assume that what happened there – or did not happen – was solely the result of British policy, implemented either by HMG's representatives on the spot or through the Rulers' British advisers, often wrongly regarded as much the same thing. Moreover, a good deal of internal Gulf opinion also took it for granted that their leaders danced to the British tune.

The reality was less simple. In my experience, the 'responsibility without power' syndrome applied with particular force to Bahrain. It was less evident in the Trucial States, where the administrations were not as sophisticated, and therefore British power more closely matched British responsibility. In the Sultanate of Muscat and Oman, which had a long tradition of constitutional independence, the syndrome should hardly have occurred at all. But Muscat's external independence was largely nominal, while the Sultan ignored our advice on internal matters.

My initiation into these mysteries concerned the reform movement in Bahrain. In the mid-1950s, the British authorities, conscious of the wind of change blowing through the region from the direction of Nasser's Cairo, were disposed at least to listen to the complaints of the self-styled 'Higher Executive Committee' which was demanding a measure of popular participation in the decision-making process. The local Government, on the other hand, was adamant that the Committee was a bunch of ambitious rabble-rousers stirred up by Nasserite propaganda and that they were best ignored, if not deported (as eventually happened).

My own modest part in all this was to maintain a discreet but by no means clandestine contact with the reformist leader, a rather unprepossessing Qatari named Abdul Rahman al Bakir. This I did on the instructions of Bernard Burrows, who had succeeded Sir Rupert Hay as Political Resident in 1953 and believed that we needed to know what was afoot in Bahrain. Unfortunately, the concept of 'Her Majesty's loyal opposition' was not widely familiar in the third world. (Sir Martin Le Quesne, once my immediate superior in Bahrain, pointed out years later in a West African context that the very term 'leader of the opposition' could be rendered in the local vernacular only as 'the chief of the enemies'.) When the Ruler sent for the Resident and informed him tartly that it had come to his ears that 'some of your young men have been hobnobbing with my opposition', the contact came to an abrupt end.

To be fair, Sir Charles Belgrave (the Ruler's adviser) and his wife had both done a great deal to put Bahrain administratively and educationally streets ahead of the other Gulf shaikhdoms. Moreover, the fact that the Al Khalifah family still presides over the island's fortunes more than 50 years later suggests that their judgement then may not have been too wide of the mark. On the other hand, perhaps those who argued in those days that the Gulf rulers needed to bend like the willow lest they be blown down like the oak had some influence on later developments. The fact remains that because of Britain's position in the Gulf in the 1950s, and the misconception about it both in the Gulf itself and outside, we often had the worst of both worlds.

So far as the 'Higher Executive Committee' was concerned, its activities were to have some far-reaching consequences. In March 1956 Selwyn Lloyd, as Foreign Secretary, flew to Karachi for a meeting of the South East Asia Treaty Organisation. On the way, he stopped in Cairo for talks with President Nasser. At Nasser's dinner in his honour, the news broke that King Hussain of Jordan had dismissed General Glubb. Lloyd believed not only that this was Nasser's doing but also that it had been timed to coincide with his own visit to Cairo. The next day he flew on to Bahrain, where he was to dine with the Ruler. Between the airport and the palace the official convoy received some rough handling by a mob. Nothing more lethal than sand was thrown, but some of the cars (in one of which I was bringing up the rear) were heftily thumped, and the crowd shouted disobliging slogans at the limousine in which Lloyd and Belgrave were riding. We had a few uncomfortable moments, but the episode hardly bore the construction which the Foreign Secretary appears to have put on it later, namely, that it was part and parcel of the Glubb sacking and once again all Nasser's doing. In fact, the Bahraini demonstrators were shouting 'Belgrave, go home'. But the experience may have helped to warp Lloyd's judgement at the time of Suez a few months afterwards.

Renewed disturbances in that connection were to result in the arrest and deportation to St Helena of the Committee's ringleaders. This action was taken under the British Colonial Prisoners (Removal) Act (sic). A technical flaw in the execution of the legal processes, however (the deportation notice was posted to the Political Agency before a piece of enabling legislation had actually come into effect), led years later to a protracted judicial battle which was finally resolved in the prisoners' favour, and they were released. This was regarded in some quarters as a triumph of British justice, though it did not look that way to the Bahraini establishment. Nevertheless, at least one of the exiles later became a respected member of it; al Bakir died of cancer shortly after release.

British influence was more evident in the Lower Gulf. The Trucial States – to which I was transferred from Bahrain early in 1953 – were far less 'developed'. Oil had not yet been discovered. The seven poor, underpopulated shaikhdoms were dependent on modest official subventions from Britain and payments made by the oil companies for their exploration concessions. Except for Dubai, whose attractive creek was lined with traditional buildings distinguished by their functional wind-towers, the coastal towns presented the appearance of a collection of 'barasti' (palm frond) huts, with a mud fort in the middle which served as the Ruler's palace. Travel was by four-wheel-drive vehicle across mud and salt flats, gravel tracks and sand dunes. Our main communication with the outside world was the weekly Gulf Aviation twin-engined Dove which plied between Bahrain and the wartime airfield at Sharjah, still occupied by the RAF. Every fortnight, a British India boat would anchor offshore on its voyage from Basra to Bombay and return to disembark passengers, cargo and mail on to lighters which could come alongside the jetties in Dubai.

It was about this time that I undertook my very first flight. It was not an encouraging experience. I was one of a party being flown from Sharjah to Bahrain in a twin-engined RAF Anson. When we were some 20 minutes out from Sharjah, with the blue-green waters of the Gulf glistening below, one of the engines stuttered and stopped. An RAF crew member emerged from the cockpit to assure us that the Anson was the safest aircraft flying, could function without difficulty on one engine, and could keep afloat for half an hour if need be. Nevertheless, it would be prudent to turn back to Sharjah and to don life-jackets 'just in case'.

So we flew back, mesmerised by the sight of the stationary starboard propeller, and uncomfortably aware of losing height every second. At one point a buzzer sounded loudly in the passenger compartment, which I took to be a signal to bale out, but in fact proved to be the pilot's indicator to lower the wheels. We eventually landed safely but in a cold sweat. The optimistic aircraftman wiped his brow and remarked, 'Phew... lucky we weren't more than 20 minutes out: we might have got our feet wet'.

Repairs were effected overnight and the next day we tried again. This time precisely the same thing happened, except that now we were 40 minutes from Sharjah. No amount of reassurance could convince us that our end was not nigh. The Anson limped back, expertly piloted, and finally landed again on one engine. Subsequent investigation revealed that the mechanics who had been repairing the plane after the original mishap had literally left a spanner in the works.

At the Political Agency in Sharjah I joined the Political Officer, Michael Weir, and the Assistant Political Officer, Martin Buckmaster. Both were of the MECAS vintage immediately before mine, and had formidable reputations as Arabists. I shared a small office with Martin: as he also happened to be a peer's son, this soon became known as 'the Hons' cupboard'. He combined devout Christian belief with deep sympathy for the Arabs. This could cause embarrassment: on arrival at the Agency each morning from the RAF camp where I was initially housed, I would have to force my way through a crowd of supplicants awaiting the Buckmaster bounty. After his departure, it was even worse: the same throng assembled in expectation of a dose of Lucas liberality. They soon learned better.

During the long hot summer of coronation year, Michael Weir was succeeded by Christopher Pirie-Gordon, one of the more memorable of all my diplomatic colleagues. He had served in Palestine during the mandate and subsequently transferred to the Foreign Service, on the strict understanding that he would not be involved with Arabs. A sympathetic Personnel Department assigned him to the Israeli desk! Christopher's abiding ambition was to be Consul-General in Florence. His way there deviated via Kuwait, the Trucial States, North Yemen and Innsbruck. When he finally reached his goal (and what was eventually to be his last resting-place), his somewhat easy-going approach to official business received a rude awakening. First, he found himself organising a British trade week; and then, during the calamitous floods of 1966, he rose even more nobly to the occasion by personally saving countless works of art.

In the Sharjah office, he soon made clear that my principal function was to 'shield me from reality'. In the flat upstairs, my role was to lend a pair of ears to his admittedly fascinating conversation, in the art of which, as Christopher would say, 'I've had a lot of practice'. Lubricated by the unvarying routine of three pink gins and two whiskies before lunch, and two pink gins and three whiskies before dinner, he would roam over the history, culture and royal families of Europe, spiced with personal reminiscences which included the curious story of Frederick Rolfe, Baron Corvo, the would-be priest with a persecution mania, in which Christopher's parents had played quite a notable part. All this was interrupted only by the occasional long, low chuckle in which he somehow managed to intersperse the last few (repeated) words of a sentence, nonchalantly swinging an elegantly crossed leg the while.

The environment in which we operated was bleak. The old-fashioned two-storey building which served as both the office and accommodation overlooked the evil-smelling Sharjah creek which did duty as the local public latrine. There was no running water in the house, nor flush toilet. A small generator provided power for lighting and some refrigeration, but we had no air-conditioning. Between March and October we suffered agonies from 'prickly heat', resulting from the inability of the sweat glands to cope with the excessive humidity. The only available remedy was to plunge into a cold bath, or as much of one's anatomy as could be immersed in the tin hip-bath filled each evening by our faithful bearers, humping the water to the primitive bathroom in disused petrol cans. But the net result was invariably to exacerbate the condition. To add insult to injury, we could hear the constant throb of the generator providing 'all mod cons' to the oil company rest-house next door.

By way of compensation, the anomalies of the British position meant that our work was probably unique in the Foreign Service for its variety. As well as diplomats, we were administrators and judges. The latter role often transgressed the time-honoured separation of powers so dear to hearts at home. I recall at least one occasion when I fell foul of my superiors by acquitting, on grounds of insufficient evidence, an alleged illegal immigrant whom they were anxious to put behind bars.

Such diplomacy as we practised largely took the form of maintaining relations between the shaikhs rather than with them. One Political Officer before my time evidently found it difficult enough to conduct British policy towards the seven rulers, so widespread were their domains and so unfamiliar their faces. He therefore devised a system whereby the Agency's 'Arab Assistant' – a kind of interpreter-cum-oriental secretary – would pop his head round the office door before any of the shaikhs was due to call, and announce confidentially, 'Ruler of X: smiling face, Sahib,' or 'Ruler of Y: frowning face, Sahib,' according to the prevailing state of our relations. This usually depended on how far the shaikhs had complied with, or contravened, the orders-in-council by which the British authorities maintained the 'truce' over a wide range of activities which constituted the local way of life. Arms dealings were sometimes a source of disagreement. Again, the rulers had accepted the abolition of the slave trade, though domestic slavery persisted, unless a slave could reach the Agency, embrace the flagpole, and claim his freedom, when we would issue him with a manumission certificate which was invariably respected by the shaikhs. In short, relations with them were generally excellent, though sometimes rather patronising and occasionally bad enough to warrant discreet influence being brought to bear to effect a change at the top.

Situations also arose when, as representatives of two rulers in dispute with each other, we were on a hiding to nothing. One of my colleagues accompanied a certain Gulf Ruler to the coronation in 1953. Uppermost in the shaikh's mind at the time was his perennial quarrel with his neighbour over some land we will call Abu Zar. During one of the social functions connected with the celebrations, the shaikh met Sir Winston Churchill. The Prime Minister opened the conversation by bidding my colleague, as interpreter, to 'tell him I'm a great friend of his father, Ibn Sa'ud'.

Since the Ruler did not happen to be among the numerous progeny of the Saudi monarch, nor were relations between them particularly cordial at the time, my friend translated this as a polite enquiry after the Ruler's health. This met with the instant rejoinder, 'Ask Sir Winston what he proposes to do about Abu Zar,' which was interpreted as a devout hope for the Prime Minister's welfare. How long this exchange at cross-purposes went on I do not know, but it certainly called for rare diplomatic as well as linguistic skills.

Another aspect of the Sharjah Agency's functions was to demonstrate to the tribal leaders in some of the farther parts of the Trucial Coast that the 'Daula' – the 'Government' (meaning Her Majesty's) – remained firmly committed to their protection. This we hoped to achieve in part through a very modest programme of economic aid. It was to lead to the establishment of the Trucial States Development Council which pointed the way to closer co-operation between the shaikhdoms, and eventually to the formation of the United Arab Emirates some 20 years later. By that time the respective economic fortunes of Britain and her protégés had been sharply reversed.

Our 'hearts and minds' campaign also included mounting 'flag-showing' expeditions in some of the remoter areas. I cut my teeth as 'political adviser' accompanying the Trucial Oman Levies on long desert trips. The Levies (later renamed the 'Scouts') were a small force of locally-recruited men under British officers, and had recently been established with Major Michael Hankin-Turvin, formerly of the Arab Legion, in command. The functions of this gendarmerie included keeping the peace by containing local rivalries (open warfare between Abu Dhabi and Dubai was recent memory); providing security for oil exploration teams; and acting as escorts for Political Officers. When the Buraimi crisis (of which more anon) blew up in 1952 the TOL was reinforced by a contingent of Aden Protectorate Levies, with whom I made a number of my excursions.

These were often exhilarating: desert dawns, ranging far and wide over the sandy wastes, and sleeping under the stars were more attractive than being deskbound in Sharjah, let alone Whitehall. But it was not roses all the way. We camped in fairly Spartan conditions, and ate frugally. Our fresh water supplies were landed by the Royal Navy's Gulf Squadron at convenient points along the coast where a frigate could get close enough to the beach to leave barrels for us to collect. A thoughtful ship's captain once invited the OC Troops and myself on board for lunch. The prospect was delicious indeed after days in the desert subsisting largely on bully-beef and dry biscuits. Even the discomfort of wading out to the dinghy which was to take us out to the frigate lying off-shore was overlaid by the thought of the sumptuous repast which awaited us. Alas, it was Saturday; and, as the captain explained with no more than a perfunctory apology as we sat down to lunch in the wardroom, the traditional Saturday midday meal in the Royal Navy since Nelson's day had been… bully-beef!

Naval occasions played quite a significant part in my life in Sharjah. The Gulf Squadron paid frequent formal visits to the shaikhdoms up and down the Gulf. These were fondly believed to boost the morale of the small British communities as well as that of the local rulers. I had once been engaged in a protracted correspondence with the Residency in Bahrain about the number of these inflictions and the short notice of them that we were sometimes given. In the course of this exchange a particular letter from headquarters had unfortunately been overlooked. One fine morning, Michael Weir sent for me in his office with its view across the creek to the open sea, and pointing dramatically to the window enquired, 'What, Mr Lucas, is that?'

'That' proved to be one of Her Majesty's ships bearing down on us for an official visit for which we had made no preparations whatever. Messages were rapidly despatched to the Ruler's palace informing him of the signal honour which was about to be done him, and suggesting with due diplomatic finesse that perhaps His Highness would wish graciously to offer the visitors lunch. Thanks to the Arab genius for improvisation, this was done and the day saved.

The United States Navy also descended on us from time to time. As custodians of the Rulers' external relations, this meant that someone from the Agency had to be present. On one occasion I had to make the long trek of several hours by Land Rover from Sharjah down desert track and across salt flats to Abu Dhabi, where Shaikh Shakhbut bin Sultan was to play host to the USS *Duxbury Bay*. Apart from the usual formal calls and informal 'mutton-grabs', the programme included an invitation to the Ruler for supper and a film on board. The movie was about a medieval pirate, not the happiest of choices in view of the early history of the erstwhile 'pirate coast'. I did my best to explain the plot to Shakhbut. At the end, I asked him how he had enjoyed it. Evidently either my Arabic or his comprehension had been unequal to the occasion.

'Well,' he replied, 'it wasn't bad, but for the life of me I can't understand why the Americans of all people want to show me a film that's 300 years old'.

In later, more prosperous, times Shakhbut was reputed to have kept the state's oil revenues under his mattress. More apocryphally, perhaps, the story was told of his first trip abroad. As his aircraft circled low over Paris he glanced out of the window and exclaimed, 'What a very rich country this must be: look at the size of that oil rig!'

In fact, though Shakhbut may – not surprisingly – have been wanting in intellectual attainments, he was among the shrewdest of the Trucial Rulers, and gave successive Political Agents a good run for his money.

But our principal preoccupation at the time was the Buraimi crisis. In August 1952 the Saudis had sent an armed force into the

Buraimi oasis, for years an area disputed between them on the one hand and the Ruler of Abu Dhabi and the Sultan of Muscat and Oman on the other. The oasis comprised nine villages, the Ruler claiming six and the Sultan three. Sovereignty in those parts tended to be based on the professed loyalties of largely nomadic bedouin to particular tribal shaikhs. Territorial boundaries were vague, and such maps as existed showed a complex patchwork quilt of competing claims. Attempts had been made – especially since the presence of oil deposits was first suspected – to define and delineate borders, but these had met with scant success. The Saudis had extended their claims over the years, their incursion into Buraimi representing their boldest move yet. The Sultan, Sa'id bin Taimur, favoured a firm and immediate response, fearing (correctly, as it turned out) that the Saudis would use their new foothold as a base from which to subvert the tribes and then argue that bedouin allegiances supported the Saudi case for expansion. Sa'id accordingly assembled a sizeable army at Sohar on the Batinah coast and prepared to march inland to evict the intruders from Buraimi.

Abu Dhabi was, of course, bound to defer to HMG's advice in such a situation. The Sultan, however, was nominally independent, though in practice Muscat's treaty relationship with Britain often approximated to that of the Trucial shaikhs. While we supported both rulers in their dispute with Saudi Arabia, we were concerned by the effect this was having on our own wider relations with the United States, already under strain as a result of the activities of Dr Mossadegh in Iran and the Free Officers in Egypt: the former had recently nationalised the Anglo-Iranian Oil Company and the latter had just kicked out King Farouk. It was an American oil company, ARAMCO, which was vitally interested in Buraimi's potential resource, and whose efficient Research Department was indeed providing the Saudis with much of the material for arguing their case. We, too, had our oil companies to support, so the quandary – typical of many we faced in maintaining our anomalous position in the Gulf – was clear.

In the event, the decision was taken to advise the Sultan not to advance on Buraimi. The Consul-General in Muscat had to travel up the coast to Sohar to carry out his instructions. When he delivered this unwelcome message, the Sultan's shrewd response was, 'I think you had better tell my troops yourself'!

Sa'id never forgave the British for what he regarded as their craven attitude, which in his view destabilised the area for the next few years.

The dispute was subsequently referred to an international arbitration tribunal. Meanwhile, the Saudi force in Buraimi was replaced by a smaller 'police detachment'. Our role in the Sharjah Agency was to monitor developments on the ground, and to give moral support to Shaikh Zaid, who represented his brother Shakhbut there. Zaid's headquarters were in a Beau Geste fort in Al Ain, one of the Abu Dhabi villages in the oasis. Michael Weir and Christopher Pirie-Gordon made regular trips there across the sand dunes from Sharjah.

The Saudis not only continued their nefarious practices in the disputed area, but even tried to pervert the course of justice in the tribunal itself. When this became clear, the British member, Sir Reader Bullard, resigned, to be followed by the neutral chairman and the collapse of the proceedings. In October 1955, the Trucial Oman Scouts and the Sultan's forces expelled the Saudis from Buraimi once and for all. In the course of this operation, sackfuls of incriminating documents were captured. These were duly despatched to the Residency in Bahrain for analysis. By this time I had been transferred back there, and supervised the examination. If we had wished to manufacture evidence after the event to justify the action taken in Buraimi, the material we found in those sacks would have been exactly what we would have produced. But this was 'for real': scores of messages exchanged between the Saudi authorities in Hofuf and their outpost in Buraimi indicating that in the next consignment of rice or dates (permitted under the arbitration agreement) there would be so many rifles, or so much cash, to be distributed to named tribes or individuals, and accounting for the largesse thus handed out.

This evidence fully vindicated the Sultan in the fears he had expressed at the outset of the crisis in 1952. For although his and Abu Dhabi's rights in the oasis had been finally upheld, seeds of subversion had been sown farther afield. These were soon to flower in the interior of the Sultanate, with far-reaching consequences not only for Sa'id bin Taimur but also for the British. We became deeply involved in the Jebel Akhdar campaigns of 1957-59, when Omani rebels ensconced in a mountain fastness were evicted with the help of the SAS, and committed more widely to the expansion of the Sultan's armed forces by virtue of agreements negotiated with Sa'id in London in 1958 by Julian Amery as Under-Secretary for War (as it happened I was by then on the Muscat desk in the Foreign Office). The agreements we reached were to set the pattern of our relations with Oman until the present time.

Meanwhile, the Sultan had decided in 1955 that, with the Buraimi issue settled and the prospects of significant oil deposits in other parts of his domains so bright, the time had come to reassert his authority in the interior. The extent of that authority had been in doubt since long before his father had abdicated in his favour in 1932. The 'campaign' in which Sa'id marched from the coast to the interior capital of Nizwa was described with characteristic flair by James Morris (as he then was) in his book *Sultan in Oman*[4]. Morris had been sent by *The Times* to cover the story, and accompanied the Sultan on the journey. En route, he called in at Bahrain, where I had the salutary experience of inadvertently providing him with some information which was no doubt of considerable interest to the oil company's shareholders when they first read it in the august columns of *The Thunderer.*

For all the anachronism, the embarrassment and the lighter side of our relationship with the Trucial States, much useful groundwork was done in fostering a sense of unity among the highly individualistic shaikhs which, as already suggested, was to stand the shaikhdoms in good stead when they became the United Arab Emirates in 1971. Twenty years later, one of the Political Agents was to write of this process and to compare it favourably with that of our withdrawal from Aden in 1967. Although Britain had more right to intervene in the internal affairs of the Aden protectorates than in those of the protected states of the Gulf, Glen Balfour-Paul's judgement is this:

> Rulers in the Aden protectorates were formally obliged by their treaties to accept advice on internal affairs but because of the curious structure of tribal society were not always able to implement it even if they wished to. Rulers of the Gulf States were explicitly absolved under their treaties from a comparable obligation, but were in general more disposed to listen to advice offered and much better able, in terms of the structure of society, to put it into effect by fiat.[5]

This, as we have seen, was less true of Bahrain. Oddly enough, it also had limited application in the Sultanate of Muscat and Oman. Here there was a paradox. The Sultanate was never under British protection. Our treaty relationship dated from 1800, some years before the first of the treaties with the shaikhdoms to the north. But, unlike theirs, it was a relationship of at least nominal independence. Later, for a variety of reasons connected on the British side with Oman's strategic location on the route to India, and on the Omani side with the need of successive sultans for help in dealing with the unruly interior, the actual relationship was somewhat different. By the early 1950s Sultan Sa'id bin Taimur was broadly content to let HMG conduct his external relations. We incurred a good deal of odium internationally in defending some of his attitudes, and on the most notable issue where we differed from him – over Buraimi in 1952 – we were proved wrong. On the internal front, the Sultan was obliged to allow us a limited role. But here again we were unable to compel the Ruler to embark on economic and social development to the extent we believed necessary.

In the spring of 1954, I had gone home on leave and to get married. Thanks to the fact that my father-in-law was Chief Harbourmaster and River Superintendent of the Port of London Authority, the wedding took place in the splendid setting of the chapel of the Royal Naval College at Greenwich. At the subsequent reception, I had chosen to start my Oxford Union-style reply to the toast of the bride and groom by telling a story about Disraeli's advice to a new and enthusiastic young MP who had asked him how often he should address the House.

'As seldom as possible,' replied the great man. 'It is far better for other Honourable Members to wonder why you do not speak than why you do.'

Unfortunately I was not to know that the proposer of the toast would raise his glass without making a speech at all, and I had not the wit to amend my contribution accordingly.

A further piece of bad luck was that on the way to (repeat to!) my stag party the previous evening, I had run my newly-acquired second-hand Hillman Minx convertible (my very first car) into the back of a lorry going down Blackheath Hill. My brother worked miracles to get a local garage he knew to patch the vehicle up overnight so that we were at least able to depart on time for our planned motoring honeymoon in Skye.

At the height of the summer, we returned to Bahrain to begin our married life in a modest two-bedroomed bungalow within the naval base of Jufair. A hare-brained journey included a nightmare drive across the Syrian desert from Damascus to Baghdad, over 700 miles in under 24 hours. Our petrol ran so low that at one stage we drove for 50 miles with the gauge reading empty and nothing in reserve, nor a sign of any other traffic in either direction. The desert heat in August was searing, and at times it almost seemed that we faced death by choking as the sand blew in the open windows or by suffocation if we closed them. On top of all this, Christine was – unbeknown to us – pregnant with our first child. I buoyed up our spirits by remembering having read in one of Freya Stark's books of a rest house at Rutba, on the other side of the Iraqi border. Alas, when we reached Rutba there was no sign of any such relief, and we had to press on and find what solace we could among the rats which kept us company in the Semiramis Hotel in Baghdad.

A week after the Selwyn Lloyd episode in 1956 we left Bahrain. The recollection of our desert trip had faded sufficiently to encourage us to make the return journey by the same route, with our eleven-month-old son. Fortunately, it was now springtime, and even Basra looked attractive. Nevertheless, we ran into a blinding sandstorm late at night approaching Rutba of blessed memory. By some miracle, through the murk and gloom a square shape suddenly emerged, which proved on closer inspection to be some kind of official doss-house. Its amenities were few and primitive, but never has any lodging been more welcome.

6

Martial Ayub

While my next posting was under consideration, I intimated to the Personnel Department that my preference was to go farther east. I was thinking in terms of Jakarta, or Kuala Lumpur (and continued to do so, without result, for the next 30 years). Shortly before leaving Bahrain I received a letter informing me that I was to be transferred to London. This was bad enough. My job was to be in the Economic Relations Department of the Foreign Office. That was worse. But perhaps most galling of all was the punchline: 'You will be dealing with the countries of South and South East Asia, which we hope will satisfy the interest you have expressed in that part of the world'.

So for 18 months I sat shuffling paper about Burmese rice and Malayan tin. 'Geographical' departments in the Foreign Office were apt to treat ERD as a suitable pending tray for papers which they wanted to clear from their own desks on a Friday afternoon and would accordingly mark to 'ERD for obs.' Another of our functions was to act as a kind of football between the geographical departments, who were the repositories of wisdom about individual countries, and Whitehall ministries, who were the experts on most of the specific subjects we dealt with. ERD's role was to ensure that in formulating policy recommendations the FO took proper account of broader Whitehall interests; that Whitehall was in turn fully aware of the foreign policy implications of its activities; and that everyone had an overall view of the economic dimension in our international diplomacy. In addition, we had specific responsibility for certain policy spheres such as oil, and the co-ordination of arms sales. Later on, the FO extended its range of 'functional' departments so that it 'shadowed' most Whitehall ministries. It therefore became increasingly difficult to tread a middle path between representing the FO to Whitehall and Whitehall to the

FO. When I subsequently joined a geographical department, I often felt that my functional colleagues had gone over to the other side. Even more irritating was the stranglehold which the Treasury seemed to exercise over the Whitehall machine: proposals were sometimes turned down not simply for financial reasons but because of the Treasury's diplomatic judgements.

All this was no doubt a necessary part of one's education in the workings of the Whitehall machine. The only task I remember undertaking with genuine enthusiasm, however, was a paper on the 'Soviet economic offensive' which was exercising ministerial minds at the time. One idea to counter it was a 'Special United Nations Fund for Economic Development'. In accordance with the prevailing passion for acronyms, my immediate superior Bill Combs dubbed it 'SUNFED for the unfed'. Nothing much was to come of it, but the work appealed to my more idealistic instincts.

The same could certainly not be said of the major foreign affairs event during this period. I was glad not to be concerned directly with Arab matters when the Suez storm broke in October 1956. But watching the drama unfold as closely as one could through the shroud of secrecy which enveloped it, I was appalled by the misjudgement, duplicity and incompetence which characterised the whole sorry business. The blatant contradictions and inconsistencies in successive statements by Government spokesmen seemed to display remarkably short memories. We were 'separating the combatants', then 'keeping the canal open' and finally 'toppling Nasser'. It reminded me of the salutary message on the nursery wall at home, 'The advantage of telling the truth is that you don't have to remember what you said'.

Those who argued that Eden's only mistake was to have stopped half-way conveniently forgot that, only months before, we had finally evacuated the Canal Zone partly because our continued occupation had become neither politically nor practically viable. How, then, could we have sustained the wider occupation which the subjugation of the Egyptian regime would have entailed? But it was not the intellectual so much as the emotional feelings aroused by our action which made me weep at the news of the bombing of Port Said.

Soon after this, I was moved to the more familiar and congenial surroundings of the Eastern Department, with responsibilities relating to Saudi Arabia and Muscat and Oman. As it happened, our relations with the former were non-existent, Jedda having broken them off over Suez, and declining to restore them until the Buraimi dispute was settled to Saudi satisfaction. We therefore had no Embassy reports to rely on, and I even found myself composing the customary ambassadorial annual reviews in the department. No wonder some of my assessments were wide of the mark. The after-effects of Suez were still reverberating around the Arab world. In the summer of 1958, a violent revolution in Iraq put a bloody end to the Hashemite monarchy there, while the head under the Hashemite crown in neighbouring Jordan lay distinctly uneasy, and the pro-Western regime in Lebanon was rocked. Some at least of these disturbing events appeared to have taken the Foreign Office by surprise. I was determined that the same fate should not befall the Saudi desk. The kingdom seemed to me to display many of the symptoms which had led to the convulsions elsewhere. I confidently predicted a revolution, and am still waiting for it to happen!

The Sultanate was altogether a different matter, and became my major preoccupation. I was involved in the weeks of preparation for the important negotiations with Sultan Sa'id mentioned in the previous chapter, and then in the talks themselves. These took place in the summer of 1958. The British side was led by Julian Amery, whose political fortunes had recovered since his time as one of the 'Suez rebels', a group of Tory MPs opposed to the 1954 agreement with Nasser on the evacuation of the Canal Zone. He was no doubt keen to score a neo-imperial diplomatic triumph. The Sultan, for his part, desperately needed assistance of various kinds, and his coffers were comparatively bare. We therefore held most of the trump cards as we gathered round the negotiating table, but it seemed to me that Sa'id, as shrewd as he was charming, took most of the tricks. The outcome was that we undertook a major commitment to the expansion of the Sultan's armed forces, and to a degree of economic development, in return for the granting of certain facilities to the RAF at Masirah and Salalah. While these arrangements certainly secured the continuation of our 'special relationship' with the Sultanate, they were to create some long-term problems.

These were some way in the future when, in February 1959, I was promoted First Secretary on secondment to the Commonwealth Relations Office and appointment to the British High Commission in Pakistan. With the family now augmented by the birth of our second son five months previously, we sailed to Karachi in some style in a P & O liner which did the voyage from Liverpool in 19 days, giving us, among other things, our first glimpse of Aden.

Shortly after our arrival, the Deputy High Commissioner and his wife were kind enough to give a party for us to meet leading Pakistanis, members of the British community and diplomatic colleagues. They were kinder still to provide beforehand a list of those invited. Mindful of the perennial problem of the diplomat – how to remember names and faces – I studied this with great care and attention. On the night, I made strenuous efforts to fit faces to names, and for several weeks afterwards, on being introduced to people who had figured on the list, I was able to say, 'Yes, of course, we met at the Walsh Atkins", even if it was the only name that I remembered.

This worked like a charm until one evening I used the formula with the Deputy Chief of Mission in the United States Embassy.

'Gee, I'm awfully sorry,' replied Mallory Brown (the name still sticks!) 'but I'm afraid we didn't get there that evening'.

My new assignment did not divorce me entirely from the Arab world. One of the first tasks with which I was entrusted was the delicate one of going round to the Iraqi Embassy to apologise for the inadvertent slip whereby the High Commissioner's congratulations had been routinely sent on the occasion of the old Iraqi national day, which commemorated the late King's birthday! The Chargé d'Affaires could not have been more charming in accepting my (correct) explanation that our records were unfortunately a year out of date.

Iraq also features in another of my Pakistan recollections. In the early 1960s, the Iraqi dictator Qassem survived an assassination attempt (in which, incidentally, one of the plotters was a young man named Saddam Hussain). Qassem was slightly wounded in the shoulder and, in order to damp down undesirable speculation, the Baghdad propaganda machine got busy flooding the world press with photographs of him sitting up in hospital, grinning broadly and with an attractive nurse in attendance. The Pakistan English-language papers duly reproduced this, with a caption which ran: 'General Qassem, Prime Minister of Iraq, seen in his hospital bed with an unidentified nurse'.

The three and a half years we spent in Pakistan were absorbing from the point of view of the job I had, the people we met and the country itself. Unfortunately, Karachi was the least representative as well as the least attractive part of it. For nine months of the year the climate rivalled the worst the Gulf had to offer. In the 12 years since independence, Karachi had grown from a pleasant fishing village of 300,000 inhabitants to a teeming metropolis of two and a half million. Apart from becoming the capital, the commercial centre and the principal port of the new state, it was the nearest point of access for the thousands of refugees who poured across the border with India and were still mouldering in the most squalid districts of the city. The needs of the exploding population had long since outstripped the amenities available, so that there were frequent power cuts and water shortages. Severe import restrictions made day-to-day living far from easy, and we were obliged to order many of our basic requirements from home six months in advance. We lived in a large modern house with adequate air-conditioning (when it worked) in a northerly suburb off the airport road. The outskirts of Karachi abounded in soulless residential areas financed by local housing societies, with addresses numbered rather than named – to the confusion of many a visitor. Ours was 43/4/G/VI PECHS (Pakistan Employees' Co-operative Housing Society). I can still feel the stifling damp heat as I drove my Morris

1000 Traveller the five miles to and from the office each day along the dreary Drigh Road. It was along this route to the airport that Vice President Johnson stopped for a folksy chat with a local camel driver. Johnson was rash enough to tell him that he would be very welcome at any time in New York. Rather to the Vice President's surprise, the camel-driver later took him up on this offer, and duly paid an official visit to the United States.

But the rest of the country was marvellous, and I was lucky to see a good deal of it either on official trips with the High Commissioner and on my own, or on local leave with the family. Lahore was the high-spot, with its impressive Moghul architecture, its refreshing expanses of greenery and the annual attraction of the Horse Show. The latter was always much more than just an equestrian gathering: its colourful events and displays, from polo to tent-pegging, drew a spectacular array of foreign dignitaries every year, including the Shah and Jackie Kennedy.

Peshawar was the gateway to the Khyber, and redolent with the turbulent history of the north-west frontier, though the famous pass itself was less spectacular than that of Garian in Libya. More exciting was the little frontier town of Landi Kotal, with its thriving market nestling under the main road and replete with every conceivable kind of contraband, from rifles to transistors smuggled in from Afghanistan or, in the case of the weaponry, manufactured locally. We had an interesting introduction to indigenous customs during an early visit to Peshawar, when we were taken round the mission hospital by the dedicated British doctor and his wife who ran it. In a small room we saw an old man lying on a charpoy, while a woman busied herself cooking a simple meal over a fire in the corner.

'You may think,' explained Jonathan Shaw, 'that the man is the patient. On the contrary, it is his wife who is in hospital: he has come to visit her – but expects his home comforts to be provided as normal!'

Islamabad, now Pakistan's capital in the Potwar Plain, not far from Rawalpindi, was then no more than a gleam in the eye of President Ayub. Apparently he considered that the Karachi climate was too debilitating for officials to work in: they spent too much time huddling over their electric fans in an effort to keep cool. Moreover, the proximity of the rapacious commercial community exposed them to undue temptation. The Ministry of External Affairs made a preliminary move to 'Pindi in my time: making calls there on one occasion I found the officials huddling over their stoves to keep warm, while it seemed doubtful whether the long arm of corruption would find the 600 miles from Karachi beyond its reach.

My travels with the High Commissioner were more often than not to East Pakistan. Curzon described Bengal as 'a low-lying land inhabited by low, lying people'. As to the topography, the contrast with West Pakistan could not have been sharper: the western province was of the Middle East, the eastern of South East Asia. Small wonder, then, that separated as they also were by race, by language and by India, the bonds of religion were to prove too fragile to hold the two parts of the country together. As for the people, whether or not they deserved Curzon's disobliging comment, they certainly merited sympathy. The province was grossly over-populated and afflicted by regular natural disasters in the shape of typhoons and cyclones. On one of our visits, we saw from the air the result of a recent massive tidal wave which had deposited a 10,000-ton vessel in a paddy field.

Despite possessing natural resources in the form of jute and rice, not to mention a native wit and diligence, East Pakistan was also pitifully poor. The Bengalis complained that although their jute was Pakistan's principal export, they did not receive a fair share of the foreign exchange proceeds, which were largely swallowed up by development expenditure in West Pakistan. Indeed their fundamental grievance was that the Government of Pakistan was a government of the West by the West and for the West (especially the Pathans and the Punjabis). The complaint was not entirely without foundation, and Ayub took some steps to meet it, including sending his trusty lieutenant, General Azam, as Governor – only to find that Azam became a convert to the Bengali cause. But it often seemed that the central Government was on a hiding to nothing: if they tried to help East Pakistan, they were accused of being patronising, while if they did nothing, they were condemned for neglect.

Chittagong was the most attractive of the places we used to visit. It was a small but busy port, built to all appearances on a series of conical hills. The lush vegetation included a nine-hole golf course which was a regular object of the High Commissioner's not very expert attention. Since it, too, was constructed on a series of pyramids, the margin of error off the tee was minimal, with the result that balls had constantly to be retrieved from the numerous valleys. This, I discovered, was the function of the First Secretary.

The High Commissioner himself was Sir Alexander Symon, a short, dynamic Yorkshire terrier who had begun his career as a boy clerk in the India Office and could never forget it. Karachi was his last post, in which he served for seven years, largely because he had become Dean of the Diplomatic Corps, and the Pakistanis wanted him to stay on until the Soviet Ambassador, who was next in seniority, had left. His working style was to draft practically nothing himself but to recount in detail to his staff conversations which needed reporting or ideas which he was developing and then to say, 'You know my mind: knock it into shape'.

This did not bother me particularly, except when I was instructed to write a St Andrew's Night speech for him. Having pored over joke books and racked my brains for some days, I eventually produced a draft which I hoped would match the occasion. Sir Alec grudgingly admitted that it was 'quite amusing, but it's not me'. His own sense of humour was illustrated at the party he and his devoted and wholly unpretentious wife 'Dodo' once gave to celebrate their joint birthday on 13 May. Most of their senior staff were present. During dinner, the buzz went round that afterwards we should all be required to do a 'party piece'. Conversation virtually came to a halt as memories were desperately searched. In due course we trooped out on to the verandah and the ghastly proceedings began. The Military Adviser proved the star turn. He commanded a wide repertoire which included a rhyme about the hazards of eating at the principal hotel in Rawalpindi.

'What will you have?' asked the waiter,
Pensively picking his nose.
'I'll have boiled eggs, you b…
You can't stick your fingers in those!'

When the recitations were over, everybody heaved a sigh of relief. Whereupon Sir Alec cheerfully announced that he had been so impressed with our performances that he was sure we would like to hear them all over again, on his hitherto concealed tape recorder!

Dodo's sense of humour was rather more refined. Some months after they left Karachi we had a delightful letter describing the perils of retirement after long years of service in the higher echelons. 'We're forever getting out of taxis,' she wrote, 'and forgetting to shut the door and pay the fare.'

Perhaps because of their common 'Indian' background, Alec Symon had more than a touch of Rupert Hay. Invited to lunch by a senior British official and his wife during a visit to Dacca, the Symons arrived before the other guests. Alec insisted on waiting in a separate room while the company assembled, so that he could make his grand entrance last of all. This put the already nervous hostess in a dither, and when everyone was finally seated at the table she enquired timorously whether the High Commissioner would care for some water.

'Never tooch the stoof,' replied Alec in a jocular tone. 'Oh – bearer, bearer,' cried the hapless lady, 'bring Lord Symon some soda!'

As the only Foreign Office member of the staff (the Foreign and Commonwealth Services being still separate entities in those days), I was naturally assigned to monitor the internal scene. This could hardly have been more fascinating. Following the disillusionment with the narrow self-seeking of the politicians who had brought the country to independence (shades of the Arab world), a military regime had taken over in October 1958 under General Ayub Khan (soon self-promoted to Field Marshal). He was an honest, straightforward soldier with little or no political guile; a devout but not a fanatical Muslim; and a warm personality once the formal military manner was discarded. I remember hearing him address a public gathering during his State Visit to Britain some time later. His subject was the economic development of Pakistan, and he read monotonously from a turgid official brief (not helped by discovering, when he reached his peroration, that the final page was missing). In the course of one particularly dull passage about the need to increase industrial output and at the same time to combat the population explosion, the real Ayub suddenly shone through. He looked up from his script and exclaimed with a smile, 'Yes, that's what we want: more production and less reproduction!'

There were, of course, many Pakistanis who lamented the failure of democracy to take root in the young nation, and numerous voices abroad who proclaimed that military dictatorships in the Commonwealth were not cricket. But in its early years at least, Ayub's martial law regime was the best government Pakistan has ever had, before or since. Stability was restored. The economy improved. Relations with big brother India reached a peak with the signing of the Indus Waters Agreements. Pandit Nehru himself came to Karachi for the occasion, and we caught a glimpse of him as he passed our front gate on his way to visit his niece, whose husband Ashok Mehta was Counsellor in the Indian High Commission and our neighbour in PECHS. Above all, after a long period of self-doubt, Pakistanis were able to hold up their heads again.

Nevertheless, the regime faced some intractable problems. The process of 'nation-building' had hardly got under way, being bogged down in arguments about the extent to which Pakistan should be a truly Islamic state, and beset by the fissiparous tendencies already mentioned. These showed only too clearly that religion may have been the necessary, but was not a sufficient, condition for the establishment of the nation in the first place. The religious opposition was led by the formidable Maulana Maudoodi and his Jama'at-i-Islami. His feathers were particularly ruffled by Ayub's Family Laws Ordinance, an attempt to modernise the legislation affecting marriage, divorce and related matters without departing too far from Islamic precepts. Maudoodi put up a spirited defence of polygamy in a newspaper debate, arguing that Muslim wives had more rights than Western mistresses. The mullahs generally had a strong hold on the illiterate village peasantry who formed the vast majority of Pakistan's population. An illustration of the extraordinary grip which outmoded traditions could exert on these simple and ignorant folk was a story I heard in Peshawar. A man had been forced to leave his village because he could not repay the debts he had incurred in connection with a family wedding (the burden of the moneylenders was a yoke borne by many such people for the rest of their lives). When asked why he had not excused himself from the crippling expense on the grounds that he could not afford it, he replied that this would have involved such loss of face that he would have been obliged to leave his village!

Another source of opposition was the legal fraternity, fretting over the arbitrary way in which martial law was often administered. Cases were frequently brought against the authorities for exceeding their powers or their jurisdictions. The judiciary showed a commendable degree of independence in dealing with such litigation. But more often than not, if they ruled against the administration on a serious issue, the result was that retrospective martial law regulations were enacted to validate the offending action. This was the unacceptable face of the regime.

Ayub tried to meet the democratic objection to his rule by introducing a home-grown brand of democracy. He called this 'basic democracy', and much of my time was spent studying it. The underlying idea was that an unsophisticated electorate was not in a position to make proper judgements on national issues or national personalities. Hence voters had fallen an easy prey to dishonest politicians with their bland promises and well-filled money-bags. Having first cleared the undergrowth by an elaborate legal process which effectively debarred the 'old guard' from both public and elective office, Ayub proceeded to erect a new structure from the grass-roots upwards. The electorate was to be confined to the limits of village issues and local personalities familiar to them. Moreover, voting would be strictly by secret ballot.

The structure began at the bottom with a village council, and worked its way upwards through area and district bodies to the Provincial Council. Each council was partly nominated and partly elected, the elected proportion increasing as the top of the pyramid was approached. The theory was almost impeccable, though the inevitable criticisms were made that the system was unacceptably condescending and too tightly controlled. But the practice was far from perfect. The former politicians may have been banned, but they had their surrogates who had slipped through the net. Nor were the provisions for secret balloting water-tight when a candidate would offer the voters 50% on account and the rest after he was elected. So the best-laid schemes did not live up to Ayub's expectations. Yet it was an interesting and praiseworthy attempt to avoid the pitfalls of transplanting Westminster-style parliamentary democracy to alien soil while adapting it to local traditions and requirements.

Despite the general improvement in relations with India, the particular problem of Kashmir continued to defy solution. The Pakistanis felt especially aggrieved that their support of the Arabs over Palestine was not rewarded by Arab help for their cause on Kashmir. On the contrary, Arab leaders of the time – not least Nasser – found a closer affinity with non-aligned India than with western-affiliated Pakistan. 'Religion,' as the Pakistan Foreign Minister Manzur Qadir remarked ruefully, 'is no basis for foreign policy'.

In the high summer of 1960 we spent an idyllic holiday in Kashmir with the two children (then aged 5 and 2). The political situation obliged us to fly first to Lahore, then to take a car to the Indian border, where we walked across to get a taxi to Amritsar, and finally caught a flight to Srinagar. The temperature there, at something in the 80s, was not much lower than in Karachi; but the absence of humidity and the clear air made it seem degrees cooler. We spent a night or two in the luxury of the Oberoi Palace Hotel, but soon realised that if we stayed there our holiday was going to be a short one. So we managed to find a vacant houseboat on the Little Nagin Lake, and spent another 12 days there at approximately the same cost as our two in the hotel. The bearded and turbaned Salama Doono was our kindly host on 'King's House' and he looked after us remarkably well. The ambience was decidedly Victorian, but comfortable for all that. Salama and his colleagues bemoaned the passing of the days when the memsahibs had come up from the plains for the long hot summer months, and spent aplenty. Then there had been 3000 houseboats on the lakes; now there were 300 – and Indian visitors were careful with their money.

We took tranquil trips by *shikara* (small rowing boats, piloted by a local) along shaded streams and across lotus-covered lakes; pony-trekked in the lush meadows of Gulmarg; picnicked in the quiet greenery of the Nashat and Shalimar Gardens; and visited the bazaars of Srinagar and the mosque of Hazratbal, complete with its inevitable relic of a hair from the Prophet's beard. We in turn were visited by a variety of water-borne merchants, including the tailor, the jeweller, 'Butterfly' with his range of local arts and crafts, and – most picturesque of all – the florist with his *shikara* festooned in a blaze of colour. The whole scene was a glorified version of the marshes of southern Iraq, this time combining the enchantment of Switzerland, Venice and the Norfolk Broads.

I must admit that I went to Pakistan equipped with various hang-ups about our imperial past. Pannikar's *Asia and Western Dominance*[6] had made a deep impression when I was engaged in the formulation of aid policy in Economic Relations Department a few years earlier. But experience of the reality convinced me that to travel in the subcontinent is almost an essential part of an Englishman's education.

Twelve years after independence the Pakistanis themselves appeared to harbour little animosity, despite British responsibility for the horrors of the partition process. Indeed, some would lament the passing of the Raj, comparing it favourably with their current circumstances. Although one had to 'aim off' for the Muslim desire to please by saying what he thought his listener wanted to hear, much of this was genuine. At its lowest level, the feeling was expressed in a leader in one of the Karachi English-language papers. It was all very well, the writer opined, to try to wipe out the past by changing street names and so on: but at least when the British ruled, the public lavatories worked properly. The positive achievements of the Raj, especially in the fields of law and administration – to say nothing of cricket – were remembered and appreciated. At the same time, removal of the colonial taint enabled relationships with the British to prosper both qualitatively and quantitatively, as they have since continued to do.

Practical expression was given to all this during the most memorable event of our time in Pakistan: the Royal Tour in the spring of 1961. Despite media problems before it began and after it ended, this was a success beyond our wildest dreams. The prelude was a reception given by the Commonwealth Press Association in London at which Prince Philip, on meeting the London correspondent of the Karachi daily *Dawn*, quipped: 'You should be behind bars, shouldn't you?'

The joke was not appreciated by *Dawn*, which went so far as to demand the cancellation of the visit. Fortunately, wiser counsels prevailed. The epilogue was the news film of the tour: although this had included both the subcontinental countries, the film was unhappily entitled 'The Royal Tour of India', which naturally did not go down well in Pakistan.

The British High Commissions in the respective capitals also had their problems. One was that while we in Karachi were beavering away drafting speeches for the Queen to say that of course we quite understood that parliamentary democracy Westminster-style did not suit everybody, and what a splendid thing it was that Ayub was inventing his own variety, our colleagues in Delhi were advising Her Majesty with equal enthusiasm to commend the Indians for maintaining the best traditions of the Mother of Parliaments. Whereas it might perhaps have been possible 50 years earlier to get away with two such contradictory pronouncements in the hope that neither capital would easily pick up what had been said in the other, this was certainly not true in 1961. The Indians were not pleased by the paeans of praise lavished on the neighbouring autocrat, while the Pakistanis expressed incredulity that anyone could seriously believe that Nehru was running a genuine two-party system.

The success of the visit owed much to the fact that although the Pakistanis had expected the Queen to be a regal figure somewhat in the Victorian mould (even if they were not, unlike our small son waving his Union Jack at the airport, disappointed that she was not wearing a crown) they were more than delighted when their royal guests proved to combine dignity and informality to such effect. My own involvement in the arrangements was minimal, Alec Symon having understandably chosen to assign these responsibilities to the Commonwealth Relations Office staff. Indeed, our experience of the visit was something of an anti-climax. The highspot in Karachi was to be at a garden party given by the Commonwealth High Commissioners on the lawns of the State Guest House at the Frere Hall. Each Commonwealth country had been allotted its own 'plot' where its nationals were to congregate, a select group of them to be presented as the Queen and the Duke walked through the assembled company. Brightly-coloured shamianas had been erected over the bars, strategically placed in various parts of the garden. Every detail had been carefully thought out, organised and rehearsed. Except one. It had not rained in Karachi in February for 87 years. There was no 'plan B'. But half an hour before the proceedings were due to begin the heavens opened. Ladies who had spent months preparing their finery for the occasion and gentlemen in dinner jackets were soon turned into a bedraggled-looking mob. The shamianas collapsed under the weight of water, trapping early imbibers beneath them: at least one of them, in the happy company of a bottle of diplomatic whisky, noisily declined to be rescued. A fair amount of duty-free liquor was purloined and later found its way on to the local black market.

A decision had to be taken. Either the party itself had to be cancelled, which might well have caused a riot; or 1500 guests had to be squeezed inside the State Guest House itself, which had room to accommodate half that number. In the event the choice fell on the great crush. Those who could obtained positions of vantage, regardless of nationality, status or decorum. The Queen and Prince Philip arrived on time, and carried on as though nothing untoward had occurred. But the Duke could not resist one characteristic pleasantry. Spotting one distinguished but dripping member of the British Community at the rear of a group, he called out, 'And how long have you been in Karachi?'

'20 years, Sir'.

'About time you knew better, then!'

Like many other regimes of its kind, Ayub's carried the seeds of its own destruction. I was to see a similar process in Gowon's Nigeria ten years later. The military come in with the best of intentions, promising to clear up the mess left by the politicians and to hand the country back to civilian rule in six months. The new brooms achieve a certain amount at first. But they soon find that the mess is even worse than they thought – and then they start to wallow in it themselves. Corruption rears its ugly head. Parliaments are abolished and the press muzzled. The essential two-way traffic between government and the governed is disrupted, and the ruling few surround themselves with a clique of sycophants who tell them what they think their masters want to hear. The soldiery, who are accustomed to giving orders and having them obeyed, grow out of touch with what people are thinking, and there is no safety-valve through which the latter can blow off steam. It is a recipe for disaster. In Pakistan's case disaster duly ensued. By 1996 the country had suffered wars, a succession of civil and military take-overs and the disintegration of the nation as it was originally conceived and created. To those who saw its 'glad confident morning' the present darkness is sad indeed.

7

Sanusi Sojourn

The Libya to which I returned in June 1962 was in many ways a very different place from the one I had left as a soldier 14 years before. After lengthy international wrangling, with various powers staking out their claims and trying to preserve their interests, the United Nations finally decided that the territory should become independent. A senior Libyan once claimed in a conversation with me that the credit for this decision was entirely his. He explained that he had been a member of the Libyan delegation in New York at the time. When the question of the future of Libya had been under consideration the result had turned on the vote of the delegate from Haiti. My informant was the only member of his team who spoke French. So did the Haitian. The two of them happened to meet one day in the men's room. The Libyan persuaded the Haitian to change his vote to one in favour of independence. Thus, according to this account, was the new state brought to birth in the gentlemen's lavatory.

Whether or not the story was apocryphal, Libya duly achieved independent statehood on 24 December 1951. The two coastal provinces of Cyrenaica and Tripolitania were joined by the inland desert area of the Fezzan to form the new monarchy under King Idris, leader of the Muslim Sanusi sect and a champion of the earlier struggle against the Italians. The King's power base was with the tribes of Cyrenaica; the more sophisticated Tripolitanians were less enthusiastic in their support. The received wisdom was that this did not matter too much since any overt opposition on the part of the intelligentsia would easily be crushed by the Cyrenaican backwoodsmen. This was not the only theory of its kind in the Middle East which was to be falsified in the event.

Meanwhile, King Idris enjoyed the strong backing of the British and the Americans, both of whom gave substantial assistance to the

Libyan economy in return for important military facilities. Britain had an air base at El Adem in the eastern part of the country, a smaller one which shared the civil airport at Idris (Castel Benito in my army days) outside Tripoli and troops stationed in Tripoli and Benghazi, the twin capitals. The United States held the major Wheelus Airfield along the coast east of Tripoli. Such was the belief of the local people in the King's dependence on Britain in particular, and in his frail state of health (which had always been exaggerated), that when Idris was regularly seen being driven round the streets of Tripoli in his Rolls Royce it was commonly said that he had in fact died some time previously but that the devious British, anxious to perpetuate their 'special relationship', had made a wax effigy which was put on show in order to deceive the populace.

All this was about to undergo some radical change when we arrived eleven years after independence (approximately the same period as in the case of Pakistan, where the local situation had also been in a state of flux). 1962 was the year in which oil began to transform the Libyan economy. Hitherto, with a population of only about one and a half million and few resources to sustain it, the country had been among the poorest in the region: hence its dependence on British and American subventions. Very soon these sources of income became nugatory. At the same time, and not altogether coincidentally with the access of oil wealth, Nasser began to display great anxiety about the shame to which his brotherly neighbour was exposed by the presence of foreign troops on his territory. A major propaganda campaign was launched from Cairo, and found some echo among nationalist opinion in Tripoli, already beginning to ask questions about where the new oil wealth was going, and to level charges of corruption against the regime. In fact, prudent plans were being laid for the disbursement of the oil revenues, but they were slow to materialise (as had happened in Iraq prior to the 1958 revolution). Suspicions were aroused, and to some extent fuelled, by certain obtrusive examples of budgetary extravagance. Meanwhile people flocked from the countryside into the main cities under the illusion that oil meant easy and plentiful jobs, and set up ugly shanty-towns on the outskirts which became festering social sores and hotbeds of political dissent.

These problems did not become evident until early in 1964. For the moment, life was interesting without being frenetic, and Tripoli was an exceedingly pleasant place to be. After the rigours of Karachi, the Mediterranean climate was a Godsend, though it could be hot and humid in the summer and the occasional sand-laden 'ghibli' – the wind that blew off the desert – was a trial. The Italians were still around in some strength, making things work and providing gastronomic delights. The British military presence (which now included military and naval training missions) yielded benefits to us in the shape of the British Forces Post Office and Broadcasting Station, the NAAFI shop and the Officers' Club on the beach at Piccola Capri. We ourselves lived in a delightful old Turkish-style house with its attractive back patio, a dining-room in a covered central courtyard (sometimes less than waterproof) and a front verandah overlooking the noisy 'lungomare' but with a magnificent view over the harbour and down to the historic and picturesque fort which dominated the waterfront – and concealed many a tale of dark deeds perpetrated within its walls during the long centuries of Ottoman rule.

My younger sister came out at an early stage of our sojourn to help look after the smaller children (our third son was born in 1963). She soon decided that she would rather look after the manager of the local branch of the British Bank of the Middle East, a friend of mine in Dubai ten years earlier. They were married from this house. When our parents flew out for the nuptials, my father and I were sitting on the verandah one evening enjoying a sundowner and contemplating the exquisite view. Suddenly he turned to me and said, 'Do you mean to tell me that they PAY you to come to places like this?' I took the point, but forebore to add that they had paid me no more to savour the smells of Sharjah creek or swelter in the stifling atmosphere of Karachi.

The attractions of the country were not, of course, confined to those attributable to the foreign presence. The tourist sites had in some respects been improved since 1948. The Roman theatre at

Sabratha now boasted musical and dramatic performances. It was fun to revisit scenes of earlier toil and tribulation. We picnicked often by the woods and streams of Tarhuna, where Norman Hall had stimulated my interest in the local way of life. I retraced my steps to the old barracks at Garian. As a regimental officer there I had barely noticed the mural executed by some bored American soldier during the war, depicting the coastline of North Africa in the agreeable shape of a nude female form reclining on her side. Now one had to pay to see 'the Lady of Garian'!

Tripoli itself still retained the atmosphere of a provincial Italian town. The second of the twin capitals, Benghazi, had a far more Arab flavour. In the early years of independence, it had been deemed necessary to preserve the balance between the two major provinces by transferring the Government lock stock and barrel from one capital to the other every second year. This meant, among other things, that the British Embassy had its headquarters in Tripoli and a Consulate-General in Benghazi for two years at a time and then vice versa. Fortunately, by 1962, we had decided to abandon this pantomine. Tripoli remained the base and Benghazi the outpost. The Consul-General there ranked second to the Ambassador in Tripoli, but as the latter's Head of Chancery I tended to be in charge *de facto* when he was away.

By 1962, the Libyans themselves had also concluded that the biennial flit was inefficient and uneconomical. Their solution was to build a third, supposedly neutral, capital in the Cyrenaican hills in a place called Baida. This appealed to the King because it had been the site of the first Sanusi 'lodge'. Unfortunately, it appealed to hardly anyone else. Libyan officials, obliged to move to the new seat of government from the comparative fleshpots of the coastal towns, resented Baida's remoteness and lack of amenities. Peripatetic ministers complained that there were now four capitals: Tripoli, Benghazi (where much of the administration remained), Baida, and 'in the air'. But at least this gave them a heaven-sent alibi when they wanted to escape from importunate diplomats: they were invariably somewhere else or on their way there. As for the long-suffering Diplomatic Corps itself, when the Foreign Ministry transferred to Baida only the Americans and the Belgians established offices there. We 'serviced' Baida from Benghazi. The Arab embassies were the most adamant of all in refusing to move.

There was a silver lining to this cloud. The British Embassy disposed of a *pied-à-terre* not far from Baida, in the shape of the Villa Graziani. This former residence of the Italian Marshal of that name overlooked the Graeco-Roman remains of Cyrene (modern Shahat) and had been taken over as a hot-weather retreat for the Ambassador and the Consul-General. But it was quite often necessary for lesser luminaries like myself to make the pilgrimage to Baida on business with the Foreign Ministry. These trips became something of a treat when we were able to combine them with a short stay in Cyrene, where a generous Ambassador made the cottage available, and to visit also the nearby beautiful site of Apollonia on the shores of the Mediterranean.

Christine's and my travels included some other memorable journeys. One was a drive from Tripoli to Tobruk and back – over 1000 miles each way – mostly along the coast road through so many places whose names were familiar from the exploits of the Eighth Army in World War II: 'Marble Arch', Agedabia and Derna, whose welcome greenery made it the most attractive town en route. Not far from Derna, in the Cyrenaican hills, there resided one of those remarkable and eccentric elderly English ladies who from time to time used to adorn the Middle Eastern scene. Miss Britten kept bees and supplied honey to the royal palace at Tobruk. Rumour had it that her fame had spread abroad as far as a Tommy serving in Benghazi who had made a pilgrimage to visit her in her mountain fastness, only to be disappointed to find that she was not, as some of his companions had told him, a former beauty queen who still retained her title of Miss Britain.

The object of our marathon drive was that I had to take a small part in a military exercise being staged at El Adem and to accompany, as interpreter, my Ambassador and a visiting General at an audience of the King. This was not a prospect I relished, since His Majesty was known to have an indistinct and piping treble voice which was none too easy to follow. I spent my off-duty hours in the days before the audience swotting up the likely vocabulary – and, when the area was deluged with rain and the Ambassador grounded in Benghazi, secretly hoping that he would not make it. His Excellency, however, was made of sterner stuff, and found alternative means of transport. In the event the royal encounter went off reasonably well, with the King indulging in reminiscences of the war and only once stumping me with an obscure joke which forced me to resort to the last refuge of the interpreter, 'I'm afraid I did not understand the last remark, but as it was clearly a funny one would you please be good enough to laugh?'

The only other item worth recording about El Adem was that the RAF station there was commanded by a Group Captain Jack Frost. The GOC-in-C Malta and Libya at the time was General Johnny Frost, of Arnhem fame, who appeared to find too little to detain him in Malta and was consequently a frequent visitor to Libya. To avoid confusion between the two, he was inevitably dubbed Ground Frost and the Group Captain Air Frost.

Another interesting trip was a flight down to Ghadames on the Algerian border and in the heartland of the Tuareg, wild desert tribesmen celebrated for veiling their men rather than their women. This was a day out thoughtfully arranged for the Diplomatic Corps by the Ministry of Foreign Affairs. We were greeted on arrival by troupes of tribal dancers who escorted us into the town with its covered streets and walkways rather like some oriental Chester; and entertained to a mammoth couscous lunch, followed by further noisy and colourful stick- and sword-dancing before returning from this glimpse of traditional Libya to the contrasting modernity of Tripoli.

A far more adventurous exploit was that undertaken by Martin Buckmaster, once again my intrepid colleague and still ploughing his own eccentric furrow. Who else would have chosen, as his last fling before transferring to his next post, to spend some local leave in the distant and remote Kufra Oasis? Much against his wishes, the British army authorities insisted on providing him with an escort. Somewhere in the parched desert, the accompanying soldiery came across what looked like a pool and stopped for a cooling dip. They later blamed Martin for allegedly misunderstanding a local Arab's warning that the pool was in fact a hot spring. At all events, some of them were scalded. First aid had to be summoned in the form of an RAF light aircraft, which then got stuck in the sand and had to be rescued in turn. Happily, no serious casualties resulted. Martin did not fail to point out that the whole episode could have been avoided if the escort had not been forced on him in the first place. However that may be, the consequent delay in his return meant that our farewell party in his honour was a case of Hamlet without the prince.

The RAF also featured in an amusing experience which befell me in Barce, a Cyrenaican town afflicted by a moderately severe earthquake in 1963. The Embassy and the British military mounted a modest relief operation, together with other humanitarian assistance which was rapidly forthcoming. This produced the remarkable phenomenon of an almost overnight quadrupling of the local population as word spread about the surrounding area that goodies were available.

Not long afterwards, I was on a routine visit to the district, and called in to see how the British reading-room – a manifestation of the Embassy's Information Section – was progressing. I found it completely deserted save for a somewhat forlorn Libyan supervisor. However, he was evidently a man of resource, for within minutes he had assembled a crowd of avid readers of our range of newspapers and magazines. As I sat chatting and drinking coffee with this audience, I noticed one old man struggling with the folds of his Arab robe. Eventually he pulled out a tattered wallet, from which he produced an even more tattered piece of paper. Smoothing it out with a gnarled hand, he proudly laid it on a table for my inspection. His demeanour suggested that the document was at least a citation for some past deed of valour. On closer examination, however, I saw that, above the signature of a Flight Lieutenant and a date in 1942, it said, 'This is to certify that Muhammad Ali al-Baruni has been of great help to the Royal Air Force, and has been amply rewarded for his services'. No doubt the unsuspecting Muhammad Ali had been carrying the chit about ever since in the belief that it represented a meal ticket when displayed to any itinerant Briton.

Although we naturally met some very agreeable Libyans, on the whole they were not my favourite Arabs. They appeared to have a marked xenophobic streak (not, perhaps, without reason in view of their history) and, like most highly sensitive people, tended to be notably insensitive to other people's sensibilities. On one occasion I was discussing with the Deputy Chief of Protocol in the Foreign Ministry the programme for a forthcoming visit by a British parliamentary delegation. They had to include a trip down to Tobruk, where the King was in residence at the time: not that they were actually going to call on him, but etiquette demanded that they sign the royal book. The Libyans themselves had few facilities in Tobruk, but British Petroleum did. In an effort to be helpful, I remarked that perhaps BP could be persuaded to give the MPs lunch.

'Mr Lucas!' exclaimed the aggrieved official, 'are you suggesting that we cannot look after our own guests?'

Mr Lucas retired with his tail between his legs. Some days later, about 24 hours before the delegation was due to arrive, the same functionary sent for me and, without batting an eyelid, informed me that the Ministry was having a little difficulty arranging suitable hospitality for the party in Tobruk, and did I think that BP might possibly help? I naturally replied that I was sure they would be delighted, and how clever he had been to think of it.

The BP terminal in Tobruk was the outlet for shipping the product of their important oil discovery in southern Cyrenaica, one of the first significant finds in the country. Before the new facilities were built, months of wrangling took place about wayleaves for the pipeline to run from the field through a multiplicity of tribal areas to the coast. The General Manager told me that when he eventually became exasperated by the slow and tortuous negotiations he went to see the King and appealed to him in these terms:

'Your Majesty, during the war I spent months in German-occupied Tobruk trying to discover ways of getting out. I never dreamed that, years later, I should find it even more difficult and time-consuming trying to get back in.' Idris promptly saw to it that the red tape was cut.

My first Ambassador in Tripoli was a congenial soul with an 'Indian' background and some Arab experience which included a spell as Consul-General in Jerusalem. Charles Stewart reminded me in some ways of my erstwhile Sharjah colleague, Christopher Pirie-Gordon. Neither was particularly zealous in the discharge of his official functions, yet when duty called both could be very effective. Stewart was the victim of a pernicious Treasury practice in those days. Members of the Service who had spent time in 'difficult' climates were entitled to count each year of such service as 18 months for the purpose of calculating pensionable age. The Treasury turned this on its head by requiring officers to retire when they reached the 'notional' age of 60. Stewart was coasting along in the belief that he still had another couple of years to go when he received, out of the blue, a letter from the Foreign Office informing him that he would be retiring within a matter of months. To add insult to injury, the day on which he finally left Tripoli and the Service was an appallingly wet one. His aircraft was diverted from Idris to Wheelus and then delayed there. By the time he eventually took off, the farewell party of friends and colleagues had gradually dwindled to one saddened Head of Chancery.

One of Charles Stewart's most endearing characteristics was the ability to tell a story against himself. I cherish two of these in particular. On 14 July one year he had promised to take his daughter to the cinema. There were, however, two national day parties on that evening – the Iraqi and the French. Since one was 'dry' and the other carried the risk of the champagne running out if one did not arrive reasonably early, priorities presented a problem. Charles decided on this occasion to leave the best till last. Reaching the French celebration a little late, he found that although the champagne had not run out, time was rapidly doing so. After doing the honours on the receiving line and walking into the garden where the party was being held, he began to look around for a way of escape which would not involve leaving by the same route and thus making it obvious to his hosts that he had given them such short shrift. He espied a small gate at the other end of the garden and started to make his way surreptitiously towards it. Just as he was reaching for the latch, he felt a light tap on his shoulder and, turning round, was horrified to see his French colleague.

'Eet's no good, mon ami,' beamed the latter, 'eet's locked'!

My opposite number in the French Embassy told me an indiscreet story about his chief. The Ambassador was being transferred. On enquiring when he would be taking up his new post (it was customary to brief our own Ambassadors about their new colleagues) I was surprised to learn that the date of arrival would be 15 July. Would this not mean, I asked, that His Excellency would miss the Quatorze Juillet?

'Oui, bien sûr – but zat ees zee point: you see, 'e 'as to pay for zee party out of 'ees own pocket if 'e is zere'.

'But would it not look better if he were to arrive, say, at the end of July?'

'Certainement – but zen 'e would lose two weeks' allowances!'

The new French Ambassador faced an even trickier problem. He began his mission as a very eligible bachelor, but during the course of it married an attractive and somewhat younger woman who was new to the diplomatic life. His Counsellor's wife, on the other hand, had been the wife of the Netherlands Ambassador in the Counsellor's previous post. Rumours reached us from the French Embassy that the two ladies did not exactly get on well together.

But I digress from the second Charles Stewart story, which is better suited to Lawrence Durrell's pen than to mine. The Chinese Nationalist Ambassador and his wife were among the most sociable and popular members of the Corps. Unfortunately they suffered the handicap of having no official relations with anyone else except the host country and the Americans: by that time the majority of the international community had recognised the Communist regime in Peking. An embarrassing possibility arose that Mr Chen, who had already been *en poste* for several years, might become the senior Head of Mission and therefore Dean of the Corps.

Charles and Caroline Stewart were among the Chens' closest friends, and they regularly played golf and bridge together – though it was, of course, impossible to invite them to any official functions, such as the Queen's Birthday. One day, Chen rang

Stewart and sought his advice over a problem of protocol which was troubling him.

'You know, Charles, that our Turkish colleague, the Dean, is leaving. In accordance with normal practice, it is up to our Egyptian colleague, as second in order of precedence, to arrange a farewell reception and to take over the papers of the Dean. But he refuses to do so because Egypt and Turkey have no diplomatic relations at present.'

'So what is bothering you about all this?' countered Stewart.

'Well, you see, as third in line I feel that I should try to mediate, but I don't quite see how to go about it.'

Stewart proposed a sensible British compromise. 'Why don't you talk to the Egyptian Ambassador, explain that you fully understand the formal position between him and the Turk, but suggest that he does the necessary on a purely personal basis?'

'Oh, but Charles, I couldn't possibly do that.'

'Why on earth not?' asked an increasingly exasperated Stewart.

'Because I myself am not in relations with the Egyptian, either'.

'If that is the difficulty, Chen,' Stewart finally exploded down the telephone, 'Why the hell are you ringing ME?'

In the brief interregnum between Charles Stewart and his successor in early 1964 a situation developed of the profoundest significance for the future of Anglo-Libyan relations, and indeed of Libya itself. The discontents described at the beginning of this chapter had rumbled on, encouraged by Cairo Radio. Not long after our arrival in September 1962, Idris saw fit to give one of his frequent shakes to the political kaleidoscope by appointing a new Prime Minister: he was rumoured to keep signed resignations in a drawer of his desk against the day when he would want to accept them. Truth to tell, this particular move suited me rather well. The outgoing premier had been a close friend of my predecessor, Bill Carden (a Sudan 'retread') who had achieved the unusual but almost fairy-tale feat for a diplomat of striking up an acquaintance with an up-and-coming politician before he became prominent, and this was an impossible act to follow. More seriously, I suspected that the change was a shrewd act on the King's part, designed to defuse the opposition by appointing a Prime Minister who was known to be more nationalistic than the previous incumbent: indeed Muhieddin Fekini was regarded by many Libyans as a surprising choice because of his radical reputation.

For a while the opposition tide, if not stemmed, at least appeared to be running less strongly. But now, in January 1964, student trouble in Benghazi spread to the streets and farther afield to Tripolitania. For the first time, demonstrations and disturbances raised slogans against the King himself. Hitherto Idris had been securely insulated from criticism, which was always directed against his Ministers. Troops were called out in Benghazi and there were casualties among the rioters, a few of them fatal.

It seemed that we might be witnessing a turning-point. In a further twist to the game of musical chairs, Idris dismissed Fekini and recalled an old retainer in Mahmud Muntasser. The Muntassers were a respected Tripolitanian family despite suspicions that they had been a little too friendly to the Italians in colonial days. They were cast in a traditional mould, as Christine and I learned when we invited to our house a younger scion of the family who worked for an oil company and was married to a well-connected and French-educated Libyan girl. We had got to know them quite well and visited their home once or twice. But a return match was acceptable only on the understanding that there should only be the four of us and no domestics. It was not, they explained, that the couple themselves had any objection to normal social contacts, but if their families came to hear of it…

Mahmud Muntasser had been prominent in negotiating the arrangements whereby Britain obtained her military facilities after independence. The scene accordingly seemed to be set for a crack-down on the opposition and the untroubled continuation of our 'special relationship' with Libya. It was at this stage that the new Ambassador arrived. Within three weeks, Muntasser announced that Libya did not intend to renew the British and American agreements when they expired. Since they still had some time to run, and the Ambassador's initial contacts with the Libyan authorities persuaded him that Muntasser's statement was only a stalling device until the heat went out of the current situation, this was not taken too tragically. Soon, however, the internal crisis reached a climax with the King's sudden and wholly unexpected decision to abdicate. In the prevailing Arab fashion of the time, he was rapidly dissuaded by 'popular acclaim' from implementing the decision.

This confirmed the Ambassador in his view that Muntasser had lost his nerve, that the King was manoeuvring to restore the position and that if we only sat tight the storm would pass. It was perhaps natural that an Ambassador taking up his first post as Head of Mission was not keen to start off by advising Whitehall that we had to accept a 'scuttle'. He therefore clutched at every available straw; and, to be fair, the messages coming from the Libyans were confused and contradictory. Nevertheless, the advice which he was getting from lower down the line in the Embassy was that, whether or not the authorities wanted the British and American bases to be liquidated and their troops withdrawn, the internal and external pressures were such that the process was not reversible. One could almost envisage the last British soldier leaving the beach while a Libyan said soothingly, 'Don't worry, old boy – we don't really mean it'.

This debate continued within the Embassy for most of my remaining time there, until July 1966. But the Libyans reaffirmed their demand for our withdrawal, protracted negotiations took place about the modalities, Prime Ministers came and went, and the King staged a second abdication crisis, with the same outcome as the first. My role in all this (apart from the ungrateful one of playing the Devil's Advocate with the Ambassador) was to co-ordinate with our own military authorities the minutiae of our negotiating position with the Libyans, and then to head the team which conducted the detailed talks with the latter. I found this a fascinating exercise, not least because the first part of it proved considerably harder work than the second. The Treasury tried to drive some ridiculous bargains about equipment which it would be impracticable to take out of the country anyway. The upshot was that some months before my departure the bulk of the facilities in Tripolitania had been closed down, and those farther east followed in due course. I left with the uncomfortable feeling that my Ambassador had never forgiven me. If so, he consoled himself by helping to negotiate a lucrative contract for the supply of a Rapier air defence system which puzzled even Libyans who were not opposed to the regime.

'If there is a threat,' they said, 'it does not come from up there but from down there' (meaning subversion from neighbouring Egypt). In the event the contract was one of the first casualties of the Qadhafi coup.

During these frenetic times, we regularly discussed among ourselves the possibility that the days of Sanusi rule were numbered, how long it might survive and who would bring about its downfall. With the wisdom of hindsight, I believe we were right to see in the Benghazi disturbances of January 1964 the writing on the wall. It took another six years or so for the coup to be mounted. When it came, in September 1969, the perpetrators were not the military men we had identified three years earlier but those one or two ranks below them. What became of the Cyrenaican 'backwoodsmen' – the tribesmen who would never let the King down – I do not know.

I cannot leave the shores of Tripoli without recalling two of those 'things that children say'. We were entertaining to lunch *en famille* one day an Embassy colleague who was visiting from Benghazi. The conversation turned to another colleague, whom we knew to be a particular friend of our guest, whereupon 10-year-old Mark interjected, 'Oh, Mummy can't stand him'.

In the stunned silence that followed he added for good measure, looking at our nanny, 'And what's more, Penny can't either'.

Christine and I drove home from Tripoli, leaving Penny to bring the two younger boys later by air. When we went to meet them at Heathrow, we asked eight-year-old Crispin about his parting from the pet dog he had acquired from the army.

'When I said good-bye to Brownie,' he announced solemnly, 'I thought I saw a great big tear rolling down her cheek'.

8

Whitehall Warrior

At the beginning of October 1966 I joined the Central Department of the Foreign Office as Assistant Head. This was another 'rag-bag' department, though in this case of a geographical nature. We covered all Europe except the Common Market and the Communist countries. In other words, we dealt with the Nordic lands; the neutrals, Austria and Switzerland; Spain and Portugal; and Greece and Turkey.

Of these, the last two groups caused the most work. This was a period when the Gibraltar issue came to one of its not infrequent heads and there were troubles in Cyprus. Although both territories were the principal responsibility of the Colonial and of the Commonwealth Relations Offices respectively, the Foreign Office were closely involved because of the Spanish claim to Gibraltar and the Greek and Turkish interests in Cyprus, not to mention the repercussions of both disputes on NATO and in the United Nations. My 15 months in the department also saw important developments on the Greek internal scene and a State Visit by the President of Turkey. Both were to contribute greatly to my education.

So did the Head of Department, Alan Davidson, a meticulous operator whose concern with detail could sometimes irritate but was an object-lesson for his juniors. He was later to take early retirement from the Service to pursue his first love, seafood, on which he produced a number of learned publications. I soon found that my role in the department was to supervise the work other than that on Gibraltar and Cyprus, which Alan made his own preserve – except, of course, that I was expected to pick up the threads whenever he was away.

Over all loomed the enigmatic and rumbustious figure of Her Majesty's Principal Secretary of State for Foreign Affairs, George Brown. Although the nature and scope of Central Department's responsibilities made it inevitable that we should work long hours and quite a few weekends, I believe that a great deal of what we – and other departments in the Office at that time – did was not so much to deal with problems as to 'be seen to be active'. Brown himself was an incorrigible activist, even when masterly inactivity would have been the wiser policy. My father told me how he had once encountered George Brown in the corridors of Westminster when the London evening papers had given him a particularly rough time. My father had commiserated with him.

'I don't give a damn for bad publicity,' George had replied robustly. 'It's no publicity that I worry about.'

As a result he had a rather pernicious influence on the Office. Officials spent an inordinate amount of time 'getting something into the Secretary of State's box' at night, even if the 'something' was a nil report.

I had a taste of this myself on one occasion. I happened to be in charge of the department late one evening in December 1967. It was the day that King Constantine had vainly attempted to unseat the hated regime of the Colonels in Athens. Our Ambassador, Sir Michael Stewart, had been in London for consultations and had returned to his post earlier that day, though due to the situation in Athens there were reports that the airport was closed. A perfectly competent Chargé d'Affaires was coping with the crisis from the Embassy end.

At about 7pm the telephone rang – a call from Brussels, where the Foreign Secretary was attending a NATO ministerial meeting. I at once recognised the far from dulcet tones.

'Where is Michael Stewart?' they barked down the line.

'We know that he took off from London this morning, Sir,' I replied, 'but there are conflicting reports about his onward journey and we cannot be quite sure where he is at the moment'.

'Are you being deliberately obstructive?' demanded the voice belligerently. 'Find out immediately where he is and tell him to get in touch with me.'

So I spent the rest of the evening, and a great deal of taxpayers' money to boot, ringing numerous points between London and Athens to enquire whether anyone had any news of the whereabouts of Michael Stewart. He was eventually tracked down in Nicosia, from where he duly telephoned Brussels, and no doubt George Brown was able to reassure his NATO colleagues at dinner that evening that he was in the closest possible touch with developments in Athens.

On the other hand, he was an extraordinarily warm-hearted character. While his somewhat unorthodox approach to diplomatic business may not always have commended itself to the more traditional envoys to the Court of St James's (any more than it did to his own officials) several third world representatives told me how much George Brown's 'informality' appealed to them: 'So different,' they said, 'from the conventional stuffed-shirt attitude we expected of the British'. Different indeed – but of that more anon.

Meanwhile I had a glimpse of his more endearing side when attending the Secretary of State while he was receiving a deputation of left-wing Labour MPs who had come to remonstrate over what they regarded as the Government's supine attitude to the tyrannical regime in Athens. How, they asked, could a Labour Government have any truck with the Colonels? We should break off diplomatic relations, and Greece should be expelled from NATO and thrown out of the West European Union.

George Brown listened patiently to this exposition. In reply, he said that there was no difference between the MPs and himself on objectives: both sides wanted Greece to return as soon as possible to the path of parliamentary democracy. But their way, far from achieving this common aim, would only make the Colonels dig their toes in. The answer was persuasion, not boycott, and if one had disagreements with a foreign government it was all the more necessary to maintain contacts with it. And more of the same, along the lines of the department's brief.

Slightly mollified by this response, the deputation took its leave. As the door closed behind his party colleagues, George Brown made for the drinks cabinet and, turning to his Private Secretary and me, said, 'You know, none of that bloody lot could run a toffee shop in this country. But they all know how to run Greece!'

Whether they did or not, Greece occupied an enormous amount of parliamentary attention throughout 1967. MPs on all sides of the House were concerned with different aspects of the internal situation there, and with its impact on Cyprus. It was interesting to observe that for some of them, practices which had been condoned during the previous, supposedly democratic, regime now became reprehensible when perpetrated by a dictatorship. The department was called upon to produce a stream of briefs, cabinet papers and answers to parliamentary questions, the large pink label attached to the latter being guaranteed to strike terror into every bureaucratic heart. Most of these documents had to be dictated under pressure of time, and noses were regularly kept to the grindstone till comparatively late at night. It was all very stimulating, and generally speaking one did not realise just how exhausting it was until the pressure eased and one came up for air. Even then, the force of habit died hard and some of my colleagues still seemed to find pressing reasons for staying at their desks till 8 and 9pm.

If officials led busy lives in these circumstances, the lot of ministers was even more hazardous. They could not possibly give their decisions the detailed attention which most issues required: there were too many problems and not enough time. The successful minister was the one who spotted the banana skin, mastered a brief rapidly and, above all, had an instinct for the answer rather than the expert knowledge. The day after my roasting by George Brown, we had to deal with a private notice question on the situation in Greece following King Constantine's failed coup. A 'PNQ' usually arrived on one's desk late in the morning and was for answer in the House early in the afternoon. There was no time to go through the normal routine in handling PQs (ie get them pronounced out of order or find some reason why they were more properly the business of another department!). On this particular occasion it fell to the Prime Minister to answer. Harold Wilson could not have received our brief much before lunchtime. I was in 'the box' in the House when he rose to his feet at 2.30. He dealt with the original question and a string of supplementaries not only without having to refer to 'the box' but as though Greece had been his meat and drink for the previous six months. It was a masterly performance – and must, of course, have been a masterly brief!

It was Turkey, however, which engaged my attention more than any other country in the departmental parish – and which provided my only 'perks', apart from *Figaro* at Covent Garden in honour of the veteran Norwegian statesman Halvard Lange (my pleasure in which was alloyed by Government Hospitality's stinginess in not including Christine in the party). In the summer of 1967 I accompanied Fred Mulley, as Minister of State in the Foreign Office, on an official visit to Ankara and Istanbul. We had only two days in each, and what with attending the Minister's calls in the morning and writing them up in the afternoon while he was on some touristic jaunt, I saw all too little of either. But it whetted my appetite for a country which had already engaged my interest as one which appeared to have thrown off the shackles of the more restrictive aspects of Islam without having lost the spirit of the faith. Nevertheless the constant paeans of praise lavished officially on the achievements of Atatürk, and the importance attached to the rituals which foreign dignitaries were required to perform in that connection (such as the obligatory wreath-laying at the hideous Germanic mausoleum visible all over Ankara) were a little irksome for comfort. It was no surprise to learn from independent observers of the local scene that there was a strong Islamic backlash in the countryside, where tradition held greater sway than in the cities. For me, this kind of background was to assume even more interest and significance ten years later when I was involved in the death throes of another reforming regime, in neighbouring Iran, and the repercussions of the revolution there.

Ankara, set in the middle of the Anatolian plain and a permanent cloud of pollution, was not an attractive capital. But Istanbul, where we had a permanent Consul-General and a peripatetic Ambassador rather on Tripoli/Benghazi lines, struck me as having all the ingredients of a satisfying post. Alive with history and bedecked with elegant architecture, it offered a range of job satisfaction in the consular, commercial and political fields as well as a variety of leisure interests which few places could match. Alas, it was never my lot to be appointed there.

The official talks concentrated largely on the Middle East, in the wake of the Six-Day War of the previous month (in which I had found my sympathies less engaged on the Arab side than in the conflict of 1956); and Cyprus, then boiling up for the crisis at the end of the year when the island was to totter on the very brink of hostilities. They included a call on Prime Minister Sulaiman Demirel, who was then presiding over one of the periodic spells of civilian rule and is now President of Turkey. Some of the informal exchanges were of a lighter kind, like the following snatch of overheard conversation.

The Minister of State, to the Secretary-General of the Turkish Foreign Ministry: 'The Commonwealth Office are a damned nuisance to us'.

The Ambassador, interjecting: 'The Commonwealth Office are even worse'.

The Minister: 'I said the Commonwealth Office'.

The Ambassador: 'Sorry, I thought you said the Commonwealth'.

In November 1967, President Sunay of Turkey paid a State Visit to Britain. I had never before been involved in the preparations for such an occasion or in their fruition, and found the experience illuminating. Apart from discussing detailed arrangements and providing extensive briefing, the department was called upon to draft a series of speeches. These were inevitably variations on an all-too-limited theme for different formal functions, including the Queen's Banquet at the Palace, the Lord Mayor's at Guildhall, and the Foreign Secretary's dinner at Hampton Court, followed by a reception and ballet performance.

The problem was, of course, to find something fresh to say, and to suit it to whoever was going to say it. We ran into snags at every turn. Research revealed that President Sunay was following in the footsteps of Sultan Abdul Aziz who had visited Queen Victoria exactly 100 years before. The Sultan had in fact travelled by train from London to Windsor for the purpose. An appropriate theme suggested itself for Her Majesty: to contrast conditions then with conditions now, with particular reference to the time taken for the journey, as an example of the extraordinary progress made over the past century. Unfortunately, we had to drop this idea when we discovered that it actually took longer to go by train from London to Windsor in 1967 than in 1867!

The Palace rejected our first draft. The Lord Mayor did not like what we submitted either. In the event he went largely his own way, which meant treading heavily on the thin ice of which he had been warned, and coming out with toe-curling references to 'the terrible Turk', harems and Turkish delight. But the Guildhall Banquet was Christine's and my first experience of such glittering occasions, and nothing could detract from the impeccable organisation and magnificent ceremonial – even if it did not quite match the dazzling impression created by Sultan Abdul Aziz who had reportedly 'arrived on a white charger, his uniform scintillating with medals, and with the traditional aigrette of diamonds on his fez'.[7]

Needless to say, the most difficult customer of all proved to be George Brown himself. The Embassy in Ankara were keen that we should include in at least one of the speeches a tale of the Mulla Nasruddin – a legendary figure of fun who appears in various guises throughout the Middle East – as a nod in the direction of Turkish culture. I chose one which seemed appropriate to the vexed question of Cyprus. Nasruddin had been appointed a magistrate. At his first case, he was deeply impressed by the eloquence of the plaintiff, and after hearing his evidence he exclaimed, 'I believe you are right!'

The clerk of the court explained that he should make no such comment until he had heard the case for the defence. Having done so, Nasruddin cried out, 'I believe you are right!'

'But they can't both be right,' expostulated the clerk.

'I believe you are right,' said the Mulla.

It so happened that a few days before his dinner for President Sunay, George Brown had behaved particularly outrageously at some diplomatic function where he had publicly castigated his Permanent Under-Secretary for not having briefed him properly, whereas he had in fact not read the papers put up to him. When he came to the Nasruddin passage, he began:

'I've been told to tell this story. I don't understand the point of it, but as I've been getting into trouble recently for not sticking to my brief I'd better tell it all the same!'

Despite these alarums, the State Visit was voted a resounding success. One of the things which nearly derailed it before it had even started, however, was a possibility that we had to exert all our diplomatic skills to avoid. This was that it might coincide with the historic visit to the Archbishop of Canterbury by His Beatitude Athenagoras III, the Ecumenical Patriarch, head of the Eastern Orthodox Church. (As it was, we had to contend with the simultaneous arrival on a private visit of King Constantine. 'All we need now,' commented Alan Davidson drily, 'is for Makarios to turn up!')

In the event, we managed to insert a week between the temporal and the spiritual. The invitation to the Patriarch was of considerable historic significance in the context of Anglican/Orthodox relations. I attended a Lambeth Palace Reception at which all the guests lined up to pay their respects to this venerable figure – and at least one of them found it difficult, on rising from the kneeling position, to avoid becoming entangled in the flowing ecumenical beard. This was followed by a most impressive solemn evensong in Westminster Abbey, celebrated in the presence of the Archbishop and the Patriarch.

These stirring events took place at a time of family sadness for me. While I was engaged in the final stages of the preparations for President Sunay, my father suffered his second stroke in 18 months, and succumbed to it a few days later without regaining consciousness. Moreover, the news of his demise reached us some hours afterwards, when the family had gathered around my mother at their flat in Victoria and I was deputed to telephone the hospital for a report on his condition. The ensuing days were fairly traumatic, helping my brother to arrange the funeral service at St Margaret's, followed by a harrowing train journey to Oxford where, in pouring rain, my father was laid to rest close to his own parents in Wolvercote Cemetery.

One faint silver lining in the cloud is the memory of the doctor calling at the flat in Roebuck House before my father was removed to hospital. Eyeing his black bag with interest, our four-year-old son enquired innocently, 'Have you come to mend my Grandpa?'

Despite the stimulus of the work, and the valuable lessons learned from it, I never felt that Whitehall was quite my scene. My pace was not suited to a system in which nearly everything had to be done yesterday, if not the day before. Nor was my temperament attuned to the office politics and inter-departmental infighting which feature so prominently in the corridors of power. I was therefore pleased as well as surprised to learn early in 1968 that I was to be promoted to Counsellor, on appointment to the newly-established Embassy in Aden, now capital of the People's Republic of South Yemen and of the first (and only) Marxist regime in the Arab world.

We rapidly dismantled some recently-concluded arrangements to buy a house near Kingston, but were not to know that the new posting was also to involve another lengthy separation to add to those of 1955 and 1963/4 when Christine had to go home from Bahrain and Tripoli respectively to produce our first and third sons.

9

Barren Rocks

A week before I was due to fly to Aden with my family, the Foreign Office telephoned to say that, owing to the local situation, I should have to go unaccompanied in the first instance, though they hoped that this would be no more than a temporary hiccup. In fact, our separation was to last for nearly three months. The original reason for it was that the newly-independent Government of the People's Republic of South Yemen had just decided to expel the British pilots who were working with the South Yemen Air Force when constraints were placed by the British authorities on their operational role. A minor crisis in our relations ensued, and it was judged inadvisable after all to rescind the ban on Embassy families proceeding to Aden which had been in force since the traumatic events leading to the British withdrawal, and South Yemeni independence, in November 1967. On several subsequent occasions the Foreign Office almost screwed its courage to the sticking point and raised the ban, but each time some new crisis supervened and they changed their minds. What made this all the more galling was that British business houses in Aden saw no problem about allowing their families to come out, so celibacy was confined to the Embassy staff. Easter holidays having come and gone with this state of suspended animation prevailing, when the summer vacation began to loom we concocted a telegram to the Office requesting an early decision since 'continued uncertainty is making family planning impossible': this evidently made someone at home sit up and take notice, and Christine and George duly joined me on June 1. I believe that the real reason for the vacillation in Whitehall was that ever since independence we had had a naval presence 'over the horizon' in case things went wrong and an emergency evacuation of the British community became necessary. In order to persuade the Ministry of Defence that HM ships should continue to be committed to this role, the Foreign Office had to demonstrate that a crisis situation persisted, and to allow Embassy families to take up residence in Aden would have undermined their argument.

However that may be, post-independence South Yemen undoubtedly was in a state of flux, and Britain's relations with the new rulers were understandably delicate. Not for the first time in the Middle East, the 'backwoodsmen' in whom we had placed our trust proved in the event to be broken reeds. When it had become clear some years earlier that withdrawal from Aden and the Protectorates was inevitable in terms of both regional and domestic politics, Britain had tried to leave behind some semblance of order in the shape of another of those ill-fated federations which were fashionable at the time. In the present case, the theory was that such a constitutional structure would enable the traditional rulers from the hinterland to counterbalance the hotheads from the trade unions in Aden. The outcome of the bloody struggle against the British, but even more between the rival factions competing for future power, had, however, been that while it was indeed the hinterland that ruled, it was the hinterland represented not by the old tribal leaders but by those who had overthrown them, and on independence emerged as the Marxist National Liberation Front regime, dedicated to 'scientific socialism' at home and the encouragement of 'liberation movements' abroad, especially in the Arabian Peninsula.

The revolution soon began to devour its own children. Only a couple of weeks after my arrival, a serious clash took place between 'leftist' and 'rightist' factions within the regime, and the pattern of 'corrective movements' – some peaceful, others violent – was to continue. To oversimplify, what happened was that a leader with impeccable revolutionary credentials, such as the first President of the Republic, Qahtan ash-Sha'abi, would assume power. He would then find that even revolutionaries had to live in the world as it is, not the world as they would like it to be. He would begin to advocate more pragmatic policies and to make tentative advances to non-revolutionary neighbours. The latter then tended to draw unreal distinctions between 'moderates' and 'extremists' in the regime, whereas the difference was a less clear-cut one between pragmatists and idealists. Eventually another 'leftist' would move to occupy the revolutionary ground, accuse the incumbent of reactionary deviationism and oust him – by fair means if possible or foul if necessary. The cycle would then start all over again.

Similar processes have occurred elsewhere. In the South Yemeni case, as we shall see, the pattern was to be repeated at frequent intervals over the next few years.

It was against this kind of background that we set about the task of building a relationship with the newly-independent state. In governmental circles – though not at the popular level – there was considerable resentment against the British. The once-flourishing economy of Aden had rested on three pillars. First, the market for goods and services represented by some 25,000 British troops and their dependants. The South Yemenis could hardly blame us for the removal of that prop, though they had some cause for complaint that the economy had been so service-based in both senses of the word. Secondly, there had been the tourist and bunkering trades connected with the traffic through the Suez Canal. The combined effects of the Suez War in 1956 and the Six-Day War of 1967, with their closure of the canal and diversion to other routes, had virtually put paid to that source of revenue. Thirdly, there was the BP refinery at Little Aden. This continued to operate, but only at a considerably reduced capacity in view of the other factors. The newly-independent state therefore faced a tight economic situation. Revolutionary fervour helped them to some extent to bear it and to deal with the inevitable privations. But enthusiasm for the new order was not widespread, nor of itself sufficient to solve the economic problems, though the regime deserved credit for its courage in introducing a belt-tightening process.

Nevertheless, the Government looked to Britain to help, by fulfilling her earlier commitment to provide £60 million in aid over the first five years of independence. But of course that promise had been to the authorities which HMG had thought would constitute the new Government. When this turned out to be the terrorists who had put such a violent end to colonial rule, there was no disposition at all in London to loosen the purse-strings, particularly at a time of economic crisis at home which had recently caused a devaluation of the pound. When, therefore, we embarked on post-independence aid talks with the South Yemenis, with the Embassy reinforced for the purpose by a strong team from the Foreign Office and the Overseas Development Administration, the offer we put on the table was no more than £1.25 million for the first year, instead of the £12 million to which the South Yemenis considered themselves entitled. They contemptuously rejected our proposals. However justified the British position, and whether or not the NLF would in any case have turned to the Eastern Bloc, the fact remains that from that moment onwards South Yemen was firmly committed to the Soviet camp. A far-ranging programme of nationalisation expropriated most of the British commercial ventures in the country, as well as long-established Indian enterprises like the celebrated firm of Bhicajee Cowasjee at Steamer Point; facilities were made available to Russian warships, which began increasingly to be seen in the harbour; a fully-staffed Soviet Embassy made its appearance; and the East Germans erected a repressive security apparatus on behalf of their new friends. During the time that I acted as Chargé d'Affaires in the interregnum between two Ambassadors from August 1968 to March 1969, the Foreign Office saw fit to ask for an official assessment of Soviet penetration: were the Russians coming? I could only reply, in effect, 'Yes – what else did you expect?'

Politically, this was a difficult time. Contacts with the authorities became few, fruitless and frustrating. We were obliged to attend endless official functions at which the British and the Americans were lampooned to the point of insult. Several times the stage was almost reached at which dignity demanded a walk-out. My US colleague in fact once essayed such a demonstration. It was at an open-air public meeting somewhere up-country. Personal insults to the American President became too much for him to bear. He rose from his seat in the front row, stalked to the back of the assembly with all eyes turned on him, and climbed into his Jeep, only to find that the wretched vehicle would not start!

An even greater irritation was the restrictions placed on private movement outside the immediate vicinity of Aden. These were applied with particular rigour to the diplomatic and consular corps. A friend of ours who was the local Shell representative, and also the Honorary Consul of the Netherlands, drove his car one day to the checkpoint about five miles along the road to Lahej. Since the vehicle carried a 'CC' plate, he was smartly turned back. Half an hour later, he returned, in his wife's car, which bore no such incriminating evidence. Despite being eminently recognisable because of a luxuriant growth of beard and thick-rimmed spectacles, he was then allowed through without question.

I protested to the Permanent Secretary in the Ministry of Foreign Affairs on one occasion about these restrictions. Was it really necessary to obtain written permission from the Ministry two weeks in advance of making even such a simple excursion as a Sunday afternoon picnic in Lahej, 25 miles away?

'Our people are very angry with you for 128 years of colonialist misrule,' the official explained gravely, 'and since we are responsible for your safety, we must know where you are going so that we can make the necessary security arrangements'.

'I am surprised to hear that,' I replied with perfect sincerity. 'On the streets of Aden, and elsewhere when I have been able to go outside, I have met nothing but courtesy and friendliness.'

'Ah,' said the Permanent Secretary, not to be outdone, 'that just shows how magnanimous our people are'.

In the autumn of 1968 we had a rare opportunity of getting to see something of the hinterland, when the Diplomatic Corps was invited to accompany President Qahtan on a series of trips – mostly by air – to some of the outlying governorates where he was distributing title deeds to the fortunate beneficiaries of his recent land reform. Although we paid a heavy price in terms of a further surfeit of revolutionary oratory, the attractive villages and green uplands were ample compensation. We were also most hospitably treated, even if the sight of the fatted calf being slaughtered for one's benefit is not guaranteed to whet the appetite. The public relations aspects, however, went somewhat awry at Zingibar, not far along the coast from Aden. Here Qahtan suffered the indignity of being rudely interrupted when part of the crowd began to fling their shoes at him – a signal insult – and to raise slogans in favour of a local hero called 'Salimin'. This proved to be the first public sign of disaffection, for 'Salimin' was the party 'alias' of Salim Rubai'a, who was to depose Qahtan a few months later.

Considering that the Aden Colony and Protectorates had been areas where, unlike the Gulf, Britain exercised both responsibility and power, our track record compared unfavourably in some respects with that in the Gulf. As already mentioned, a thriving service economy had been built up in Aden itself, but by its very nature was not destined to survive the withdrawal of those who sustained it. We bequeathed an efficient port and a profitable oil refinery, but both these depended on uncontrollable outside factors. Some modest economic development had taken place in the Protectorates; and we could claim to have kept the peace until the warring factions turned against us as well as each other. But by and large Aden was not a monument to imperial endeavour, and the circumstances of our departure left some bitter legacies.

One with which I became particularly concerned was the payment of pensions to Adeni officials who had given long and faithful service to the colonial administration, and many of whom had been persuaded to stay on to oversee the transition to independence, even when the going had become extremely rough. The end had come so rapidly and chaotically that the normal post-colonial arrangements had not been negotiated, so that these unfortunate officials had found themselves between the devil and the deep blue sea: HMG firmly maintained the principle that their pensions were the responsibility of the successor Government, while the South Yemenis argued forcefully that they could not be expected to reward services of which they had strongly disapproved; and in any case, thanks to British parsimony, they could not afford to do so. It took several years before Whitehall could be persuaded to honour its moral commitment, and even then the payments in question were made in the form of 'loan advances' in order to preserve the sacred principle. The resolution of few problems in my diplomatic experience gave me greater satisfaction than this.

Having been promoted Counsellor in an Embassy which at the time seemed likely to be a fairly busy one, I found after the first few months that I was spending a certain amount of my time writing to the Foreign Office to say that there was not really enough to do, and the Embassy could be drastically pruned. The reason was that following the failure of the aid talks the South Yemenis ceased to take much interest in the British. Apart from trying to follow the intricacies of local politics, which in the nature of things was very difficult, and to preserve what one could of the British commercial stake in the country, which became increasingly so, we acted as a listening post for events in North Yemen, then still in the grip of civil war. During the colonial era, it had been the constant complaint of Arab nationalists and others that it was only the diabolical British, with their traditional policy of 'divide and rule', who were keeping the two Yemens apart. The irony was that following the British departure from Aden the gap between them grew wider. The Republicans in San'a were middle-of-the-road rulers, conscious of their powerful Saudi neighbours and adept in the art of attracting aid from all quarters. Despite their continuing struggle against the Royalists they had little in common with the Marxists in Aden.

In 1967, Egypt's defeat in the Six-Day War with Israel compelled Nasser to withdraw his troops, who had been supporting the Republicans. The civil war ended in the emergence of a moderate republic in San'a. The ritual rhetoric on both sides of the border continued to proclaim the unity of the two Yemens, and occasionally talks were held about translating the principle into practice. But it was largely a case of kissing one day and killing the next. When, as one offshoot of the collapse of the Soviet Union, the Yemens finally merged in 1990, San'a gradually asserted itself as the senior partner. Another, briefer, civil war took place in 1994. This was not, as previously, among the northern factions but between the old north and the old south and resulted in San'a confirming its supremacy within the union.

My tour in Aden lasted only 15 months and, despite the drawbacks, it was a happy time for us. Aden has the reputation of being a thoroughly disagreeable place. But for those whose acquaintance is longer than that of the transit passengers we ourselves had been ten years before on the way to Karachi, it has a number of attractions. Even the celebrated 'barren rocks' had their moments. One retired Governor entitled his memoirs of a lifetime of service in Aden and the Protectorates *Shades of Amber*[8]. He explained this by recounting how, prior to their first posting, he and his wife had asked an Archbishop who knew Aden well if it was true that there was nothing green there at all?

'Green?' the Archbishop mused. 'No, I wouldn't say so; but there really are the most delightful shades of amber.'

We had a good view of the changing hues of the rocks at different times of day, and of the pleasant aspect across Steamer Point and the harbour to Little Aden, from our house on the hill at Tarshyne. The Embassy had been fortunate in inheriting a prime site for its compound, which included offices previously the regional headquarters of the Ministry of Works, and senior staff housing previously occupied by the top military brass (our own had been the residence of the Air Office Commanding). Down the hill and across the road were staff flats and houses of impressive quality; and a statue of Queen Victoria which had stood in public gardens at Steamer Point but had been rescued by some heroic exploit shortly before withdrawal. It must have been about the same time as departing troops with a sense of humour had placed on one of the highest of the barren rocks two large spherical objects which remained visible for miles round. The compound also boasted an excellent club with an air-conditioned restaurant and facilities for open-air film shows which became a focal point for the British and diplomatic communities on Sunday evenings. We owed much of this to an enterprising Ministry of Works official named Fred

Rummer who was one of those rare birds prepared to bend the rules if not actually to break them.

Morale in the Embassy, as often happens in the more 'difficult' posts, was as high as I knew it anywhere in the Service. One reason for this was that it was run in an unusually democratic way: I recall, for example, that when the internal crisis erupted a week or two after my arrival, almost the entire staff gathered round the club bar at lunchtime to discuss the latest developments and how we should report them to London! Another reason was that we were lucky in our Ambassadors. The first British Ambassador to the People's Republic of South Yemen (subsequently named the People's Democratic Republic of Yemen, known to the cognoscenti, somewhat incongruously, as 'P-DRY') was Robin Hooper. For a man with such a remarkable war record (DSO, DFC, Legion of Honour and Croix de Guerre with two palms) he was equally remarkable for his modesty, amounting at times to actual shyness. My only previous encounter with him had been in 1951 when, as Head of the Personnel Department, he had given me my 'new boy's jaw'. It would be difficult to say which of us was the more embarrassed. Robin shifted from one foot to the other, and finally gave a deferential sort of cough as a preliminary to whispering, 'I've been trying to think of the best advice I can give you... On the whole, I think you shouldn't get married until you've been at least five years in the Service'. I forebore to remind him in Aden that I had in fact ignored this piece of counsel, with excellent results!

This wise, experienced and delightful man left on transfer in August 1968, and I held the fort until the arrival of his successor in March 1969. Part of the reason for the long interregnum was a characteristic misunderstanding in the Ministry of Foreign Affairs. The new Ambassador whom I was to propose to them was John Phillips, a former rugby international and member of the Sudan Political Service (one of a number of 're-treads' who joined the Foreign Service when Sudan – among other territories – became independent). Currently Deputy High Commissioner in Cyprus, he had as Consul-General in Muscat some years before written a classic despatch reporting his attempts to identify, at the request of the Foreign Office, the music of the National Salute to the Sultan (known in the vernacular of the British soldiery at the time as 'Gawd Strike the Sultan Blind'). The quest was complicated by the fact that the only known version of the anthem was on a gramophone record last played at an evening reception in honour of Sultan Sa'id bin Taimur, who had afterwards inadvertently sat on it.

I duly requested *agrément* from the South Yemenis. Their governmental processes dragged on for weeks. Rumours started circulating about the identity of the new Ambassador. An aunt of a member of the Embassy staff wrote from Nicosia saying that she had seen baggage belonging to John Phillips – addressed to Aden. A Sudanese adviser in the Foreign Ministry approached me at a party and demanded in a loud voice to know when his old friend Phillips was arriving. The look on my face evoked the rapid follow-up: 'Oh – have I said something wrong?'

I began to have visions of a situation in which *agrément* would be refused on the grounds of a premature leak. Eventually I was instructed to press for an answer. I went to see my old friend the Permanent Secretary to enquire the reason for the delay. He looked at me sheepishly, and finally admitted that the Ministry were afraid that Phillips might be the same who had been turned down by the Saudis some years previously, following publication in a Jewish journal of a report that he would be the first Jew to be appointed British Ambassador. I was able to reassure him that this had been the luckless Horace of that ilk, and not even a relation of John.

Hardly had John arrived when he was faced with a new crisis, less important perhaps than those which we had already survived but destined to make a far greater impact on the Embassy's prospects in Aden. For some time the delights of the compound had been impaired by the attentions of the South Yemeni guards who were stationed at the gates, ostensibly to keep out intruders but in practice to ensure that we ourselves did not remove from the premises items which they regarded as part of the 'national heritage'. Even the innocent and simple business of transferring a refrigerator from one side of the compound to the other across the road became a hazardous occupation because of the interference of these zealots. But the real blow fell when the newly-arrived Ambassador was summoned to the Foreign Ministry to be told that the Embassy must leave the desirable properties at Tarshyne –'for security reasons' (the President's house was in the vicinity). The demand was not entirely unexpected, nor for that matter unreasonable. John Phillips was accordingly in a position to respond diplomatically that while of course the South Yemenis were perfectly within their rights in making the request, HMG would wish to discuss the question of compensation. The Foreign Minister agreed readily enough, adding, however, that by 'compensation' he meant our compensating them for occupying their property from the time of independence to the time we moved to new premises on Ho Chi Minh Street in the sandy wastes of Khormaksar.

Luckily for us, the move took place after our own departure from Aden. In the meantime, we continued to enjoy the very agreeable life we had known there. The two elder boys came out for school holidays, a great part of which were spent swimming and snorkelling at Gold Mohur, or going on launch trips from Little Aden. I played more tennis and cricket than I had done since leaving school, or have done to this day. There was a flourishing British expatriate team called the Venturers with whom I enjoyed a modest Indian summer with the bat, mostly against sides composed mainly of Indians and Pakistanis. I top scored in a representative match in connection with Youth Week, which subsequently involved participation in a ceremonial parade and march-past of all those taking part in the Week, a curious pastime for the Counsellor in the British Embassy to indulge in, according to some people (including the British Counsellor!).

Memories of Aden combine cricket with church. Steamer Point boasted a rather splendid Victorian edifice which had no doubt accommodated a host of worshippers in the heyday of Empire. Now we could muster only enough to fill the choir-stalls on a Sunday evening (and when I last saw it in 1985 it had descended to the level of a warehouse). In the absence of a parson, services were run by a couple of worthy laymen from the British community, Malcolm Merrett of Stalco and Bob Sims of the Port Authority. The Embassy contributed a fair proportion of the 'congregation', including the redoubtable figure of the Defence Attaché, Colonel John Paley (whom we had known when he was in the British Military Mission in Libya and who later commanded the Abu Dhabi Defence Force). John was possessed of a stentorian voice, but no sense of music. One evening when the rest of us were battling with the Nunc Dimittis, John was for some reason giving his own rendering of the Magnificat. Although heavily outnumbered, he eventually succeeded in drowning the majority, and the entire proceedings ground to a halt. The deafening silence which followed was suddenly broken by an anguished military cry: 'Oh, my God!'

The Embassy made two further contributions to the church. One was small George's invariably late 'Amens', which became quite a feature of our worship. The other was his father's appointment as 'Bishop's Warden', which seemed to have been some sort of penance following the Remembrance Sunday visit of Bishop Oliver Allison from Khartoum in 1968. ('Have you been a good Bishop today?' enquired George innocently over tea in our garden one afternoon.)

Down the road was a Missions to Seamen establishment in the charge of an ordained Congregationalist priest. His tiny chapel was usually filled to capacity, and we ourselves attended a couple of weddings on his territory. The poor fellow, who had been in Aden for some time, was probably more familiar with the funeral than with the marriage service. On the first occasion, he intoned solemnly in his Scottish brogue, 'Those whom God has put asunderrr…' The second time we waited with bated breath to hear whether he would repeat the error. Evidently unnerved by his earlier performance, he was determined to do better, and pronounced firmly, 'Those whom God has joined asunderrr...'. Nevertheless I always thought it a sad commentary, in the circumstances, that the Anglicans resisted any idea of merging the two, except for inviting the mission chaplain to administer communion in our church once a month.

These two aspects of our life in Aden were brought together in a rather moving way on our last Sunday there. In the afternoon I was accorded the honour by the Aden Cricket Board of Control of a 'farewell match', an agreeable custom which they observed on occasions. I had to leave before the end (in which 'my' side lost by six runs) to dash to church for evensong. Appropriately enough, it was Trinity Sunday. After the service, Malcolm Merrett made a kind but embarrassing little farewell speech, concluding by presenting us with a family Bible. It contained a generous inscription, thanking us *inter alia* for George's 'loud Amens'.

10

Among the Hausa

We left Aden in June 1969 not knowing our next destination. I learned on reliable authority that it might have been Muscat, where the first British Ambassador was about to be appointed. But someone had had cold feet at the last moment, fearing that the appointment might have attracted some publicity, in which my mother's maiden name could have been an embarrassment. This probably had little effect on my subsequent career, since it was decided not to upgrade the Muscat post at that stage, and it remained a Consulate-General until 1971. So it was that in September I found myself flying to Lagos to make my number with the British High Commission there prior to embarking on my new assignment as Deputy High Commissioner in Kaduna, a post which was to prove as fascinating as any I had filled up to then, and in many ways since.

My knowledge of Nigeria was largely confined to a vague recollection that in the early years of independence after 1960 it had been a model of the transition from colonialism, but that since the traumatic events in 1966 when the underlying tribal and regional rivalries had come to the surface, the country had embarked on a slippery slope. The first of numerous military coups had resulted in the assassination of the federal Prime Minister, Sir Abubakar Tafawa Balewa, and the northern Premier, Sir Ahmadu Bello, the Sardauna of Sokoto. I had met the latter briefly when he visited Libya a year or two earlier and made a splendid impression with his imposing figure, magnificent robes and impeccable Oxford English. (A brief sent to us at the time by the British High Commission in Lagos had described how 'the Sardauna's self-esteem, soaring steadily since independence, has now reached the limits of outer space and is safely in orbit.')

Now Nigeria was plunged into civil war, with the attempt of Col. Ojukwu to take the oil-rich eastern region – Biafra – out of the federation. The would-be secessionists had gained a good deal of sympathy in Britain and elsewhere. Apart from a natural inclination towards the underdog and the efforts of the Roman Catholic lobby (the Ibos of the eastern region were mainly Christians), this owed much to a Swiss-based public relations firm named Markpress. Television was flooded with pictures of starving Biafran babies in a population apparently forced to resort to revolting-looking sausage-flies as a staple diet, and accounts of atrocities said to have been perpetrated by the federal troops. Soon after arriving in Kaduna we found that sausage-flies were regarded as delicacies by shoppers in the local market, while many of the horror stories were filed from the comfort of the Ikoyi Hotel in Lagos by correspondents who knew only too well what their editors wanted.

The remarkable effect which this propaganda had on the most innocent minds was brought home to me when I travelled to Kano (on what was to become a familiar 160-mile trek from Kaduna) to meet Christine and six-year-old George, newly arrived in Nigeria. On the drive down to Kaduna, we stopped for refreshment at one of the catering rest houses which lighten the burden of travel in those parts. As we sat sipping cold drinks George eyed with some trepidation a group of tough-looking soldiers who were similarly occupied.

'Daddy,' he finally enquired, 'are those Biafrans?' A premature end to our Nigerian experiences was fortunately avoided.

In fact the civil war, then in its last six months, had little impact in the north, apart from a shortage of goods in the shops. So much so that when it ended there were no noticeable celebrations in the streets. I remarked to a Nigerian friend that this surprised me, since I had been long enough in Kaduna by then to know that Nigerians needed little excuse for a party; it almost seemed that they had not realised that the war was over.

'Don't worry,' he replied: 'most of them had not realised that it had started'.

One side-effect of the hostilities which did make a deep impression on us was the Maxillo-Facial Unit, a British aid project.

The unit had been set up locally by some remarkably dedicated plastic surgery experts from Sir Archibald McIndoe's establishment in East Grinstead, for the tending of war victims. The dry climate in the north was more conducive than that nearer the war zone to the treatment and healing of the terrible wounds which resulted from the fighting. We paid the hospital a number of visits. Some of the sights had to be seen to be believed. Bullets had made holes which enabled you to see daylight through one side of the jaw to the other. Flaps of flesh were being grafted on to injured faces, and often looked worse than the original wounds, which were themselves so horrendous that few normal human beings could have survived them in the first place. On one of the visits, Christine was actually obliged to 'retire hurt' herself.

Despite the weight of political and public opinion at home, it was greatly to the credit of the Labour Government under Harold Wilson, and especially to the Foreign and Commonwealth Secretary at the time, Michael Stewart, that they remained unwavering in their support of the federal cause. There were, of course, cogent reasons for doing so. We had a vested interest – as did many other, particularly African, countries – in 'One Nigeria': a successful secession could open a Pandora's Box all over the continent. It was also important that Nigeria's potential oil wealth should remain available to the whole of that populous nation. Amid steady criticism and biased reporting throughout the war, HMG stuck literally and metaphorically to its guns. When, therefore, the federal authorities finally achieved victory early in 1970, the British had every reason to look forward to receiving their reward in terms of goodwill, not to mention the commercial orders which would flow from the requirements of reconstruction. But the cup was very nearly dashed from their lips by the familiar combination of the free British press and the perverse British courts.

Some time before the end of the war the Defence Adviser in the High Commission in Lagos had written a report critical of the federal armed forces. He subsequently had the oversight to mislay the document, which came into the hands of Jonathan Aitken and the *Sunday Telegraph.* The latter published it. The Nigerians were naturally furious. Proceedings were brought under the Official

Secrets Act against those who had divulged the contents of what had been classified as a 'secret' communication. The defence maintained that there was nothing secret about it at all; everyone knew that the federal armed forces were every bit as chaotic as Colonel Scott had said, and the security classification of his report had been overgraded. The court accepted this argument – oblivious of the fact that what mattered was not so much whether the Defence Adviser's strictures were public knowledge as that their disclosure as the formal views of a representative of a friendly government could only do serious harm to that government's relations with the host nation. Apparently such considerations do not fall within the purview of the British courts. Sixteen years later similar circumstances arose (without getting as far as the courts) when a valedictory despatch from the British Ambassador in Jedda, containing some fairly frank views about Saudi Arabia, was leaked to the press. Although no upholder of bureaucratic obstruction of the democratic 'right to know', it seems to me to strike at the very roots of diplomatic intercourse to claim that communications of this nature should be exposed to the public gaze.

A more enduring – and far more important – source of misunderstanding between Britain and Nigeria was our attitude to Rhodesia and South Africa. It soured relations almost as much as our relationship with Israel undermined those with the Arabs. There were calls in the Nigerian press for withdrawal from the Commonwealth, which was alleged to embarrass Nigeria by association while giving her nothing positive in return. We spent a good deal of time and effort explaining the British position on southern Africa and pointing out the solid practical worth of the Commonwealth link. At the official level, these arguments appeared to have some effect. But neither the federal nor the state authorities made any attempt to guide their own public opinion in this context, and I suppose that we can count ourselves fortunate that Lagos remained in the Commonwealth, albeit without any great enthusiasm. Kaduna did, however, witness a student demonstration which was the only occasion in my experience when a diplomatic mission was subjected to a physical attack. Compared with later examples of the genre it was only a mild affair, resulting in a few broken windows. I received a deputation of the disaffected, who proved to be less concerned with British policy towards Rhodesia than with the fact that an over-zealous member of my staff had been taking photographs of the demonstration. We destroyed the film, and honour was satisfied.

These minor hiccups apart, relations with the Nigerians were amicable enough. Feelings at the official level still appeared to be based on Tafawa Balewa's gracious dictum at the time of independence: 'We are grateful to the British officers whom we have known, first as masters and then as leaders and, finally, as partners – but always as friends'.

There were few post-colonial hang-ups. I found that wherever I went on tour the local Military Governor would give a reception, or occasionally a lunch, in my honour which would be attended by dignitaries of the state as well as senior members of the British community. Unfortunately, these stereotyped gatherings seldom afforded any opportunity to talk at length to the guests, partly because a conversation-stopping band would be blaring away close at hand, and partly because most of the time was spent standing in an official receiving-line saying hello and goodbye, while protocol demanded that the proceedings be brought to an abrupt conclusion precisely one hour after they had begun.

Happily, there were less formal opportunities of meeting the British communities in outlying areas. More often than not, a local resident expatriate would arrange a party at which I was the host (and provider of the hard liquor). The logistics were not always easy, and this kind of operation was further complicated by the bureaucratic rule that I was not permitted to take Christine on tour with me at public expense except once a year to each state capital – and then only with the specific approval of the High Commissioner in Lagos. Such economy was not readily understood by the expatriates, especially the wives, who wondered what sort of Deputy High Commissioner it was who so often travelled unaccompanied.

These frequent tours sometimes gave me the considerable pleasure of implementing what was called the Heads of Mission Gift Scheme. This was a modest arrangement whereby we could donate to deserving causes or institutions minor items which fell outside the scope of the official aid programmes. Such presentations might include, for example, medical equipment for a maternity hospital or sports gear for a boys' club. They demonstrated, as I used to make a point of telling the recipients of these gifts, that governments can be human. They also gave us a certain amount of favourable publicity at the popular level, and did something to advertise the quality of British products.

Most of the presentations I made in this connection were undertaken in the course of routine visits in my area. But during my very last tour, in the southernmost part of the parish, the Gift Scheme tail was permitted to wag the touring programme dog. Had it not been for an irresistible request by the Holy Rosary Sisters at a distant Roman Catholic Mission I doubt whether I should ever have made a detour of nearly 300 miles from Ilorin, my most southerly capital, in Kwara State, to visit the remote, isolated and neglected town of Idah; and to make the acquaintance of its tribal chief, an understandably sad character who rejoiced at least in the title of His Highness the Atta of Igala. The request was for a sewing machine for the local social welfare centre, and I was able to combine it with presentations of table-tennis equipment to a couple of recreation clubs in Idah and in Bida – my one and only venture into ping-pong diplomacy!

It was on this journey that I was travelling on the narrow single-track Kaduna-Lagos road, on which accidents were not an unusual occurrence, when I came across a monumental pile-up, even by Nigerian standards. Four or five vehicles had collided to form a kind of grisly pyramid, almost blocking the carriageway. In the middle of them was an oil-transporter, lying on its side with a slogan clearly visible in the surrounding confusion: 'Esso means happy motoring'. I sent a photograph of the scene to Esso, and some time later received a dead-pan letter thanking me for my trouble, and assuring me that the snap had been widely circulated as a warning to the company's drivers to take greater care on the roads.

Less rewarding aspects of the job in some ways were the annual Queen's Birthday Party and the inevitable Foreign Office Inspection. Here as elsewhere the 'QBP' was a major headache. Whitehall was increasingly indisposed to provide the wherewithal for such celebrations, but the local pressures to maintain the custom were considerable. They came mainly from the British expatriates, but also from the need to keep up with the diplomatic Joneses. The British Community in the northern states was too large for everybody to be invited, yet not large enough for those excluded to be unaware of the fact. The net result was invariably that the Party created less goodwill among those who came than ill-will among those who did not. The expatriates tended to regard the occasion as very much 'their' affair, regardless of our obligations to diplomatic colleagues and to representatives of the host country. The situation was not entirely dissimilar to that so charmingly described by Sir Ronald Storrs in *Orientations*[9], where he is comparing the social experiences of two of his chiefs in pre-World War I Cairo.

> Lord Cromer during his last years in Egypt had, after the death of his wife, and under the weight of his labours and his age, no longer entertained on a large scale; and though the invitations that did issue from him conferred such distinction as to be retained on the mantelpiece long after the entertainment, the complaints of the far more numerous uninvited were as deep as they felt and as loud as they dared. Sir Eldon Gorst, aware of this, assisted by a young and charming wife, with the means and the desire to show a large hospitality, was at great pains to give pleasure by taking the utmost trouble with the numbers, the frequency and the arrangement of his luncheon and dinner parties, which indeed could not have been improved either materially, or in the choice and placing of the guests. As a reward for his solicitude the same critics pronounced that it was really no compliment to be asked to the Agency now; you

seemed to meet everybody there. And his attempts to stem the rising flood of insularity by the judicious mingling of elements served but to evoke the classic dialogue:

'Were you at the Agency last night?'

'No; but then you see I'm not a foreigner; I'm only British'.

Our own predicament was fortunately less serious. Although Nigerians formed the majority of the guest list, they rarely dominated the party by their numbers. The Consular Corps in Kaduna was small, consisting of only an American, a West German, an Egyptian and a Sudanese apart from myself (even so, for most of my time I was the only one in official relations with all the others!). So although the circumstances of Kaduna required long-term planning and Herculean labours by our wives and secretaries, not to mention the DHC's being out of pocket at the end of the day, we usually managed to satisfy a fair number of customers, assisted by a spacious garden in which the spectacular flame-of-the-forest trees invariably burst into flower at just the right time.

My introduction to the Kaduna British community was illuminating in more ways than one. A few days after I arrived, a young expatriate businessman called on me and said he was a member of the local Rotary Club. They held a weekly dinner meeting and would be grateful if I would address them the following week. Assuming that the Rotarians, who were mainly, though not exclusively, British, wanted to have a look at the new DHC, I accepted with pleasure and not a little pride, devoted the weekend to working on a talk, and duly appeared on the Tuesday evening.

'Thank God you've come,' the young man greeted me. 'You see, we nominate a speaker-finder each week, and if he can't produce someone, he has to give the talk himself. It's my turn this week!'

The subject I had chosen was the recently-published Duncan Report on the role of the Diplomatic Service (as it was now called) in export promotion, which I used as a peg on which to hang a general exposition on the functions of a diplomatic mission, with particular emphasis on the commercial side. The response was gratifying, but somewhat surprising, in that the local business community found this approach rather novel: they were evidently accustomed to a situation in which the three circles – government (including diplomacy), commerce and the military – operated in completely watertight compartments.

So far as Foreign Office Inspections are concerned, worthy institutions though these are, I suffered at least one in each of my posts abroad except the last. As Head of Chancery in Tripoli I had boned up on oil production statistics and other facts and figures in order to impress the visiting inquisitor. His very first question, alas, bowled me middle stump: 'When did you last inspect the Embassy lavatories?'

In vain did I explain that I left that sort of thing to the Administration Officer. It was made painfully clear that this was among the H of C's major responsibilities. We embarked immediately on a tour of the facilities. Truth to tell, they were not in a very happy state. Not for the first time, a promising career appeared to have been nipped in the bud. A few years later, the inevitable inspection loomed in Aden. I told the foregoing cautionary tale to my Head of Chancery, who took it so much to heart that he had the Embassy toilets entirely re-equipped throughout. This time, of course, the Inspector did not call. In Kaduna, the whole exercise seemed to have gone altogether better. On his last evening, I dined with the Inspector – a particularly agreeable colleague with a deliciously dry sense of humour (who unhappily died young). I was rash enough to recount my earlier experiences by way of contrast with his own examination. He gave me a long and thoughtful look, and finally said, 'I'm sorry to disappoint you, but as a matter of fact before leaving the office this evening I did tell your secretary that I would like to see you tomorrow morning – at your convenience!'

None of this is meant to detract from the fact that over the years the internal inspection system practised by the Diplomatic Service has ensured a high standard of 'good housekeeping' as well as a continuing review of objectives and achievements. The pity is that it has not obviated consistent cuts across-the-board when cold economic winds have blown, so that the Service has suffered a succession of double doses of economies. Nor has it prevented a series of uneven external enquiries, perhaps justifiable in themselves and doubtless serving some political purpose, but nevertheless hardly conducive to morale.

But to return to Nigeria. The country was fortunate – as Pakistan had been in Ayub – to have in General Gowon a leader of honesty and integrity who was determined to heal the ugly scars of civil war and to adopt 'magnanimity in victory' as part of his object to create a national identity among the diverse peoples whom the accidents of geography and history had thrown together to make one nation. The fundamental problem was to get away from the ancient rivalries between the Ibo of the east, the Yoruba of the west and the Hausa of the north. The first were almost wholly Christian, the second mainly Christian with a substantial Muslim minority, and the third predominantly Muslim. The first two were educationally far ahead of the third who, however, formed the majority of the total population and were seen by the others as abusing this position to gain an undue preponderance of political power in the country as a whole.

As one of the comparatively rare breed of Christian Hausas from the 'middle belt' – that part of central Nigeria which was northern, but on the fringes of the southern regions – Gowon was well placed to exert a moderating influence. In addition to preaching the doctrine of 'one Nigeria', he also introduced some practical reforms designed to undermine the old feelings of loyalty to the three regions. The federation was now divided into twelve states, six in the north (which covered 75% of the land area of Nigeria) and three each in the east and west, including Lagos. Each state had its own Government, headed by a Military Governor and up to a dozen civilian Commissioners, with a good deal of responsibility devolved from the federal Government, particularly in matters related to economic and social development. The hope was that new enthusiasms and fresh loyalties would be created which would override the traditional rivalries.

It was a brave effort, and looked at first as though it might succeed. But old habits died hard, especially when reinforced by the religious affiliations already mentioned. It has to be added that another reinforcing factor – or so it often seemed to me – was the continued presence of a number of colonial administrators who had 'stayed on' after independence but who had found it difficult to make some of the adjustments necessary. While there was no doubting the administrative competence which most of them brought to their new masters – and which were sorely needed in the north – their tribal loyalties sometimes appeared to exceed those of the Nigerians themselves. In vain did one try to promote the concept of 'one Nigeria': for many of this old guard, who had for the most part been posted in colonial times to one of the three regions and stayed there (not least, perhaps, because transfer elsewhere would have involved learning a new language, or languages) the rest of the country was nowhere, and Lagos devoted only to its own nefarious interests. It was not difficult to share the view of some Nigerians that the tribal problems of the country owed much to the colonial administration.

Nevertheless, they cannot all be put down to that. One northern acquaintance of mine once explained to me how the Hausa saw the difference between the Ibo and the Yoruba. If you were discussing a business deal with an Ibo, he would argue the hind leg off a donkey for weeks on end. But once you had convinced him that the proposition was in his interest, he would sign the papers and you could be certain that he would abide by the agreement thereafter, come what might. A Yoruba, on the other hand, would clinch the deal straight away, sign on the dotted line – and tear it up half an hour later if he got a better offer.

It was certainly the Yoruba who emerged as the bogey-men in my early discussions with Nigerian officials in connection with the important topic of our aid programme in the northern states. This included an educational element, and a degree of supplementation of the local salaries paid to Britons working in ministries, schools and other institutions. The northerners made it clear that they would rather employ British than anyone else in these capacities; but if need be, they would recruit Pakistanis, Egyptians or any other nationality rather than their compatriots, the Yoruba. Given half a chance, the latter would be only too ready to bring their sisters, their cousins and their aunts and swamp the north altogether. The hidden premise was, of course, that there were not enough qualified northerners to fill the posts; and the reason for that was a vexed question of history.

When Lugard established the system of 'indirect rule' at the turn of the century, he made a pact with the traditional rulers of the northern emirates. They were prepared to let him set up his 'dual administration' to supervise the existing local authorities, provided that he did not allow a single Christian mission to venture beyond the Niger. The Emirs were afraid (and rightly so) that the educational activities of the missions would eventually lead to their own demise. Northern education in those early days of British rule accordingly tended to be a matter of Quranic instruction dispensed under palm trees. Meanwhile, Ibos and Yorubas prospered in the mission schools. Come independence 60 years later, it was they who had a monopoly of skills and hence the ability to acquire the best jobs, whether in government, education or commerce. The officials to whom I spoke therefore blamed the British for not having prepared the northerners for independence and putting them at the mercy of their own countrymen. When I endeavoured to put the matter in its historical perspective their invariable answer was, 'But you should have forced us to be educated!'

As though this was not bad enough, I received precisely the opposite complaint from students at the Ahmadu Bello University at Zaria. This admirable institution would not have existed at all without British (and to some extent American) money, staff and building. It was another of the monuments of our aid programme. While I was not so naive as to expect the gratitude of its incumbents, I was certainly not prepared for the swingeing criticism levelled at us for what we had done and were doing. It was 'blood-money': repayment for the wrongs we had perpetrated during the days of slave trade (in vain did I argue that it was we who had put an end to that infamy). It was 'neo-colonialism': having lost our political predominance, we were trying to replace it by cultural and economic means. In vain did I reply that we were trying to meet the genuine educational needs of the north, and that without us there would probably have been no university for them to go to. 'You should have let us work out our own salvation,' they said, 'instead of forcing your values and your culture down our throats'. Even their seniors were calling for a renaissance of learning about African history and culture. This plea at least found a ready echo in a temporary exile from the Arab world. As I wrote at the time, it was symptomatic of the dilemma facing those trying to establish a national identity based on their own traditions while at the same time seeking to import what they wanted of alien technology and ideology and to discard the rest. The resulting psychological confusion all too often produced a dangerously inward-looking mentality, as it did a decade later in Iran.

Attention can often be diverted from problems of this kind by the prospect of substantial material advancement. Since the creation of states in Nigeria, the emphasis had been on development generally and the correction of economic and educational imbalances in particular. For three or four years the information media had poured out promises of better conditions, especially in the impoverished rural areas. Improved communications (in the 'information' sense) and crash education programmes had spread the realisation that the gap between living standards in town and country was increasing. But with the best will in the world, the backwardness of the northern states, deriving from the historical factors described above and exacerbated by resistance to ethnic integration, had resulted in a grave shortage of administrative expertise and middle-level manpower which would have frustrated the most carefully laid plans.

Unfortunately the North exhibited neither the best will in the world nor carefully laid plans. Outside the 'extended family' – which admittedly constituted something akin to a welfare state on its own – there was little social conscience or even consciousness. Corruption, which the military claimed to have moved in to uproot, still flourished: indeed, Nigerians complained that it was now worse than before because whereas the politicians devoted at least some of their ill-gotten gains to vote-catching projects, the soldiers kept the proceeds in their pockets. 'Good works' were inspired mostly by foreigners, and some of their deeds were well-meant but misguided. At the agricultural research station attached to the Ahmadu Bello University, I remember being told how foreign experts had expended enormous effort trying to persuade local farmers to grow their guinea-corn shorter: the long stalks absorbed too much of the goodness of the soil and resulted in poorer corn yields. The farmers stubbornly refused to change their methods – and it was some time before the experts accepted that one of the reasons was that guinea-corn was much more than just a food-producing crop: it was put to a variety of uses, including fuel and hut-building, for which the longer stalk was required. As for planning, it was all too often a matter of 'going through the motions' rather than of hard, clear thinking ahead.

These were some of the obstacles which eventually defeated the best endeavours of General Gowon and his more able lieutenants to bring about a thoroughgoing regeneration of this potentially prosperous country. Yet they – and especially he – must be given credit for the fact that the war of unity was won and the seeds of post-war vindictiveness were not allowed to grow. A number of parallels suggest themselves between Gowon and Ayub, the least fortunate among them being the almost inevitable failure of military regimes to avoid the very pitfalls which they claim to take power to remove. When Gowon was deposed in 1975 in – unusually for Nigeria – a bloodless coup, the British High Commissioner of the time wrote that 'Jack Gowon was a thoroughly nice guy: which all goes to show what happens to thoroughly nice guys'.

One of the most interesting features of life in the northern states was the religious aspect. The North was commonly, and rightly, regarded as a predominantly Muslim area. But it was by no means as solidly Islamic as was often supposed. Although reliable statistics were hard to come by, researches by others and myself led me to conclude that perhaps 45-50% of northerners were Muslims, 5-10% Christians and as many as 40-50% pagans. Both the monotheistic religions exhibited characteristics different from those they displayed elsewhere. Islam was originally introduced into Nigeria by merchants from North Africa, where the religion was influenced by the unorthodoxy of certain Sufi orders. It gradually percolated downwards from the ruling elites (who were the principal customers of the merchants with their luxury goods) and its impact was further shaped by contacts with traditional cultures and social systems. The resulting hybrid religion inspired the reformist Uthman dan Fodio to launch his 'jihad' in the early 1800s, which saw the establishment of the Fulani Empire whose theocratic states represented the first uniform popular acceptance of Islam. In more recent times, the forces of modernisation and secularisation had faced Muslims in Nigeria, as elsewhere, with the familiar problem: how 'to straddle… the world of the Qur'an and the Sunnah and the world of computers and planning,' as one of my superiors put it. Nationalism, social change and the growth of secular authority combined in the North with a decline in religion, which tended to become more of a personal matter. Thus it came as something of a surprise to find an Alhaji presiding over a beauty contest in Kaduna and exhorting the bloom of Nigerian womanhood to participate more readily in such exhibitions. (The Alhaji in question was the State Commissioner for Labour Affairs, Umaro Dikko, who later achieved fame in a packing-case at Stansted Airport. His exhortation evoked one of those endearingly ambiguous headlines in the local press: 'Commissioner calls on Nigerian girls to keep abreast of modern times').

The history of Christianity in the north covered a much shorter span – 150 years against 1000 – but, like that of Islam, passed through various phases. In its original African form as introduced to southern Nigeria by 'the first black bishop', Samuel Crowther

1A. ABOVE. Author's father and mother. Nashdom, 1947. *Country Life*

1B. LEFT. "And then the schoolboy". Nashdom, 1937. *Private*

2A. ABOVE. Saiqal, 1952. *Author*

2B. BELOW. "Mutton Grab": USS Greenwich Bay and Shaikh Shakhbut, Ruler of Abu Dhabi. 1953. *Private*

3A. ABOVE. Political Agency Sharjah. 1953. *Christine*

3B. BELOW. Interpreting for Shaikh Abdullah bin Isa and UN Secretary-General Dag Hammarskjold. Bahrain, 1955. *Private*

4A. ABOVE. Presenting Mobile Information Unit to North Central State Government, Kaduna, on behalf of Freedom from Hunger Campaign. 1969.
(L to R: Sani Zangon Daura, Commissioner for Information; Nuhu Bamalli, Commissioner for Works; Deputy High Commissioner; Muhammadu Dan Mallam, Commissioner for Agriculture; Baba Jimeta, Commissioner of Police).
Nigerian official photograph

4B. BELOW. Nigerian Independence Day Garden Party, Lugard Hall, Kaduna. 1 October 1971. Christine; author; Col. Abba Kyari, Military Governor, North Central State. *Nigerian official photograph*

5A. ABOVE. Royal Mosque, Isfahan. October 1975. Third, fourth and fifth from left: author, Denis Healey, Edna Healey. *Private*

5B. LEFT. Christine and friend at Baihan. October 1968. *Author*

6A. ABOVE. Presenting credentials to HM Sultan Qaboos. Muscat, 17 May 1979. *Omani official photograph*

6B. LEFT. Investiture, 1980. *Private*

7A. ABOVE. Qatar Ambassador presenting farewell gift to the author on behalf of the Diplomatic Corps. Muscat, December 1981. *Private*

7B. LEFT. Author with Christine. Kuria Muria Islands, 1981. *Author*

8A. ABOVE. Audience at Salalah, Oman. April 1981.
(L to R: author; Douglas Hurd, Minister of State, FCO; Margaret Thatcher, Prime Minister; HM Sultan Qaboos). *Omani official photograph*

8B. BELOW. Presenting credentials to President Asad of Syria. 11 February 1982. To the right of President Asad, Abdul Halim Khaddam, Foreign Minister.
Syrian official photograph

in the mid-1800s, Christianity was seen as a broad civilising influence which would lead to acceptance of the Christian faith. The emphasis was on education and agriculture: 'The Bible and plough must regenerate Africa'. Later on, European missionaries arrived to evangelise on the basis of 'the deep conversion of individuals', with no allowances made for practices like polygamy. The conflict between these two attitudes retarded missionary activity. The latter also suffered from the taint of association with colonialism, and in the north, of course, was largely disallowed under Lugard's self-denying ordinance. A notable exception, however, was the CMS Mission in Zaria, founders of the Hausa Anglican community to which the Gowon family belonged.

By the time I was studying these developments in the late 1960s, the wheel had turned full circle. The churches, like other institutions, were becoming increasingly Nigerianised. The first Nigerian to be appointed Anglican Bishop of Northern Nigeria arrived in Kaduna, in the ample shape and the charming person of Festus Oluwole Segun, a Yoruba who admitted at his induction that he had never before been north of the Niger. Proselytisation, particularly by the Protestants, was more and more in the hands of the Nigerian evangelists who met with greater success in making individual conversions because they were divorcing Christianity from its foreign associations. The European (and American) missionaries, receding into the background, were taking the original broad view of missionary activity. This was especially true of the Roman Catholics who, while appearing to be more in tune with local conditions and requirements, were regarded by their Protestant counterparts as too flexible in their approach and unscrupulous in their competition.

Despite the handicap of their southern connections, the indigenous African churches, generally founded in revolt against the more puritanical aspects of the Western missions and appealing to African emotions, were growing in authority, sometimes with curious results in the eyes of the more 'orthodox' Christians. The Spiritual Father of the Cherubim and Seraphim Movement in Kaduna had three wives and 18 children. Advertisements for the wares of a religious bookshop included 'the best prayer books containing 110 elaborated and efficacious prayers, with selected psalms for protection against enemies and evil occurrences'. We attended the dedication of a new church built by and for the Hausa section of the Anglican cathedral. For fully an hour, various groups jigged and danced their way up the aisle, singing at the tops of their voices, to present their offerings at the altar in a kind of fund-raising sing-song which seemed to belie the Bishop's earlier declaration that henceforth the premises were 'for ever set apart from profane, common and ordinary uses'. Different the form of worship may have been: but there was no doubting its vigour or its enthusiasm.

To the limited extent that Islam and Christianity were competing for the allegiance of the pagans, the former appeared to have the advantage of being a 'Third World religion' and closer to their way of life. But flexibility and indigenisation were perhaps giving Christianity the edge. Fortunately both displayed commendable tolerance and restraint at that time; Islamic extremism was to rear its ugly head only later.

Meanwhile, discomforts and frustrations notwithstanding, Kaduna was a post to be enjoyed – especially during the remaining months of civil war, which kept the High Commissioner firmly in Lagos and therefore left me very much my own master. Accredited as I was to six military Governments in the northern states, some of whose capitals were 300 to 400 miles from Kaduna, I had plenty of travelling to do. Within a couple of weeks of arrival, Christine and I found ourselves driving 360 miles to the Kainji Dam on the Niger to meet a hovercraft expedition led by David Smithers which was exploring the length of the river – as new to us as it was to them. A more regular journey was that between Kaduna and Kano – a mere 320-mile return trip by road. Kano was our nearest international airport where we would meet and see off our holidaying children. More important, it was the north's commercial centre, and as such had a strong claim to be the location of the Deputy High Commissioner's office. A protracted but indecisive debate on this continued throughout my two years in Kaduna:

inertia, the fact that Kaduna had been the capital of the old Northern Region, and its more central position, dictated that we never advanced beyond establishing a *pied-à-terre* in Kano.

On my very first visit there, I went to pay a call on one of the Kano State Commissioners who was about to make an official visit to Britain. Finding him not 'on seat', as the local expression had it, I left my card, with an appropriate message. Later in the day, my driver, a charming but somewhat feckless young man from the Jos area, came to my room in the Central Hotel to announce that the gentleman on whom I had called in the morning had arrived to see me. We greeted each other as effusively as strangers can, and I was a little surprised to be addressed as 'Your Excellency'. When my interlocutor's conversation begun to turn on matters which identified him as someone other than my visitor to Britain, it dawned on me that each of us was under the impression that he was talking to someone different, but by that time it seemed too embarrassing to admit it. We accordingly parted on excellent terms and in mutual ignorance. I eventually discovered that he was a prominent politician named Maitama Sule, while he had come to see the Pakistani Ambassador from Lagos! We were to meet quite often thereafter, and never failed to have a laugh over our first encounter.

My travels in northern Nigeria took me more than 23,000 miles by road and 3000 by air, to places more fascinating than any I had seen since southern Iraq in 1952 – and sometimes equally uncomfortable. Fortunately, what lingers in the mind is not so much the penetrating red dust of the laterite roads along which we drove, the unspeakable ugliness of some of the shanty-towns through which we passed, or the sweltering heat and the indifferent cuisine of the catering rest houses where we stayed, but more agreeable and more amusing recollections: the tribal dancers who entertained me one warm October morning by the shores of Lake Chad; and the colourful and spectacular displays at the 'Sallahs' held on Muslim festivals, or at the installation of the Etsu Nupe, the tribal chieftain in Bida in the south-west, when horsemen, trumpeters and gaily caparisoned local dignitaries combined to produce something between Bertram Mills' Circus and the Royal

Tournament. Bida, some four and a half hours drive from Kaduna and a centre through which we often passed on the way to the south, exercised a particular fascination. Nowhere else was the thin Islamic veneer so evident, underlaid as it was by customs and traditions not far removed from witchcraft; nor the efforts of the Church Missionary Society better rewarded, even though I was not myself greatly in favour of proselytisation.

Other memories crowd in. One of my tours took me to the middle reaches of the Niger to Pategi, which was the venue of an annual regatta. As I was sitting enjoying the passing scene, with elaborate 'floats' proceeding on their majestic way down the river, a friend of mine from the United Africa Company hurried up to me with a pressing invitation to participate in the next event, which was to be the expatriate canoe race. I expostulated that I was hardly dressed for the occasion in my official-looking lightweight suit.

'Don't be so stuffy,' he said; 'take off your jacket, roll up your trouser-legs and off we go!'

And off we went, to perch precariously in a kind of dugout, just the two of us with a paddle apiece. The problem of how to start was resolved by a muscular Nigerian who gave us a mighty shove into the mainstream, after which we went helter-skelter down the fast-flowing river, to plaudits from the bank. The problem of how to stop was less easy: I began to have visions of finishing up in the delta, hundreds of miles to the south. However, willing hands were there to bring us to a halt when we reached the finishing-line – to discover that we had come in third. Admittedly, there were only four 'crews' in the race, but the satisfying feature was that the pair which had come last consisted of my American colleague in Kaduna – who happened to be an Olympic sculler – and a British official from Jos, and I learned later that they had been practising for the event for weeks beforehand!

Then I remember an official visit to the northern emirates of Gumel and Hadejia. My colleague Richard Parsons, Head of Chancery in Lagos, had come up to join me for the tour. As we drove into the first town on our route, the roadside was lined with colourful tribesmen on horseback, while above us the street had flags strung up between the treetops and a large banner bearing the inscription 'Welcome, Your Excellencies!' Richard was as impressed as I was (secretly) surprised, and remarked that, although he knew that we had got things 'buttoned up' in the north, he had hardly expected quite such a demonstration of the relationship. It was no more than a minor disappointment when we discovered, inevitably, that the decorations at least had been left on display following a State Visit from across the border the week before.

Another of my official visits gave me a useful lesson (not exactly my first!) in dealing with the press. Shortly before travelling to Jos – then the capital of Benue-Plateau State, centre of the tin-mining industry and an attractive hill-station – to pay my respects to the Military Governor, I learned that his brother, a diplomat in the Nigerian High Commission in London, had had an unfortunate brush with the police. The incident involved a parking offence, in which the police claimed that the diplomat had been unco-operative while he in turn complained that they had been violent. On arrival at the airport, I was approached by a little man who told me he represented a local newspaper and demanded to know what I thought about 'the brutal, disgusting and inhuman treatment handed out' to the Nigerian diplomat in London. I replied that, since the matter was *sub judice* it would be improper for me to make any comment. This diplomatic response was duly reported next day: 'On arrival in Jos yesterday, the British Deputy High Commissioner said that he had no comment to make on the brutal, disgusting and inhuman treatment...'

After all these excitements, our eventual departure from Kaduna was something of an anti-climax. We took the familiar road to Kano to catch an international flight. The dust-laden 'harmattan' looked ominously thick as we drove north, and sure enough when we reached Kano it was to discover that there was no aircraft. We repaired to the habitual haven provided by St Elmo Nelson, a flamboyant 'retread' official of the Kano Government, and his wife Lynette, who had so often dispensed the hospitality of their charming and unusual mud-built home called Gidan Dan Hausa.

The next day we tried again, but the harmattan prevented a Boeing from landing and a Fokker from taking off. We returned to Kaduna, much to the perturbation of our houseboy, who was celebrating our departure by a ceremonial ride round the front drive on his bicycle and was most put out to find that he had not got rid of us after all. The following day, the small airfield at Kaduna was operative, and we boarded a flight for Lagos and took leave of Nigeria from there.

The parallels with Pakistan have unhappily persisted, in the sense that both countries have since chopped and changed between military and civil regimes but neither type has been able to arrest a general decline. If religious differences have been at the root of Pakistan's troubles, Nigeria's have been tribal rivalries which have helped to frustrate the potential represented by the country's rich natural resources. Each is a land of sadly unfulfilled promise, and we were fortunate to see them in better days.

11

Danish Delight

At the beginning of each year the FCO (as the merged Foreign and Commonwealth Office was now known) would distribute a post preference form. Members of the Service were invited to tell a benevolent administration how they viewed their current assignment, whether any particular factors should be taken into account in deciding their next one, and, above all, where they would like this to be. Few people took this very seriously, any more than they did Personnel Department's pretensions to 'career planning'. Experience showed that the exigencies of the Service more often than not turned the best-laid schemes into a game of musical chairs. Unwelcome transfers were resisted, if at all, with varying degrees of success – perhaps in the belief that expressing a positive preference could be the kiss of death, as had happened with my own South-East Asian ambitions.

Nevertheless, after a succession of posts in hot, Muslim, developing countries, I thought that we – especially Christine – needed a break. Our assignments had been professionally fascinating but domestically difficult; and for the most part while I had the fascination, she coped with the difficulties. At the start of our last year in Kaduna, therefore, I treated the post preference exercise with more care and attention than hitherto. Going religiously through the FCO list I worked out where suitable vacancies appeared likely to crop up from the standpoints of my seniority and their desirability. Eventually, by a process of elimination, I narrowed the possibilities to three. To our agreeable surprise, one of them duly came out of the hat, and in the spring of 1972 we found ourselves crossing the North Sea bound for Copenhagen, where I had been appointed Counsellor and Head of Chancery, which meant being second-in-command to my colleague of German Political Department days, Andrew Stark. The prospect was a pleasant one, and the reality confirmed it.

The Nordic scene was not altogether unfamiliar, having been one of my responsibilities in Central Department, and though I had never visited the area I had learned something of the foibles of the Scandinavian peoples from Donald Connery's excellent book on the subject[10], which among other virtues contained a fund of amusing stories illustrating the different national characteristics. One of those relevant to the present context told of a referendum held among the Scandinavians to elicit which of the four nations was the most popular in their own estimation. Each voted by varying majorities in favour of one of the others: except that the Danes voted overwhelmingly – for the Danes.

But the first discovery we made about them came as something of a shock. Among the drudgeries of which I had hoped Christine would now be relieved was that of running a household with the handicap of having admittedly plentiful but invariably indifferent domestic staff. Even this problem had not been without its lighter side on occasions. In the subcontinent we had become familiar with the standard plea for work, pay rises or other favours which ended with the punch-line, 'Finally, Sir, may I say that I am a great admirer of J. Christ Esq. whom Your Honour so closely resembles'.

In Nigeria, aspiring employees would come armed with a whole dossier of references. Sometimes they would be blissfully ignorant of the actual contents. Among one such sheaf of papers we came across the explanation that the applicant had been a cook in a local army unit, but had 'been dismissed for using foul language to the Commanding Officer's wife'.

We soon found that even unreliable servants could be preferable to no servants at all. The available Danish cooks and waiters, while admirable in themselves, were in such short supply for parties that the hapless diplomatic hostess would first have to ascertain when they were free to come before turning to the relatively minor matter of inviting guests.

This hazard apart, entertaining and being entertained in Copenhagen both took on a new dimension compared with our experiences hitherto. We did, however, retain and refine one particular family tradition which had originated in Karachi, where we used to give a joint annual staff party with our colleagues and neighbours Tony and Suzanne Golds. This was the Scavenge, a convenient way of getting rid of one's guests for a couple of hours soon after their arrival, while they scoured the neighbourhood for specific objects (such as 'a figment of the imagination' or, more down to earth, a fried tomato – disguised anagrammatically as 'I'm food treat'); and answers to questions also framed in crossword-style clues which could be solved only by going to particular places. Over the years we had repeated the dose in our various posts, with the necessary injunction in most cases that scavengers should take great care to avoid offending local susceptibilities. Even so, the wife of 2nd Lt Samson of 1 Div. Rear HQ in Kaduna had been understandably suspicious when she received a telephone call from a strange man enquiring whether her husband was duty officer that night!

One of the joys of scavenging in Copenhagen was that there was a great deal more scope. Nowhere else had we been able to set questions like 'Where are Meunier, Rodin, Falgiere, Carpeaux, Dubois, Jerichau, Bissen, Freund, Wiedeweldt and Stein?' (statues around Ny Carlsberg Glyptotek). Nor had the proprietors of that excellent hostelry the Søllerød Kro ever experienced such a rush on their menus. Scavengers who were first to arrive at the offices of *Berlingske Tidende* reported that the night staff were interested to be asked for a copy of the newspaper's issue for Constitution Day 1974; later visitors found that the joke was wearing a little thin; those who brought up the rear were none too politely turned away! Another Copenhagen refinement was to extend the range of our guests on these occasions to the families of friends made by the children, which proved not only rewarding in itself but that the most stolid of Danes could unbend in the right atmosphere.

Their own socialising, while charming and civilised, still tended at times to be a trifle formal. Dinner parties started early – and exactly on time – but finished late. Moreover, there was occasionally the worry about perhaps having to offer the traditional vote of thanks at the end of the meal – and whether it was the gentleman on the left (Danish-style) or the right (British-style) of the hostess to whom this somewhat daunting honour should fall. Then there were the other ritual courtesies: thanking for the invitation on arrival, for the meal after eating, for the evening when leaving and, by no means least, 'tak for sidst' ('thanks for the last time') when next you met your host – even if it was a year later. All this is not, of course, unknown elsewhere, but we were quite new to it.

Partly to make the appropriate welcoming noises at our own table, as well as for more important reasons, I made a serious effort to learn the language, attending lunch-time courses at the Folk-Universität and struggling with tapes before breakfast. Although this was not strictly necessary in the course of official or private business in Copenhagen, English was not always widely spoken outside the capital, and in any case reading the vernacular press was essential. Danes reacted far more kindly to one's faltering attempts at conversation than the French in similar circumstances. Nevertheless, since there were only about 5,000,000 of them, and their language was not exactly universal, in addition to being difficult to pronounce as they pronounced it, they were unaccustomed to foreigners who tried, and with the best will in the world an approximation which sounded near enough the mark to us but was a little off beam in accent or accentuation would be impossible for them to grasp. Conversations with Danes therefore tended to be brief before they remarked how wonderful one's Danish was, and should we now continue in English... The net result of my efforts was to scrape through the Civil Service Commission's Lower Standard Examination, which brought me the princely sum of £80 a year (taxable) so long as I was in Denmark: after I qualified for the allowance, this turned out to be only a few months.

We lived in a well-appointed house in the northern suburb of Hellerup, not far from the attractive Gentofte Lake, which was a delight to walk around in summer and across in winter. Copenhagen's streets and shops, its parks and waterways, its restaurants and concert-halls were sheer joy to the oriental traveller. Christmastime was out of this world so far as window decorations and displays were concerned, though one could not help noticing that for the shopkeepers the festive season began exceptionally early and ended abruptly directly after Boxing Day. The Danish Ballet at the Royal Theatre was a source of endless pleasure, and at the subsidised rate which seemed to apply to everybody irrespective of need, which struck us as somewhat hard on the Danish taxpayer in the provinces. We were lucky, too, in experiencing fine summers and wonderfully tinted autumns, when trips to elegant castles and beautiful gardens all over Denmark put this posting in a class of its own.

The Danes themselves, while often displaying a reserve generally attributed to the British, were so well-disposed towards Britain that one literally felt at home. Despite the fact that Denmark was a NATO ally of Germany, and soon to be an EEC partner, flags were flown at half-mast every year on 9 April, the anniversary of the occupation, and candles lit in the windows on 4 May, to commemorate the liberation. During our two-and-a-half years there, I think that the typical Danish feeling was changing from 'good old Britain' to 'poor old Britain', on account of the economic difficulties we were then experiencing. This was somewhat irritating because the Danes were living even further beyond their means than we were: but international indebtedness did not seem to affect the krone, which was not a world currency, as seriously as sterling, which was still the medium of a large proportion of world trade.

Before going there, I had heard of the crippling burden of taxation in Denmark, but this was usually coupled with the proviso that, on the whole, Danes accepted this as a price worth paying for the range of welfare benefits available to them. In fact, most of them we met – admittedly from the better-off sections of society – preferred fewer benefits and lower taxes. Indeed this became one of the dominant themes of Danish politics, resulting among other things in the emergence of a *poujadiste* party led by an eccentric lawyer named Mogens Glistrup. He actually refused to pay taxes (for which he later served a prison sentence) and his Progress Party's policy included such novel proposals as the reduction of defence expenditure to the cost of a telephone line from Copenhagen to Moscow with a single recorded message: 'We surrender'. This kind of programme made quite a strong appeal to the Danish electorate, and won Glistrup a handful of seats at the first election which his party contested, in 1973.

The election was more remarkable for doubling the number of parties represented in the Folketing to 11. The Social Democrats remained the predominant group, as they had been for years, but the modest size of their majority – and the prevailing system of proportional representation – obliged them to engage in protracted haggling with other parties to maintain their rule. I remember remarking patronisingly to a Danish friend that while, of course, this system was admirably fair and just, we in Britain preferred something which worked. A few months later the laugh was on me, when we had the two elections in 1974 resulting in miniscule Labour majorities which were hardly the stuff of which 'strong government' was made. As time went on – and following a further election which produced a Venstre Government under Poul Hartling, who commanded no more than a score of the 174 seats in the Folketing – I began to see certain virtues in the Danish set-up. One was that no single party, or group of parties, was able to ride roughshod over the views of the others, so that the more important policies, such as defence or housing, were hammered out and a compromise eventually reached which made most voters feel that, although the outcome was not wholly to their liking, at least their views had been taken into account. Moreover, these agreed policies would remain in force for a period of time, often regardless of changes of government meanwhile. The advantages of this were that policies were conducted on a basis of consensus rather than confrontation, and of continuity rather than the drastic swings of the pendulum which can be so ruinous – particularly for the businessman – in our own system. Danish Governments tended, of course, to be regarded by outsiders as 'weak', but I am not sure that their achievements, at least in the first half of the 1970s, compared particularly ill with those of British administrations of the time.

A feature of Danish society which took more getting used to was its extreme liberality. By this I do not mean in particular the sexual permissiveness exemplified in 'live shows' and other forms of entertainment. Although the Danes tend to rationalise this phenomenon by claiming that it catered largely for the tourist market, and anyway that the forbidden was attractive only so long as it was forbidden, a backlash had already started against such facile thinking. More extraordinary were the local attitudes to what Danes regarded as innate 'liberty' but we would probably characterise as blatant 'licence'. For example, an obscene and offensive film was produced about the life of Christ. Although Danes in general were not noted for their religious ardour, this was deeply repugnant to a large section of public opinion. Their feelings were only exacerbated when it became known that the producer had actually obtained a government grant to enable him to make the film. The consequent furore resulted in a typical Danish compromise: the Government withdrew the grant – on the specious pretext that the film had been shot against a different background from that originally approved – but stoutly defended the producer's right to go ahead with the film, on the principle that nothing must be done to infringe 'artistic freedom'.

Another instance which came to my attention concerned the lax supervision of university students. This was part and parcel of the belief that higher education was virtually a human right (despite the fact that no more than 15% of children from humbler backgrounds aspired to it), with the result that the universities were overcrowded, academic standards low and graduate unemployment rife. So much was freely admitted to us when we visited a provisional university and were shown round by a scruffy-looking individual who complained bitterly of the adverse circumstances in which the staff had to operate. We could not help thinking that if he was anything to go by there was indeed cause for alarm: it was not until half-way through our tour of inspection that we discovered that he was the Rector!

Some time later, an Embassy colleague told me that a Danish student who was enrolled at Copenhagen University and with whom he was exchanging Danish lessons for English had 'disappeared' for a year, during which time, while continuing to draw his Danish allowance, he was pursuing a course of study at a British seat of learning. I found this so difficult to believe that I took the opportunity of a cocktail-party encounter with the Rector of Copenhagen University to enquire whether such a thing was possible. He did not attempt to deny it.

'But,' I persisted, 'what would the Danish taxpayer have to say if he knew?'

The Rector agreed that more should be done to ensure that students worked – but added that 'freedom is a very valuable thing'!

The Venstre (meaning 'left' but in fact more akin to our Liberal Party) Government tried in 1974 to introduce some order into this jungle by proposing a system of 'study norms' and the tailoring of admissions to available resources and employment opportunities. But both ideas were rejected by the student bodies, who regarded them as aiming at the suppression of criticisms of the 'establishment' and as an attack on academic freedom. The minority Government failed in any case to survive the general election later that year.

There was also at this time a vigorous public debate about another aspect of the Danish educational system. It was sparked off by a Ministry of Education official who gave a newspaper interview in which he complained of 'indoctrination' being carried out in primary schools and kindergartens by a well-organised minority of Marxist teachers. This unleashed an impassioned argument in press and parliamentary circles. On one side there were those who raised the cry of 'McCarthyism' and maintained that indoctrination was not confined to supporters of the left. On the other, there were those who said that the problem itself was not confined to the schools, but was perhaps more serious still in the universities. In the middle stood those who applauded the official for drawing attention to the danger but claimed that it was less critical than he believed, because it affected only a small proportion of teachers and pupils; or because it did no more than reflect the conflicts in society itself; or because puritanical indoctrination by narrow-minded Christian teachers was equally reprehensible. As a generalisation, it was probably fair to say that parents welcomed the matter being aired, while educationists regretted it as likely to lead to unacceptable restrictions being placed on all teachers (which the Marxists would probably succeed in evading). At all events, we were aware in the Embassy of parental anxieties about certain attitudes and materials being displayed in the classrooms. The outstanding example was a history book which emanated from a left-wing publishing house in Copenhagen. It portrayed, in cartoon form and classic Marxist terms, world history from the medieval class struggle between the land-owning squires and priests and the landless peasants and labourers, to the present day when all were exploited by the capitalists – the principal offenders in Denmark being named in the book.

The debate was perhaps symptomatic of the struggle going on at the time in the Danish mind between innate conservatism and increasing liberalism. The 1973 election sounded a warning to the Social Democrats, who had become the 'natural party of government'; in 1974 the voters seemed to be saying that the Social Democrats, having been duly rapped on the knuckles, could now resume their traditional role. They have since done so, but not without a lengthy interregnum during which a Conservative Prime Minister held sway. This was Poul Schlüter, who had been a frequent guest at the Starks' table in the early 1970s.

The Ambassador's Residence was then still in the palatial old building in Bredgade, near the central square of Copenhagen. Controversy raged over whether it was a priceless asset or an uneconomic anachronism. Successive Ambassadors tended to take opposing views, with the result that no firm decision was taken until, I believe, the crumbling foundations eventually had the last word. Meanwhile the Starks presided over as elegant a diplomatic establishment as I ever encountered.

My first experience of it was when, shortly after our arrival, the Duke and Duchess of Kent came on an official visit in connection with a big British trade drive in Denmark. They stayed in Bredgade, and the high point for us was the evening on which Queen Margrethe and Prince Henrik came to dine. This would have been a mark of singular distinction for the Starks at any time, but was particularly so on this occasion because it was the first time the Queen had emerged from the period of mourning following the death of her father, King Frederick VII, earlier in 1972.

The Ambassador detailed me to ensure that the Kents met the other guests assembling in the ballroom after he and his wife had gone downstairs to greet the Danish royals. Being so new, of course, I was unlikely to know many of those invited. Nevertheless, once the gathering got under way, with the Starks still in the ballroom and the Kents not yet having entered from their suite off one end of it, I made it my business to repair this omission as rapidly and completely as possible. Suddenly I was aware of an Ambassador and his Ambassadress literally skating across the ballroom floor in a great flurry and heading for the staircase: Her Majesty and her consort had arrived unexpectedly early! My own problem assumed a new dimension: would the Duke and Duchess appear before the Danes did so, as protocol certainly required? Urgent messages were despatched. But we need not have worried. As the Queen and the Prince, escorted by the Starks, swept into the ballroom at one end, the Duke and Duchess swept into it at the other, with perfect timing – and elegance to match!

The Embassy office occupied three very graceful buildings in Kastelsvej, the back of which overlooked a large cemetery. So did the Embassies of the United States and the Soviet Union, thus giving rise to the pleasantry that our three Missions were situated in the 'dead centre' of Copenhagen. I soon discovered that by far the largest part of the British Embassy was the Commercial Section, presided over by a Counsellor named George Marshall. George was a big man in every sense of the adjective, seconded from the Department of Trade and an export promoter to his fingertips. Whatever he may have thought about a younger colleague with direct responsibility for a much smaller political section yet being the Ambassador's deputy, he never showed the slightest resentment, and proved delightfully easy to get on with, both officially and personally. This might not have been so, for I succeeded in affronting him at the outset of our relationship, when he was conducting me round his expansive and well-staffed domain. I asked how all this was justified. George expostulated that

I was presumably aware that British exports to Denmark were topping the £80 million mark. There did not seem to be any necessary connection between the size of our staff and the amount of our exports, but this was sacrilege. In fact, I was to come to the view – despite what I had told the Rotary Club in Kaduna – that the pendulum had swung too far in the direction of trade promotion as the be-all and end-all of the professional diplomat. Where strong Commercial Sections were needed was in areas like the Middle East, because of the complexities of the market, political uncertainty and linguistic barriers. Even there, we were to learn in Iran five or six years later that concentration in the Embassy on recycling petro-dollars was achieved at the expense of the more traditional diplomatic role, that of finding out what is going on in the country to which you are accredited. But in a place like Denmark, where there is virtually no language problem, a businessman can pick up the telephone and talk direct to his opposite number, and it is hardly any trouble to pay him a visit, the need for large-scale commercial diplomacy is far from obvious.

Of that more anon. Meanwhile, from the point of view of political/economic work in the Copenhagen Embassy, my time there was divided into two. During the first half, we were trying to persuade the Danes to join the European Community with us; during the second, the Danes were trying to persuade us to stay in the European Community with them. The latter period was that of the Callaghan 'renegotiation'; the former was the more interesting. For reasons connected with our respective, and complementary, trading patterns, there was little doubt that, from the economic angle, Danish entry to the Community depended very much on whether Britain joined. This was particularly true of the Danish farmers, who had a great deal to lose if the British market were to become inaccessible for them. Politically, however, the Danes had considerable reservations. They were torn between their Nordic associations and the new vista opening up to the south: for this reason, the Norwegian decision whether or not to join the

Community was almost as important as the way the British went. They were chary of submerging their cherished independence in a grouping of larger and more powerful European states, including particularly the old enemy Germany. When the Danish people were eventually asked to make their choice in a referendum, the arguments seemed nicely balanced between the economic pros and the political cons.

Before that stage was reached, however, the most persuasive campaigner for the European cause proved to be the British Prime Minister. When Edward Heath visited Copenhagen in June 1972, I think it is fair to say that he was a revelation to many of us. Even his admirers admitted that he was not the warmest or the most humorous of politicians. But on this occasion he belied that reputation. He made the friendliest of impressions on the Embassy staff when he came round to meet them. Much more important, he established a close rapport with the Danes in general and with Prime Minister Jens Otto Krag in particular. When they took him to Frederiksborg Castle outside Copenhagen, Heath was invited to play the ancient Compenius organ in the chapel, evoking remarks that this might be the first time a country had been played into the Common Market on a church organ. Apart from a slightly testy TV interview, he hardly put a foot wrong.

The climax of the visit took place on the last evening, when the Social Democrat Prime Minister of Denmark played host to the Conservative Prime Minister of Great Britain at a lavish banquet in the magnificent setting of Christiansborg Castle (the first time, I think, that the former royal apartments had been used for such an occasion). Towards the end of the meal, Krag rose to propose a toast to his guest. It was a brilliant and witty speech in the best British after-dinner style – and in perfect English – based on the experiences of King Christian IV of Denmark when he visited King James I of England in 1604: the retinue he brought, the revelries they enjoyed, and so on. I sat listening with mixed admiration and trepidation – for I knew what a turgid, if worthy, script we had prepared for Heath and could not see how he was going to match this. But when Krag eventually sat down, Heath got up and began, 'Mr. Prime Minister, we have all listened with amusement and instruction to your fascinating excursion into history. I only wish, Mr Krag, that I had the staff to do the same for me!'

He then proceeded in similar vein, recounting in turn a visit to London paid by Per Haekkerup – the Danish George Brown – when there had been a riotous trip down the Thames, ending in a sing-song with the assembled company rendering at the tops of their voices a ditty to the tune of 'John Brown's Body' which included the line: 'We'll make Nancy Astor sweep the steps of Transport House'. By the time the Prime Minister got to the serious part of his speech he had the audience in the palm of his hand. Among my mementoes I still have the turgid script with scribbles all over it containing the notes of the jocular remarks.

This was, of course, not the end of the story. After a sort of slow bicycle race in which the Danes and the Norwegians each strove mightily to have the other hold their referendum first, the Danish voters went to the polls. There was a last-minute panic, when Peter Shore was widely reported in the Danish press as having stated that the Danes should take into account that a future Labour Government in Britain would take us out of the Common Market. The authorities in Copenhagen looked around desperately to find some Labour figure of repute who would counter this potentially damaging statement. They hit upon George Brown – and, so the story goes, got him out of a lunch at the British Embassy in Paris, where he was *en route* from a Mediterranean holiday, to urge him to come straight to Copenhagen. As Chargé d'Affaires at the time, it fell to me to give him a briefing over breakfast at the Hotel d'Angleterre. Later that morning George Brown gave one of his most rumbustious performances at a press conference at which he made clear that whoever this Peter Shore might be, he certainly had no authority to make such statements or to commit a future Labour Government to any such policy.

As it turned out, the Danes voted convincingly in favour of joining the Community. Perhaps the most surprising thing about the referendum was that immediately the result was announced Jens Otto Krag resigned as Prime Minister – a rare example of a leading politician with the wisdom to leave the stage while still at the peak of his performance. The Norwegians did, in the event, vote after the Danes, and against joining. Pro-market Danes breathed a sigh of relief that their referendum had been held first: some felt that the Norwegian vote would have had more effect on the Danish than the Danish had evidently had on the Norwegian.

Once Britain and Denmark became members of the European Communities, together with the Republic of Ireland, on 1 January 1973, the work of the Embassy shifted into a higher gear. One found oneself involved in abstruse discussions on obscure topics with officials in the Market Secretariat who seemed remarkably young but at the same time to have been dealing with Community matters all their lives. The Danes tended to follow the French example of maintaining a strict division between the political and the economic aspects of the Community, the former being regarded as outside the scope of the Rome Treaty. On one famous occasion during the first Danish presidency, Community Foreign Ministers met in Copenhagen in the morning to discuss political matters, but the French Minister, M. Jobert, insisted that they adjourn to Brussels in the afternoon to continue with the economic part of their agenda. The British took a characteristically pragmatic view: it was this inconvenience which prompted Sir Alec Douglas-Home to observe that although he was obliged to wear two hats he found that he had only one head.

In the Danish case, the separation manifested itself in a division of responsibility. The Foreign Ministry 'proper' dealt with 'political co-operation', while the Market Secretariat handled the economic issues. In the early days of our common membership, Kenneth Baker, as Minister for the Civil Service, came over with a strong team of officials to compare notes with the Danes on the machinery for coping with Community affairs. In the course of conversation with the Permanent Secretary in the Market Secretariat, I mentioned that we tended to take the view that political and economic issues were usually inextricably linked, citing the Middle East as an example.

'Don't worry, Mr Lucas,' he gently chided. 'Even in the Market Secretariat we've heard of the Arab-Israeli problem'!

The six-monthly presidency of the Community rotates on an alphabetical basis. The luckless Danes accordingly found themselves in the hot seat for the second half of 1973, only six months after joining. This presented them with a number of problems. There is inevitably an ambition on the part of the presidency to make its mark by promoting Community aims as well as its own national interests. In the Danish case, these objectives conflicted more than in that of most of their partners: talk of economic union and a common foreign policy was in the air, and these were not what the Danish electors had voted for in the referendum. They were probably the least 'communautaire' of all the Community peoples, with the British not far behind, though at least we were in the vanguard of the movement towards closer 'political co-operation'. The Folketing created effective machinery designed to tie the Government's hands and ensure that no initiatives were taken without exhaustive debate and the Market Committee's approval. Though it is probably fair to say that the Social Democrat administration of the day – now led by a relatively obscure trade unionist named Anker Joergensen who had little experience of the international scene – was not bursting with enthusiasm for a united Europe, it was in any case placed under severe constraint by these considerations.

A further problem was that Copenhagen became the venue for a series of meetings of the Nine at ministerial and, more often, at official level, which could stretch the logistical resources of a small capital. In fact, they managed this remarkably well. The apogee of the Danish presidency was the ill-fated summit of December 1973. This had been called at six weeks' notice by President Pompidou following the outbreak of the Yom Kippur War in the Middle East in October and the subsequent threat to Western oil supplies. The physical arrangements for the summit were admirable, but the wretched Danes were beset by an accumulation of political disasters. In between the calling of the meeting and its taking place, Anker Joergensen had lost an election and was only a caretaker Prime Minister as well as a caretaker Chairman of an unfamiliar gathering. Pompidou arrived in an indifferent temper for some reason I cannot now recall, while Edward Heath, under siege at home from the miners who were to bring about his downfall a few months later, was not in the sunny mood of the summer of 1972.

To cap it all, the summit was hardly under way when a bevy of Arab ministers descended on Copenhagen demanding discussions with the assembled Community leaders. The harassed Danish Foreign Minister, a delightful man called K.B. Andersen (whom I got to know quite well at a Wilton Park conference we persuaded him to attend the following year) told them in effect that the Community would be pleased to talk about anything any time – except the present, when they had their hands so full. In such inauspicious circumstances was the Euro-Arab dialogue conceived: small wonder that it was eventually still-born.

Through no fault of their own, therefore, the Danes became associated with the summit that went wrong. Nevertheless, many of them individually enormously enhanced their reputations, and we happily found ourselves close to them on most of the issues which arose at the time. For us in the Embassy, the great bonus of the Danish presidency was the frequent visits of senior ministers and officials. Andrew Stark was particularly good to me in ensuring my attendance at the briefing sessions, usually held over dinner at the Residence the night before the more important meetings, where one was able to observe at close quarters the skills of such luminaries as Sir Alec Douglas-Home, the Foreign and Commonwealth Secretary; Sir Michael Palliser, UK representative to the European Communities; and Sir Oliver Wright, Deputy Under-Secretary in charge of economic matters in the FCO. The latter two were then in contention for the top job of Permanent Under-Secretary and Head of the Diplomatic Service: Palliser won, but it must have been a close-run thing.

Andrew Stark and I had at the end of October tasted the joys of political co-operation on our own account when we participated in the very first meeting of ambassadors of the Nine in a presidency capital, called to discuss the Middle East situation and to draft a declaration for submission to our respective governments. We foregathered at 3pm. It soon became apparent that agreement was not going to be reached easily, with the French Ambassador in particular holding up proceedings by frequent recourse to the telephone to consult the Quai d'Orsay on abstruse points of drafting (which was being done in French). At 7.15, we were served dinner in an adjoining room, and it was not until 11.15 that we had finally hammered out a text to be telegraphed to capitals, and which eventually saw the light of day as the first statement to be issued by the Nine in the political co-operation machinery.

The declaration was also something of a landmark in the Middle Eastern context, setting out as it did the principles on which the EEC believed the Arab/Israeli dispute should be settled, ie: inadmissibility of the acquisition of territory by force; ending the Israeli 1967 territorial occupation; respect for the sovereignty of all states in the area; and recognition of the legitimate rights of the Palestinians.

This morale-booster coincided with a less happy experience from my point of view. On the day the statement was issued, I flew to Aarhus to give a talk to the English Club on 'Britain and the European Community'. In the light of events twenty years later, it is curious to recall that my brief included – on instructions – a fairly detailed argument in favour of economic and monetary union. The Heath Government supported this at the time, and even expected it to materalise within the next few years. The preparation of the talk had taken a good deal of time and effort, and I looked forward eagerly to the engagement. Imagine my chagrin when I arrived at the Aarhus venue to find that it was a small BP canteen, and my audience consisted of about 15 to 16 Danes, mostly women, to whom my text was entirely unsuited. My attempt to adapt it *ad lib* inevitably fell completely flat, and EMU never took off!

After the Danish presidency, however, the Embassy came increasingly to sit on the touchline while the Community games were played directly between the experts in London and their counterparts in Copenhagen, either on the telephone or in the course of regular meetings in Brussels or in the presidency capital. I began to feel a little nostalgic for the posts where, although the work one was doing might not be of earth-shaking importance, one was the person who needed to be consulted if London wanted to know what was going on: the 'big fish, little pool' syndrome. My return to that world was to come rather sooner than I expected, and in a somewhat different form. One morning towards the end of November 1974 I woke with a feeling in the subconscious that something unforeseen was about to occur. I did not immediately connect this with the announcement I read in *The Times* on arrival in the Chancery that Patrick Wright had been appointed Foreign Affairs Adviser at No. 10. But an hour later Andrew Stark bustled in, brandishing a telegram saying that I was to succeed Patrick as Head of Middle East Department at the end of January.

This on the whole unwelcome news just gave us time for a last Christmas holiday for the boys in Copenhagen, and for the trip to Stockholm which we had long promised them but had expected to undertake at greater leisure. We had an exciting train journey and a hurried weekend in the Swedish capital between Christmas and New Year, which we thoroughly enjoyed but which left us feeling that we had been luckier to have spent nearly three years in Copenhagen. There was something almost too clinically efficient about the socialist paradise in Sweden. Its less attractive aspects had recently been chillingly described by Roland Huntford in *The New Totalitarians*[11]. Her Majesty's Ambassador in Stockholm for most of our time in Denmark, however, took a much rosier view of his parish. So much so that the Chancery in Copenhagen, on receipt of a copy of Sir Sam Falle's 'First Impressions' despatch entitled 'Return to Paradise', ran a little competition for the best limerick on it. The winning entry (the authorship of which modesty does not allow me to reveal) was:

There once was a seer named Falle
Who got out his old crystal ball,
Put on rose-coloured specs
And, ignoring the sex,
Proclaimed Sweden the best place of all.

Three years later, Sir Sam (an admirable man of leftish persuasions who had spent a long time in a prisoner-of-war camp learning a variety of difficult languages and subsequently had a distinguished diplomatic career in the Middle East) wrote a valedictory despatch on his departure from Stockholm. This was entitled 'Au Revoir to Paradise', and was only slightly less euphoric than the earlier effusion. The limerick competition was revived, this time between the Middle East and the Western European departments (the latter under my Trinity contemporary David Goodall). I had to give the palm to Francis Richards (son of my erstwhile Head of Chancery in Bahrain at the time of the James Morris *contretemps*) whose contribution ran:

Theologians have never agreed on
The site of the Garden of Eden.
But there's no doubt at all
That the scene of the Falle
Has been rediscovered in Sweden.

We left Denmark on 25 January 1975 in even more traumatic circumstances than those attending our departure from Nigeria three years before. We joined the brand-new DFDS ferry, the *Dana Regina*, at Esbjerg that evening. Gale-force winds were already blowing as we slipped anchor. We retired with the ship pitching and tossing, but confident in the up-to-date stabilisers with which it was fitted. I woke in the small hours and was vaguely conscious that complete calm prevailed. It was not until the next morning that I realised why: weather conditions had deteriorated so badly during the crossing that the ship had turned back and was now anchored just outside Esbjerg, though the seas were still too high to allow us to enter harbour. Meanwhile, there was a list of some 7-8°, a great deal of water having been shipped; new sheets and pillow-cases were strewn all over the place in an attempt to mop it up; and the large, thick observation window at the front of the first-class lounge was smashed. Fortunately for us, the list was away from our side of the vessel, but cabins on the other side of the corridor were flooded.

Once we regained port that afternoon, DFDS acted with commendable efficiency. Repairs were effected, vehicles off-loaded and surveyed on the quayside. A hapless public relations official addressed the passengers in the lounge, assuring them that the ship was the safest on the North Sea run (voice from the back: 'That's the sort of thing they said about the *Titanic*!') but adding that of course the company would fly any passengers who preferred not to sail to Harwich. We elected to stay put, and duly set off again that evening, the ship pursuing a reasonably steady, if still rather lop-sided, course to England, home and duty.

12

Four Years Hard

We landed safely at Harwich on the afternoon of 27 January 1975. I had to start work in Middle East Department on January 29. On the intervening day we went to look at a house in Wimbledon which Christine had seen advertised in the press while she was confined to her bunk during the crossing. Acting with rare speed and decision I made an offer the same evening. Three months later we moved there from the Blackheath flat which had been our home base since 1966, having initiated both sale and purchase through the personal column of *The Times* and without any estate agents!

The reason for the FCO's indecent haste was that both my Assistant Head, Terry Clark, and the supervising Assistant Under-Secretary, Michael Weir (again!), were due to leave on trips abroad. It was Terry who was soon to win my notional prize for the Witticism of the Month. A report came in from the Military Attaché in one of our posts abroad. It recounted how a local senior army officer had sought his help in obtaining medical treatment in London for his wife and himself, who had been unable to produce any children. The report concluded: 'I offered him the usual visa facilities'. In the margin Terry had scribbled: 'Multiple entry, I assume'.

Fortunately my new parish was reasonably familiar. Of the ten countries covered by the department I knew nine: the Arabian Peninsula states and Iraq. It was my bad luck that the 'odd man out' should prove to be the one that blew up in our faces – Iran.

But it was from elsewhere that my first 'crisis' hit me. In late March the much-respected King Faisal of Saudi Arabia was assassinated by a disgruntled junior member of the royal family. My immediate reaction was that my superiors would expect an instant appraisal of the event and its possible consequences. I set to work on this at once, without the benefit of a reporting telegram from our Embassy in Jedda, which had not yet arrived. By a stroke of luck, however, there was some interruption in the Danish communications between Jedda and Copenhagen. Their London Embassy had received an assessment from the Danish Ambassador to Saudi Arabia, and rang me to ask if we could transmit this to Copenhagen on their behalf. I was only too glad to oblige – and to pick the Danish brains en route!

In fact, precious little interest was displayed at a higher level in my views on the significance of the murder. Practical details rather than political analyses were the order of the day. Official messages of condolence had to be drafted and tributes paid that afternoon in the House, where a foreign affairs debate happened to be taking place. Instructions had to be issued for the half-masting of flags and other manifestations of mourning for a friendly head of state. In the middle of all this, who should ring me but George Brown, to announce that he proposed to make an immediate trip to the area to keep the temperature down!

The following month I accompanied the Defence Secretary, Roy Mason, on an official visit to Saudi Arabia and Oman, returning alone via the other Gulf states on a refamiliarisation tour. The Saudi leg was predictably low-key in the aftermath of Faisal's death. As for Oman, it was the first time I had set foot in Muscat. One of the main items in the programme was Roy Mason's audience of Sultan Qaboos in the garden of the latter's palace at Seeb. At the top of the agenda for their talks was the future of the British troops who had been helping Qaboos to put down the ten-year-old rebellion in his southern province of Dhofar, aided and abetted since 1967 by the Marxist regime in neighbouring South Yemen. A combination of military operations and a 'hearts and minds' campaign had finally succeeded in bringing the civil war to the brink of conclusion. At home, the Ministry of Defence foresaw that economic and morale difficulties would arise if the soldiers remained for any length of time. The Foreign Office, on the other hand, argued that it would send the wrong signal to the Sultan if, the moment the war was over, we were to withdraw them and give him the impression that he could no longer count on British support. In the course of the tea-party at Seeb, a select group of those present repaired to the summer-house to acquaint the Sultan with HMG's views. Whether it was due to the force of the FCO arguments; or the powerful plea which had just been made to Mr Mason in Riyadh by both King Khalid and Crown Prince Fahd that Britain should 'not do an Aden in Oman'; or the charm of Sultan Qaboos (who, like his father before him, had an impressive track record of undermining British ministerial resolution), the Secretary of State for Defence came down firmly on the right side from my point of view, though some of his own officials were looking a trifle glum by the end of the proceedings.

My return journey up the Gulf was a revelation. It was nearly 20 years since I had last set eyes on what were now the United Arab Emirates. Instead of clusters of barasti huts with mud forts in the middle which served as palaces for the Rulers, there were now luxurious modern houses, apartment and office blocks, and Hilton hotels. The salt flats and sand dunes had eight-lane carriageways driven through them, and grass verges planted alongside. The perimeters of the international airports at Dubai and Sharjah overlapped each other. The places were virtually unrecognisable, but most of the faces were familiar. Despite the physical evidence of wasteful expenditure on prestige projects, one marvelled at the adjustments which had been made in human terms to adapt in a couple of decades to an economic and social transformation involving the kinds of change that had taken western countries generations to absorb.

Of course, this had not been achieved without strains and stresses in the process of accommodating the requirements of rapid and wholesale economic development within the framework of traditional societies. Though oil wealth was percolating downwards, gaps between the haves and have-nots were expanding. Old rivalries among the highly individualistic shaikhdoms were to surface in the summer of 1978, when for a time the federal links looked like being stretched to breaking-point. These problems were now being exacerbated by the massive influx of foreigners – European, American, Asian – required at various levels to meet the shortage of manpower, and especially skilled workers. The expatriates brought with them different values and life-styles of a kind which conflicted with local customs and ways of thinking. The result, repeated elsewhere in the Gulf region, was a major culture clash. Nevertheless, the wonder was not that the Gulf States in general had encountered such problems but that they had coped with them so well.

In October I had a still more exciting trip. The Chancellor of the Exchequer, Denis Healey, was to co-chair a financial conference in Tehran with the Iranian Minister of Finance, Hushang Ansary. As part of my education on Iran I was allowed to join the impressive array of Treasury talent which accompanied the Chancellor and Mrs Healey. The conference itself was scheduled to occupy a weekend, and on the two days preceding it our Iranian hosts took the entire delegation on a marvellous tour of Isfahan, Shiraz and Persepolis. The weather was perfect, the sites fabulous, and the Chancellor on the top of his form. Whereas most politicians in that situation would soon tire of the touristic attractions and want to go off and talk politics, Healey was an avid sightseer and keen photographer – and even stopped the convoy on occasions to snap a scene which I was dying to photograph myself! He had the knack of getting to first base with everyone he met within 30 seconds of meeting them, and a great sense of humour. He seemed to me hardly to put a foot wrong, except that his Achilles heel was imagining himself an even better linguist than he was. He was (commendably) determined to address the forthcoming conference, at least partly, in Farsi. Throughout our southern tour he would elicit phrases from our hosts, record them in a notebook and practise them on the unsuspecting. Come the opening of the conference, and he duly trotted out a few appropriate remarks at the beginning of his speech. The assembled company was dutifully impressed, if a little uncomprehending.

The Chancellor decided to repeat the performance at the formal banquet marking the end of the conference. Unfortunately, inebriated with the exuberance of his own Farsibosity, he completely forgot to include the ritual reference to the Shahinshah, Light of the Aryans etc etc. As he sat down, somebody (perhaps the British Ambassador) must have kicked him under the table, for he suddenly shot to his feet again and, compounding the error, added:

'And, by the way, if it had not been for His Imperial Majesty, whose inspiration this conference was...'

The ritual references were rather a nauseating feature of our calls on various Iranian dignitaries. There seemed to be a prescribed scale in the inverse order of their importance. The Prime Minister made at least one allusion to His Imperial Majesty, and there was a steadily increasing number the lower down the pecking-order one went. Our meeting with Prime Minister Hoveyda (who was to perish tragically at the hands of the revolution) was nevertheless particularly convivial. The conversation turned to the recently-arrived American Ambassador, a man named Helms who had previously been Director of the CIA. Hoveyda recounted how the Soviet Ambassador had accosted him at a reception and remarked:

'Mr Prime Minister, I find it difficult to understand why you have allowed the United States to send their No. 1 spy as Ambassador'.

'Well, Your Excellency,' Hoveyda had replied, 'our relations with the United States are very good. Some countries send us only their No. 3 or No. 4 spies.'

My major preoccupation with Iran was to come later, as described in the next chapter. Meanwhile the department's responsibilities in that area included the Central Treaty Organisation (CENTO). This was the residue of the old Baghdad Pact, from which Iraq had withdrawn following the 1958 revolution. It now comprised Britain, Iran, Turkey and Pakistan, with the United States as a sort of non-playing captain. Since we belonged to other defence pacts which bound us to the last three of these, the principal *raison d'être* of CENTO from our point of view was to maintain a link of that kind with Iran: hence the allocation of responsibility to MED, and the collapse of CENTO when Iran left it. But it was not the part of my job which enthused me the most; and it was very time-consuming, not least because the less relevant it became, the more loudly we had to proclaim our devotion to it, for the sake of the regional members.

The devotion was exhibited particularly on the occasions of the annual CENTO Ministerial Council. It fell to the department to organise two of these during my tenure, when they took place in London – in 1976 out of Anthony Crosland's consideration for Henry Kissinger, whose tight itinerary at the time made London the most convenient venue, and in 1978 because it was our turn. My principal recollection of both meetings was of the virtuoso performance of an individual. The highlight of these gatherings was the restricted session in which the Foreign Ministers of the member countries let their hair down and gave their confidential assessments of the politico-strategic situation in the CENTO area. In 1976 the star was undoubtedly Kissinger, who outshone even my former economics tutor (whose premature death nine months later was a great sadness as well as grievous loss of talent). Kissinger's exposition was so brilliant, yet so comprehensible, that I began to understand why the Foreign Ministers of the regional members took the trouble to attend.

In 1978, David Owen was in the chair. At one of the sessions, when the other ministers were presenting their somewhat pedestrian annual reports, I happened to be at the table sitting on his right. I noticed that he was busy scribbling away, and assumed that he was making notes for his summing-up of the meeting. Then I saw that he was consulting some books on the table in front of him, and glancing at these I realised that they were hardly germane to the topics under discussion: one of them was Paul Johnson's *History of Christianity*[12]. I could not decipher what the Foreign Secretary was writing, but whatever it was it did not distract him from taking a proper part in the proceedings, injecting the appropriate comment here and there, and finally summarising the debate as if his mind had been concentrating on nothing else throughout. I was none the wiser (about the subsidiary preoccupation, that is) at the end of the session. But the mystery was solved a few days later when I opened my *Times* to read an extract from an address given by Dr Owen in a Plymouth church on the subject of 'The Morality of Compromise': in the course of it, he quoted Paul Johnson! In its way this was hardly less impressive an intellectual *tour de force* than Kissinger's two years earlier.

Another subsidiary issue which occupied an inordinate amount of our time, particularly in the autumn of 1977, was the Randel case. Lt Col Randel was a signals officer who had been concerned in sales of equipment to Iran and other Middle Eastern countries. Earlier that year he had been arrested on charges of accepting bribes. Towards the end of October it became apparent that part of the defence submission at the forthcoming trial would be that Randel had been doing nothing out of the ordinary: indeed, evidence would be placed before the court to show that the Shah himself condoned, and even benefited from, such practices. The evidence in question had been gleaned from certain Whitehall files which had been opened to the defence lawyers in misguided zeal for the principle that the accused should be enabled to pray in aid all possible mitigating factors. On learning this, our first concern was that our Embassies abroad should be forewarned of what might emerge from this Pandora's Box. The reaction was predictably fierce, not least from Tehran, where the disclosures in open court of confidential discussions between the Shah and our Ambassador was not exactly calculated to ease the latter's already delicate task at the time.

At this point, the issue became one of singular importance, not to say fascination, as I realised fully late one Friday evening when the Treasury Solicitor himself called on me. The question was whether we should advise Ministers that the damage likely to be done by disclosure to the vital relationship of confidentiality between the Shah and the Ambassador was so great as to justify refusing permission for the documents to be used as evidence, on grounds of national security. This would have been a grave step for the Foreign Secretary to take, with all its constitutional implications for the relationship between executive and judiciary. Eventually Ministers and the legal pundits evolved a satisfactory compromise, but in the process David Owen earned my esteem for upholding the constitutional proprieties – even if this was a little inconvenient for me. The Foreign Secretary understandably directed that I should personally inspect the relevant Whitehall files with a view to giving him a solemn assurance that no further skeletons lurked in the cupboards of the offending ministry. This somewhat Herculean task was duly accomplished, but not without my having to postpone for a few hours a long-standing engagement to go into hospital for a minor operation.

So David Owen emerged smelling of roses, an aroma not invariably associated with him in the august precincts of the Foreign and Commonwealth Office.

Immediately after the trip to Iran in the autumn of 1975 we were busy preparing for the important visit to London of Crown Prince Fahd of Saudi Arabia. This nearly backfired when it emerged at a late stage of the planning process that as First Deputy Prime Minister, His Royal Highness would expect to be met on arrival at the airport by his opposite number, whom he considered to be Harold Wilson. The latter needed some persuasion before agreeing to establish such a precedent. Perhaps he knew that with only another six months in office any adverse consequences would not affect him. He certainly knew that 'we needed the money'. At all events the gesture was duly made and started the visit on a high note which was happily maintained throughout.

One of its fruits was the signature of a memorandum of understanding which led to the creation of a Joint Saudi-British Economic Commission, with a British 'branch office' in Riyadh. This was a valuable extension of the Embassy in Jedda before diplomatic missions were themselves permitted to set up in Riyadh some time later.

So pleased was Harold Wilson with the outcome of the visit that he decided to see off Crown Prince Fahd as well. As the two leaders were chatting in the south side VIP lounge an airline official came in with the unwelcome news that fog had descended and take-off would be delayed indefinitely. His Highness rose to his feet and the occasion: 'With your permission, Prime Minister', he said graciously, 'I think I will go and rest on board the aircraft'.

The problem of meeting-and-greeting Arab dignitaries was to exercise me a good deal. British Ministers have so many calls on their time that it was difficult for them to match the level of Arab courtesies in this context. But Arab protocol often has to prevail. I once went out to Heathrow at lunchtime on a summer Sunday to greet a Gulf Ruler coming on a private visit. His aircraft had been delayed, and an impressive crowd of senior businessmen had spent the better part of the morning waiting for it. The Amir eventually arrived, descended the gangway, took a quick glance around him, stepped into his waiting Rolls and was off.

'I hope,' I said to a banker who was there, 'you feel that your morning was well spent. I don't suppose His Highness had time even to see who was here to meet him.'

The banker was wiser than me. 'Don't worry,' he replied, 'these chaps have an uncanny knack of spotting who isn't!'

The memorandum of understanding signed during the Fahd visit involved us in a whole new area of work, in conjunction with the Department of Trade and Industry. We were determined to play as big a part as possible in the burgeoning Saudi economic development. New techniques were devised. One of them was designed to meet the Saudi feeling that in awarding contracts for major projects they were handicapped by being unable to evaluate the competing offers from so many firms and consortia and then to monitor their performance. Our response was to select a 'chosen instrument' for a specific project, and to sign a government-to government agreement accepting responsibility for the satisfactory completion of the contract. This was complemented by a back-to-back agreement with the company concerned, whose performance thus also became an official responsibility.

The procedure brought us more resentment than contracts. I recall one project in particular involving a package deal of construction, equipment and educational components. Our horse failed to win, whereupon the representative (a prominent ex-minister, as it happened) of another of the runners came to complain bitterly to me that if his group had had a fair run they might well have made it, but because the Government had backed their competitors, the Saudis had not even allowed their entry into the race. It was really a 'no-win situation' – and the fact is that during the Saudi boom period in the late '70s and early '80s, whether or not for that reason, Britain was markedly unsuccessful in landing the 'jumbo projects'.

I was again in trouble over Saudi Arabia early in 1978. One morning in January, the British press headlined the story of 'a Jedda Romeo and Juliet': a Saudi Princess and her illicit lover had been executed for their adulterous association, and the more lurid newspapers vented their moral indignation in no uncertain terms. At midday I was telephoned by the News Department, who wanted an appropriate statement ready for use at the daily press briefing half an hour later. Normally my reaction to such a request would have been 'No comment'. But having been well and truly indoctrinated with the current ministerial passion for human rights, I could envisage all too clearly the coals of fire which would be heaped on my head if we said nothing at all: feeble officials pussy-footing as usual etc. So we hastily drafted what seemed to me a suitably diplomatic form of words, to the effect that HMG naturally shared the feelings which had been expressed about this human tragedy: no criticism of the Saudi authorities, nor of Islamic customs. The text was duly used at the press conference. The Saudi Ambassador heard it broadcast shortly afterwards, and was round in a flash, protesting strongly to the Foreign Secretary against this unwarranted interference in Saudi Arabia's internal affairs. The Foreign Secretary was in the comparatively comfortable position of not having been consulted about the statement, and could therefore take up a position of magisterial disapproval.

The matter then ascended into the stratosphere, where wiser heads than mine decided that the appropriate response was to express regret that the Saudi Government should have been offended by a broadcast news report. At this, David Owen was out of the frying pan and into the fire, for the House of Commons – particularly some members on his own side of it – were even more outraged by what they considered 'kow-towing to the oil-rich' than they had been by the execution itself. I finished up with egg on my face thrown from all directions, some of it by a Mrs Joyce Boyce of Tooting, to whose letter criticising the official line I replied in suitably mollifying terms, only to receive the further pithy comment: 'Rubbish!'

It was a couple of years before I had the doubtful satisfaction of watching from abroad while the drama was re-enacted with the showing of the television film of the episode, 'Death of a Princess', when Lord Carrington suffered the even greater indignity than Dr Owen of having to withdraw our Ambassador in Jedda for a time. To be fair to the Saudis, I believe that what upset them most on both occasions was not so much the foreign criticism of their royal family's handling of the affair as the fact that the family itself was divided on the issue and therefore anxious to avoid having it blazoned forth.

The Whitehall routine was relieved for me twice in 1976 by trips abroad. In the spring I crossed the Atlantic for the first time, to take part with Michael Weir in talks with the Americans about the Middle East. My particular topic was the future of the RAF airfield on Masirah Island off the southern coast of Oman. On this occasion HMG believed it neither necessary nor desirable to maintain a presence there, and it was the Americans who were trying to get this decision reversed.

Apart from this, I squeezed in as much sight-seeing as possible in the course of two days each in Washington and New York. The capital exceeded my expectations, the 'Big Apple' my fears. The eastern seaboard was experiencing an April heatwave, but the greenery and blossoms of Washington were a glorious sight. The consensus of expatriate opinion was that it was nevertheless a dull place, populated mostly by politicians, diplomats and journalists, while New York was vibrant and exciting. What I saw was a noisy, dirty metropolis where it was possible to move from extreme affluence to utter squalor more rapidly than in any other place in my experience.

In November I undertook a fortnight's pastoral tour of the Yemens. My journey involved an overnight stop in Jedda, where I spent the evening listening to Her Majesty's Ambassador locked in combat with the visiting inquisitors from the Central Policy Review Staff, then engaged in producing what was to be the highly controversial Berrill Report on the future pattern of Britain's overseas representation. I flew on to San'a, where it was unseasonably and unusually wet. But the unique local architecture, with its multi-storeyed gingerbread houses, was a striking feature to the newcomer. More unexpected, however, was the prevalent air of prosperity. Sitting in London reading official reports about the Yemen Arab Republic, the salient fact was that it was, according to the United Nations league table, one of the 25 least developed countries in the world. On the ground, it was not difficult to see why it should have this lowly status. Administration was rudimentary, public services elementary (we were told that not more than 40% of the population had access to a clean water supply), and the pervasive addiction to the narcotic plant 'qat' both uneconomic and debilitating. Yet of one thing there was no shortage – money. Moreover, unlike every other country in the Arabian Peninsula which boasted an abundance of this commodity, it was in private pockets rather than national treasuries: as a San'a Chamber of Commerce official put it, 'In Yemen the citizens subsidise the Government rather than the opposite'. For the Republic's wealth came from oil not directly and therefore to the Government, but indirectly through remittances from the one and a half million Yemenis sending their earnings from the oil fields of the neighbouring lands to their families at home. The consequence was plenty of goods in the shops, a thriving private enterprise economy, rocketing land prices – alongside a largely impoverished Government whose writ did not run far beyond the major towns. Society therefore remained mainly tribal in character, which not only gave certain outside powers scope for interference but was anathema to the process of economic development. This required planning on a national scale, which in turn called for public resources. But public resources were not forthcoming where the administration was not sophisticated enough to be able to tap private affluence through such advanced methods as income tax.

This vicious circle was only partly alleviated by the astuteness of the authorities in soliciting aid from every conceivable quarter. The Chinese made roads and built hospitals (as well as endearing themselves to the local populace by living under the latter's conditions). The Saudis tried with limited success to reconcile their anxiety to prevent North Yemen going the way of the South with their fear of making the more populous republic strong enough to challenge the kingdom itself, and inevitably tended to fall between these two stools in their aid and arms programmes. The Soviet Union was a principal supplier of military equipment and training. Western powers and the United Nations were also among aid donors; we ourselves were prominent in a modest way in helping agriculture through technical co-operation schemes.

Apart from the intrinsic strategic importance which the YAR possessed by virtue of its location on the Red Sea and its proximity to sensitive parts of the African continent, the country owed something of its international popularity to the prestige of its President, Colonel Hamdi. Under his rule, the country had emerged from the troubled period of the 1962-70 civil war between republicans and royalists, supported by their respective foreign backers, with a moderate republican regime and a brand of non-alignment which enabled Hamdi to be to a considerable extent all things to all men. Certainly the Western Ambassadors on whom I called were characteristically effusive in their praises, giving the impression that the incumbent leader was effective, respected and irreplaceable. Be that as it may, he certainly had the benefit of some exceptionally able lieutenants.

Of these, none was more outstanding than Abdul Karim Iriyani. I first had the opportunity of recognising his qualities when he attended a reception given by the British Ambassador, Bill Carden (my erstwhile predecessor in Tripoli), for a visiting trade mission from the London Chamber of Commerce. Iriyani was of diminutive stature but capacious intellect. At this time, he was a veritable Pooh-Bah of the YAR, combining the roles of Governor of the Central Bank, Head of the Central Planning Organisation and Minister of Education. Later, after a period in the wilderness (partly connected, I believe, with the fact that the Saudis held him responsible for the presence in the local schools of atlases containing maps of the peninsula which depicted the Saudi/Yemen border in a way unacceptable to the Kingdom) he became Foreign Minister and Prime Minister. The highlight of my visit was undoubtedly the Muslim weekend which the Cardens, another colleague named Hugh Leach and I spent with Iriyani in his native village of Iriyan, perched spectacularly on the side of a mountain, with magnificent views over range upon range of rocky hills, some of them decorated with tiny dwellings and terraces of sorghum. None of this, however, was visible as we arrived in heavy fog which made the ascent from the plain a somewhat hazardous process. We turned off the main road from San'a to Ta'iz at Yarim, where a bumpy winding track signalled that it was time for the Ambassador to hand over the Range Rover's controls to his wife! We first suffered a puncture; then ran into rain and mist which fortunately for our peace of mind obscured the sheer drop to our left at 'Bain al Dahatain', 'between the two cliffs': the other one was a massive wall immediately on our right.

The following morning, with bright sunshine revealing our surroundings in all their glory, we embarked on a long walk around the village of Iriyan and its environs. They were idyllic in their simplicity, with children playing football on what could have passed for an English village green, or bathing in the Himyaritic pool; animals grazing; the road being repaired after the ravages of the rain; and the entire scene dominated by an old fort. We climbed up to this and surveyed the panorama below, set against the backdrop of the Hubaish mountains and looking down over the breathtaking view of the Wadi Huwar with its lush coffee plantations.

Dr Iriyani told us that until the age of 16 he had not set foot outside this village nor spoken any language but Arabic. He had then been lucky enough to be one of the favoured few allowed by the old Imam to go to Cairo for further education. Subsequently he had pursued his studies in the United States, gaining a degree in sciences. It was a remarkable achievement and, though not matched by many of his compatriots, nevertheless a tribute to the native ability of the Yemenis.

While the remainder of the weekend party returned north to San'a, Hugh Leach and I proceeded south to Ta'iz, the old capital of the country and headquarters of the Imams. Their former palace had been turned into a rather gruesome museum by way of reminding the populace – and any curious visitors – of the horrors of the *ancien régime.* Photographs and relics of public executions and methods of torture were on display. The *pièce de résistance* was the Imam Ahmed's bedroom, preserved as it had been when he died in 1962, and complete with its electronic bed fitted with flashing coloured lights and a vibrating mechanism. The room was viewed through a glass panel, which bore brief notes in Arabic, French and English explaining that it was on this couch that the Imam had taken 'a lot of tranquillisers and morphine which ended his life in the most fabulous and mythical manners'.

Hugh Leach eventually dropped me off at the frontier with South Yemen, or the People's Democratic Republic of Yemen, where I was met by the British Chargé d'Affaires, John Roberts. The tone was set by the first sight to meet our eyes after crossing the border: a platoon of uniformed small boys, armed with Kalashnikovs and being drilled by the side of the road. And so to Aden and Lawn House, which seven years before had been the home of our good friend Brian Levick, the bearded and bespectacled local manager of Shell Marketing, but was now the British diplomatic residence.

Much else had changed, too. In the old Embassy compound, the Chancery had become the Prime Minister's office, and our houses on top of the hill were now deserted state guest houses. Bhicajee Cowasjee's shop at Steamer Point was the nationalised Victory Trading Store. However, I had not come on a nostalgia trip but to try to assess the local situation and the prospects of our restoring diplomatic relations to ambassadorial level: the previous incumbent had been replaced by an officer of more modest rank.

With the tough bunch of ministers I called on I had the same old dialogue of the deaf. The heads of Diplomatic Missions I met expressed diametrically opposed views on whether it was possible or even desirable to get on terms with the still Soviet-oriented regime. At the back of my mind, too, was the thought of a friend of ours from the earlier days who was languishing in a local gaol. He was an employee of the National Cash Register Company who had apparently been arrested on suspicion of using equipment with which the PDRY security sleuths believed he was communicating with American satellites. We had mounted an intensive diplomatic campaign to secure his release, and I had had a number of distressing interviews with his wife in London. Eventually he was set free in September of that year, but I gathered that he was in such a poor psychological state that the marriage itself was in jeopardy.

Another of my objectives was to see a part of the country we had not been able to visit during our time in the Embassy. Accordingly, John Roberts and I drove the 400 miles along the Chinese road to Mukalla, whence we had been promised an officially-sponsored tour of Wadi Hadhramaut, with its celebrated skyscraper towns of Tarim and Shibam. As if to ensure that this trip materialised – but in fact for less charitable reasons – the Ministry of Foreign Affairs was good enough to send the head of its Western Europe Department, one Azzam Shadly, to accompany us throughout our journey. Things began to go wrong immediately we arrived in Mukalla. First, there was no accommodation at the government guest house, as supposedly arranged; secondly, there would be no plane to fly us the next day to Saiyun in the Wadi Hadhramaut because, most unfortunately and quite unpredictably, all available aircraft had been diverted to transport pilgrims to the Hajj! There was not enough time to do the trip by car, so once again I failed to see the Wadi. Meanwhile, we were all kindly put up in Mukalla by the Hunting Survey people who were engaged on a mineral project in the area. Their presence, and that of the Crown Agents who were involved in preliminary work on the proposed Mukalla-Saiyun road, was encouraging proof that the British were still welcome where they had something to offer. The main problem for the expatriates was that the authorities in Aden, in their obsessive zeal for security, had recently decreed that outside working hours there must be absolutely no kind of social contact between them and the Yemenis with whom they worked.

It clearly behoved us, therefore, to be suitably guarded in our conversations with Azzam Shadly, all the more so when he posed as someone doing his best to improve relations with the West but continually thwarted by the regime with which he affected to have little sympathy. It was difficult to judge whether this was a disingenuous sham or a genuine approach, not to mention more sinister possibilities. At the time, it seemed best to be prudent. Some months later, Shadly visited me in London, where I formed a slightly more positive opinion of him – which may or may not have been confirmed by the rumour reaching me a couple of years afterwards that he had come to a sticky end.

Such was certainly the fate of a number of more exalted players on the Yemeni stage during this period. On 25 March 1977, I lunched at the YAR Embassy in South Street, where the Ambassador was entertaining his Prime Minister, Abdul Ghani. Among the other guests was a saintly-looking man named Abdullah Al Hijri, an ex-Prime Minister of Yemen. A fortnight later, on Easter Sunday, he and the agreeable No. 2 in the Embassy, Hammani, were shot dead outside the Royal Lancaster Hotel. Although probably the result of some tribal feud or other, the crime was never solved, and our failure to make any arrest became a continuing sore in our relations with the YAR – as well as adding considerably to the workload of my department. In October of the same year, the redoubtable Colonel Hamdi was assassinated in San'a in particularly macabre circumstances, together with his brother and two French girls of dubious reputation who may well have been 'plants'.

In the course of a dramatic weekend the following June, President Ghashmi of the YAR (Hamdi's successor and, according to some accounts, also his murderer) was blown up in his office by an emissary from Aden bearing, unwittingly or not, a booby-trapped briefcase. This sparked off a coup in Aden involving the demise of President Salim Rubai'a, which was something of a classic double. Once again, my feeling that these events were of sufficient significance to warrant ministerial concern was not shared at a higher level. But Ministers were admittedly apt to adopt a rather ambivalent attitude, at least towards the PDRY. On one occasion in 1977, two ministerial comments on papers submitted by the department arrived on my desk simultaneously. One said, in effect, that it was difficult to understand why we were considering improving our relations with a regime which had such an appalling human rights record. The other said that what we were proposing was the least we could do, and complained that officials seemed to have a built-in prejudice against regimes of a leftish persuasion!

For all that, Iraq was the country which, with one notable exception, was causing me the most headaches. Curiously, while our relations with Baghdad were far from cordial in the late 1970s, (involving *inter alia* police incidents and diplomatic expulsions in both capitals), our contacts with the Embassy in London were probably closer than those with any other of my 'clients'. The Minister-Counsellor, Issam Mahboub, was a frequent caller on the department, an example which I wished our Gulf diplomatic colleagues would follow. But despite our excellent official relations with them, and their protestations of admiration at our alleged expertise in their area, they were conspicuously absent from the queue of diplomats who beat a path to my door in 1978 to glean our assessments of the deteriorating situation in Tehran. To be fair, part of the explanation for this was almost certainly that the Gulf Embassies were geared to act more as travel agencies and welfare centres for the growing flood of visitors from their countries than as Embassies in our sense of the term.

With Issam it was possible to discuss problems and to share jokes. Leaving the former aside for the moment, the best laugh we ever had was over an official dinner given by his Ambassador for a visiting Iraqi Minister. I was telephoned by the Embassy some days before this function, to be asked whether Christine and I could attend, and replied affirmatively. Several further calls ensued with anxious enquiries whether an invitation card had reached me; I said that as a matter of fact it had not, but that in any case we needed no such reminder and were looking forward to the occasion. Then a card did arrive: and glancing at it I saw something rather puzzling which I thought might have something to do with the anxiety, for the venue of the dinner was given as the Carlton Tower Hotel – in the Baked Alaska Room. Not having heard of this part of that august hostelry, I caused some low-level enquiries to be made. It emerged that a junior functionary in the Embassy who was making out the invitation cards had rung the Carlton Tower to ask the name of the suite, and had inadvertently been given the name of the sweet! Driving up that evening, Christine and I made a pact to desist from pulling Issam's leg. The meal was proceeding according to plan, and the main course had just been removed, when he leaned across the table to where Christine was sitting and, beaming broadly, said in a loud voice, 'Ah, Mrs Lucas, you know what's coming next, don't you?'

Alas, not all our exchanges were so jocular. An unhappy event which impaired our relations with Baghdad for a long time in the autumn of 1978 was the arrest and incarceration of an employee of a British firm operating there who had evidently fallen foul of the authorities for some reason. To us, it was a familiar but particularly painful matter of a probably trumped-up allegation, no formal charge, and limited consular access. To the distressed family members whom I saw on a number of occasions, it was an issue which demanded the personal attention of the Prime Minister (who was not the only person in Whitehall at the time preoccupied with the deteriorating situation in Iran). Being ground between the upper and nether millstones was a disagreeable bureaucratic experience, especially as the accused's wife was a lady of unusual courage (who actually accepted an Iraqi invitation to visit her husband in prison). At one point during the protracted dispute, the Iraqi Ambassador was summoned to the Foreign Office for a dressing-down by the Minister concerned, who happened to be a mild, soft-spoken Welshman named Lord Goronwy-Roberts. As the official in attendance, I doubted whether the strong speaking-note drafted by the department was likely to prove very effective. The Ambassador, a breezy Oxford-educated character with an English accent to match, sought to minimise the affair by dismissing it as 'a summer cloud which will soon blow over'; but what nearly blew over was the Ambassador himself, as Lord Goronwy-Roberts rejoined sternly: 'Unfortunately, Your Excellency, in this country summer clouds do not disappear so easily' – and proceeded to roast the hapless envoy with a string of wholly unexpected invective.

On another occasion I was myself the target of some barbed comments at the hands of the Iraqis. It all began when I was invited to give the 'keynote' talk at a gathering of businessmen whom both the Foreign Office and the Department of Trade were keen to persuade of the potential of the Iraqi market. My task was to paint a general background picture of the country, its politics, society and external relations. In the course of describing the latter, I mentioned the curious fact that Iraq and Syria did not get on too well together, despite both regimes being Ba'thist and drawn from minority communities in their own countries, the Alawites in Damascus and the Tikritis in Baghdad. As I sat down next to a young man, who turned out to be the Second Secretary (Commercial) from the Iraqi Embassy, he made some conversationally polite remarks, adding, 'you seem to know a lot about our country'.

I thought no more about this until some weeks later I was invited to lunch *à deux* with the Iraqi Ambassador (not he of the Oxford accent) who, in the course of a rather lavish repast, suddenly said, 'We were not very pleased with what you said about the Tikritis: it's quite untrue, you know'.

I replied that I was sorry if this had given offence, but that it had been no more than a passing comment in a talk the rest of which was a highly favourable account of the climate for doing business in Iraq. The Ambassador indicated that he was prepared to forgive and forget, and once again I thought no more about the matter.

Five months later, in October 1977, I happened to accompany Frank Judd, Minister of State in the Foreign Office, on an official visit to Baghdad. Judd was a warm-hearted extrovert, and on one of our first calls on an Iraqi Minister, characteristically slapped him on the back and declared that he would be very welcome in London whenever he liked to come. The Minister replied sourly that the last time he wanted to come he had been refused a visa; and added for good measure, 'Anyway, how can you expect us to have good relations when your senior officials tell lies about us in public?'

Judd turned to me for elucidation, which I promised to give later – when he was extremely understanding about the snub. But I was amazed that this tiny grievance should have found its way back to such high authorities in Baghdad at all, let alone be stored up and trotted out in these circumstances: it was the only time in my experience when an Arab deliberately went out of his way to embarrass a guest.

The Judd trip also included Kuwait. As we were leaving Baghdad news reached us of the aforementioned assassination of President Hamdi. The consequent official mourning in Kuwait cramped our visit there. More important from my point of view, the unsettled situation in the Yemens caused me to cancel my onward journey to Aden, where I was to have explored once more the possibility of improving our relations with the Salim Rubai'a regime. Meanwhile, a hijack further down the Gulf led to the closure of Kuwait airport, which enabled me to attend the seventh birthday party of my God-daughter, Emma Denny, whose parents had been colleagues in Kaduna and were now in the Kuwait Embassy. One way and another, however, this trip had not gone quite according to schedule.

Happily, the same could not be said of the enterprise which gave me much the greatest satisfaction of all the work I did in four years in Middle East Department. This was the launching of the Queen's and Prince Philip's tour of the Gulf in February/March 1979. The original idea had been David Ennals', when he was Minister of State, and suggested one day that a royal visit to South America in *Britannia* which had been a roaring success in both political and commercial terms might well provide a suitable precedent for the Gulf. My efforts to interest the proper quarters in the proposal in June 1975 fell on stony ground. But by the spring of 1977 the climate seemed more favourable, and we began to canvass opinion first within the Office, then with the Palace and finally with our Ambassadors in the area. The plan was to include Iran – to bolster the Shah, who was in need of encouragement at the time – Saudi Arabia, and the states along the eastern seaboard of the Gulf, some of whom appeared to be under the misapprehension that Britain had turned her back on them since the 'withdrawal' in 1971. The visit would embrace seven countries in all, which in itself would be something of a new departure for a royal visit, quite apart from the fact that it would be for the most part completely new ground for the Queen. The Ambassadors reacted with predictable enthusiasm, and with equally predictable determination that their own particular patch should have its fair share of the action. Their replies having been analysed, further consultations were required with the Palace and in Whitehall before we embarked on the next stage – consulting the States to be visited. Here the element of competition naturally exceeded even that of Her Majesty's representatives, tempered only by the consideration that, in the nature of things, variety in the programmes to be arranged was at a premium: oil, camels and horses reappeared with monotonous regularity.

We also ran into other difficulties, some expected, some not. One problem was the terms in which the visit should be described. 'The Royal Tour of the Gulf' was the obvious, pithy choice. But the Iranians were sensitive on the point that in their eyes the waterway was, as it had always been, 'The Persian Gulf': momentous diplomatic gaffes had been known to be perpetrated by ignoring this simple truth. The Arabs were slightly less concerned: on no account would they accept 'the Persian Gulf', and they preferred 'the Arabian Gulf'; but they were prepared to settle for 'The Gulf'.

In the end, if memory serves, we plumped for the rather ponderous 'The Royal Tour of Iran and Eastern Arabia'. It was also somewhat misleading, in that the Queen was to visit only part of the Gulf coast of Iran. But in the event the problem was resolved by the unhappy circumstance that the Shah was no longer around when the visit materialised, so Iran was omitted from the itinerary altogether. Sad though this was, there was a bonus: in the aftermath of the Shah's fall, the Rulers on the Arab side of the Gulf were left wondering who their friends now were. Within a few weeks of the Iranian revolution, the royal tour took place: there could have been no more appropriate answer to the question nor a better ambassador to convey it. Whether the Gulf authorities gave us their customary credit for having foreseen exactly how events would develop I do not know. In fact, of course, the timing was largely fortuitous, royal visits having to be fitted into a full schedule and organised long in advance. In this case the wheels had first been set in motion early in April 1977; and it was not until May 1978 that we were able to make an official announcement that the visit would take place in the following February. Account can rarely be taken of minor matters like coups and revolutions.

I was able to watch on the television at home the unfolding of the plans so laboriously laid over that period of nearly two years, and now being translated into a triumphal progress. By that time I had left the department and, though disappointed not to have been included in the entourage, I could at least look forward to our imminent move to Muscat. My visit there with Roy Mason had reinforced a growing ambition to be appointed Ambassador there. The current incumbent, Jim Treadwell, was clinging on tenaciously before retirement – and for the royal tour (and who could blame him?). Knowing that I had my eye on his job, he sent me a card one Christmas containing an old print of Muscat Bay, showing the picturesque sixteenth-century Portuguese forts at either end. Below the print Jim had written, 'The forts are still there to repel invaders'.

But by Christmas 1978 I had been able to tell the family that the invasion was on.

13

Decline and Fall

The Iranian Revolution of 1978/9 has been ranked by some experts with the Russian revolution of 1917 and the Chinese of 1949 as major historical events of the twentieth century. In its first flush, comparisons were even made with 1789. Certainly Ayatollah Khomeini's ousting of the Shah was an extraordinary example of how an apparently solidly entrenched autocracy can be overthrown by determined and largely peaceful popular action, a precedent that did not go unnoticed elsewhere in the region.

It was also important for bringing religion back into the forefront of Middle Eastern politics. The revolution was a Shi'a action, but it had a far wider appeal which embraced Sunnis the world over. Whether these political and religious effects will be of lasting significance it is perhaps too early to say. Nearly two decades after the Revolution, there are signs that it is losing its original ardour. From my own perspective, they were to dominate my remaining five years in the Diplomatic Service. During the heady days of the decline and fall of the Pahlavi Empire a good deal of my own thinking about the area crystallised, and it was later distilled in other contexts.

Both objectively and subjectively, therefore, this particular aspect of my Middle East Department years and its repercussions seem to merit a separate chapter. In it I shall try to describe the drama and reactions to it in London; and to draw some personal conclusions.

By the time I came to take an interest in Iran in January 1975, the main factors shaping events there had been two. The Shah's modernising zeal, first manifested in the 'Shah – people' or 'white' revolution of 1963, and later in his quest for what he called 'the Great Civilisation' (to make the country by the end of the 1980s a modern industrialised power of the second rank), had been pursued at the expense of civil and political liberties and without the approval of the religious fraternity. But opposition had been largely muted so long as the oil-based economic boom, which reached major proportions after the dramatic price rise initiated by the Shah himself in the early 1970s and accelerated following the Arab/Israeli war of October 1973, maintained its momentum. Unfortunately, the authorities in Tehran mishandled the boom by embarking on over-ambitious development plans. By 1976 these were generating serious inflation, congestion in the ports, administrative and manpower blockages, a massive exodus from the villages to the towns, and widespread corruption. At the same time, world recession and inflation, and the consequent oil glut, had falsified the assumptions of buoyant oil revenues on which the expanded development plans had been based.

The consequent slowing-down of the economy coincided with the Shah's introduction of limited measures of political liberalisation, in particular allowing greater freedom of expression and easing policies towards, and the treatment of, political prisoners. Thus economic discontent (especially among the under-privileged and rootless urban proletariat and the disillusioned middle class) combined with wider and louder criticism of the authorities to produce a situation by August 1977 in which the Shah felt obliged to jettison his trusty Prime Minister of twelve years' standing, Amir Abbas Hoveyda, and to replace him with a technocrat, Jamshed Amuzegar, hitherto Finance Minister and Iran's principal spokesman in OPEC.

Dr Amuzegar grappled successfully with the economy, reducing inflation and stabilising the situation generally, albeit at a lower level of activity. But pressure for further political liberalisation continued, and the Shah to some extent bowed to it, for a number of reasons. In the first place, he recognised the need to establish broadly-based and effectively-functioning political institutions by the time he planned to hand over to the Crown Prince some time in the 1980s: Prince Reza was then 18, and his father, as we now know, was already afflicted by incurable cancer. Secondly, the Shah genuinely believed in controlled liberalisation as part of 'the Great Civilisation', and was not insensitive to foreign opinion in general and the human rights concerns of certain of his allies in particular. Thirdly, his experiment in a single-party system in the shape of the Rastakhiz, or Resurgence Party, set up in March 1975 had proved a failure.

At this point there occurred a development which Amuzegar proved unable to handle. Hitherto the active opposition to the Government had come largely from the 'intellectual left' – writers, journalists, lawyers and academics – who criticised the autocratic basis of the regime and wanted to move farther and faster along the path of Western-style democracy and social progress. This was to some extent exploited by the underground and proscribed Tudeh, or Communist Party. But from the beginning of 1978 the main opposition role was increasingly assumed by religious elements who, while they certainly contested the legitimacy of the Shah's rule, stood for precisely the converse of what the 'liberal' opposition wanted. They believed that the Shah had already moved too far and too fast in his pursuit of modernisation, to the detriment of the country's traditions and the neglect of its religion. They preached a return to the fundamental precepts of Islam; demanded the revival of the 1906 constitution when (after a similar movement against the monarchy) provision was made for a committee of five mullahs to exercise veto powers over all legislation; and were strongly opposed to the Shah's Atatürk-type secularisation policies and to the 'Westoxification' of Iranian society. They reflected the Iranian tendency to dislike and distrust foreigners, which had been accentuated by an influx of large numbers of Americans and Europeans in the wake of the oil boom, and which also found expression in hostility to the Jewish and Bahai communities.

Although the religious leaders, or ayatollahs, professed the Shi'a version of Islam, their appeal was a broader one in the light of the world-wide revival of Islamic self-consciousness and self-confidence, and of regard for traditional values in the face of the onrush of materialism, which had been a feature of Muslim societies since Allah had blessed the faithful with the gift of oil. They undoubtedly commanded a wide respect and following throughout Iran, where Shi'a Islam was the state religion and the faith of 90% of the population.

The rising tide of opposition in 1978 began with demonstrations in the holy city of Qom in January, against what was believed to be an officially-inspired newspaper article critical of the Ayatollah Khomeini, who at the time had been in exile in Iraq since 1963. These disturbances resulted in a number of fatalities, and thus set in train a 40-day cycle (the Muslim period of mourning) of riots, violence and deaths. The cycle reached its climax during the fasting month of Ramadan (early August to early September in 1978) when the crowds gathered in the mosques to hear inflammatory sermons – some of them by Khomeini on smuggled tapes – and then debouched on to the streets to damage and destroy in particular such symbols of Western civilisation as cinemas, banks, restaurants and casinos. The culmination of these troubles was the gutting of a cinema in Abadan on 19 August with the loss of some 400 lives.

By this time the liberal and religious streams had come together to form a current which was soon to become a flood sweeping the regime away. For the moment, the Shah tried to stem it by further concessions to public opinion. In June he had replaced the head of the hated security police (SAVAK). On 5 August, free elections had been promised for June 1979 and the ban on political parties lifted, with the result that a score of flowers bloomed. Now on 26 August the Shah dismissed Amuzegar after a year in office and appointed the more traditional figure of Ja'afar Sharif-Emami as Prime Minister, with a belated mandate to open up a dialogue with at least the more moderate of the religious leaders. Sharif-Emami announced concessions designed to appeal to them: casinos were to be closed, the Islamic calendar was reinstated and pledges were made of adherence to the tenets of Islam. At the same time, to placate the other wing of the opposition, press censorship was relaxed, the intention to hold free elections reaffirmed and a fresh purge of corrupt practices announced. Less admirably, action was taken against certain minority groups, especially the 'heretical' Bahai sect.

Despite these measures and promises, demonstrations continued, and displayed a new and bolder hostility to the Shah himself. Probably on the prompting of the armed forces, the Shah proclaimed martial law in Tehran and eleven other major cities late on 7 September. The following day, whether in defiance or in ignorance of the proclamation, crowds assembled in Jaleh Square in the capital, and troops opened fire with considerable loss of life, officially stated at the time as 58 but later admitted to be more than that, and popularly believed to be greatly in excess of the official figure. This catastrophe was to prove a milestone on the road to revolution. Hardly had the Iranian public recovered from it when it was visited on 16 September with the natural disaster of a major earthquake at Tabas. The Government's attempts at relief operations were upstaged by those of the religious authorities. The regime's credit sank so low that Sharif-Emami, speaking in the televised Majles debate in which the martial law legislation was approved, remarked ruefully that he would not have been surprised had the Government been charged with responsibility for the earthquake.

The imposition of martial law was accompanied by a continuing conciliatory mood on the part of the Shah and his Prime Minister. This served only to encourage the outbreak of widespread strikes for higher wages, which were promptly granted. Further stoppages were called with political demands, among them the return from exile of Ayatollah Khomeini who, expelled by Iraq and denied entry by Kuwait, was now ensconced outside Paris, blandly ignoring the French stipulation that he should not engage in political activities. By the end of October, the strikes had spread to the oilfields. Faced with this ominous development, and a renewal of disturbances in the towns, the Shah tried to persuade some of the opposition National Front leaders to join an administration. This failed, evidently on Khomeini's instructions, and after renewed violence in Tehran on 5 November, including an attack on the British Embassy, the Shah appointed the following day a predominantly military Government under General Azhari.

Still this did not herald a period of repression. The Shah adopted a moderate, even apologetic, tone on television; and accompanied it with the disreputable gesture of having Hoveyda arrested.

Strikes and demonstrations were now reinforced by power cuts in Tehran: the economy was being wrecked. On the occasion of the important Shi'a festival of Muharram on 10 and 11 December peaceful marches of some one million people through the streets of the capital attested to the opposition's strength even more than the earlier violence. Nevertheless this was resumed later in the month: morale in the security forces showed the first signs of cracking, and oil production plummeted again. The Shah made a last-ditch approach to the National Front politician, Shahpour Bakhtiar, to form a government. Bakhtiar agreed, on condition that the Shah left the country. A fateful period of ten days elapsed between the Shah's acceptance of this condition and his fulfilling it, which effectively undermined Bakhtiar's position by making it appear that he was 'the Shah's man'. The Shah left, ostensibly on holiday, on 16 January 1979, and in the final *dénouement* Khomeini returned in triumph on 1 February, declaring the Bakhtiar administration null and void. When shortly afterwards the latter's military support suddenly disintegrated in an internecine confrontation, the new order had arrived.

Whether we knew it or not, we were witnessing during this traumatic period a classic case of an authoritarian regime unscrewing the valve in an effort to let some of the steam escape but finding that the lid blew off. De Tocqueville had words for it:

> It oftener happens that when a people which has put up with an oppressive rule over a long period without protest suddenly finds the Government relaxing its pressures it takes up arms against it... Only consummate statecraft can enable a King to save his throne when after a long spell of oppressive rule he sets out to improve the lot of his subjects.[13]

The argument raged whether the Shah's problem was that he liberalised too late or that he liberalised at all. I inclined to the former view: the Shah had failed to ensure that social and economic change was accompanied by a commensurate degree of political change. But it is of course open to question whether earlier improvement of the lot of his people would simply have triggered off an earlier religious backlash. At all events, when the crunch came the Shah showed clearly enough that he had no stomach for a blood-bath, and I believe that he was at least right in this.

But I anticipate. Back in January 1975, as I have already mentioned, we had, on any rational calculation, no cause for alarm. The furthest we went was to scrap a defensive brief highlighting the 'better side' of the regime, on the grounds that there was a danger of 'going overboard in defending Iran'. In certain ministerial quarters, factors of instability began to give rise to concern at the beginning of 1977. Economic problems led the department to comment in April that further serious set-backs to the Shah's plans could change the mood of Iranian society from passive acquiescence into active resentment. The level of anxiety rose perceptibly following the Qom disturbances of January 1978 and their aftermath, when we noted that if popular opposition became a widespread phenomenon the will to rule of the Shah himself might be sapped. As the 40-day cycle continued, we posed the question how long it could go on without the Shah either 'cracking up or cracking down'. In mid-August we sounded alarm-bells at under-secretary level, and early in September recommended that Ministers be warned of the gravity of the situation. On the day of the Jaleh Square massacre in September, we had an interesting discussion with the Ambassador (who was about to return to Tehran from his summer leave) on whether the Shah was facing the greatest challenge to his authority since the opposition to his White Revolution in 1963, or since he was forced into temporary exile by Mossadegh in 1953. I tended to the gloomier view: and after reviewing the situation at his post a few days later, the Ambassador expressed himself in much the same terms. In early October we commented that if the opposition steamroller continued on its path the dynasty would be lucky to survive until Christmas. A month later, following the establishment of the military

Government in Tehran, we saw the unfolding drama in terms of an inexorable Greek tragedy, and found it difficult to see how the Shah was going to get out of the corner into which he had painted himself.

While the record would not sustain any claim to prescience, it does perhaps show that distance lent disenchantment: in London we were sometimes as optimistic as our colleagues in Tehran, but never less pessimistic. Such differences as there might have been in analysis, however, were seldom reflected in recommendations on policy, for the simple reason that we did not have much choice. Iran had inherited Britain's mantle as protector of security and stability in the Gulf. Through this vital waterway at the time there flowed 70% of Japan's oil imports, 60% of Western Europe's and 44% of the United States'. With her 1200-mile border with the Soviet Union, Iran formed an important barrier to any ideas the Kremlin might be harbouring of expanding to the warm-water ports of the Gulf and the Indian Ocean.

Finally, Iran had become not only a significant source of oil but a major export market, not least for defence equipment. In short, we had a good thing going with the Shah. We were perhaps over-apprehensive of spoiling it by frank speaking on topics like human rights and liberalisation (though admittedly it was none too easy to tell the Shah how he should be running his own country when he was busy lecturing us on how we should be running ours); and dire prognostications that to do so would 'lose us the next contract' were not borne out in the event. The calculation we did get broadly correct was that any conceivable successor regime was likely to be inimical to our interests as well as being worse for Iran. The prospects for comparatively efficient administration and orderly progress would be poor; a force for regional stability would be removed; a barrier to Soviet expansion could be breached; and a major British market might be lost. We should, on the other hand, score few points by changing to another horse, even if a suitable runner could be identified, and our other friends in the area would be discouraged and demoralised were we to try. The prescription therefore tended to be 'support for the Shah, warts and all, while occasionally offering treatment for the warts'.

These assessments, modified as time went on and especially when it became clear in the autumn of 1978 that whether we liked it or not the Shah was doomed, were duly reflected in our various policy refinements. For example, the human rights issue was dear to ministerial hearts at the time, and one which stimulated a great deal of interest among MPs, their constituents and other correspondents from the public; we spent what I think was a commendable amount of time and trouble composing replies to the flood of letters we received – far more than on any other topic I was concerned with. Our line was inevitably rather stereotyped, and rarely convinced our interlocutors, but we tried hard to avoid too bureaucratic an approach. (I was always mindful of the story of the passenger on the Orient Express who had the misfortune to be bitten by a bed-bug. He wrote to the Chairman of the company, complaining bitterly about this experience at the hands of so reputable an organisation and after paying such an exorbitant sum for his ticket etc. etc. In due course he received a soothing reply from the Chairman: he was deeply sorry to learn of the complaint, such a thing had never happened before, steps had been taken to ensure that it did not occur again, and meanwhile he could only offer unqualified regret, and so on. Unfortunately, the effect of this abject apology was spoiled by the recipient's finding, inadvertently attached to it, an instruction in the Chairman's handwriting: 'Usual bug letter please'.)

In the early stages of public interest, we adopted the attitude that the Iranian authorities were well aware of the British Government's views on human rights, but that diplomatic representations were likely to prove counter-productive since, unless British subjects were involved, we had no standing to intervene in Iran's internal affairs and such action would be resented. Later on we were able to take the more positive line that the Shah was trying to liberate his regime and deserved encouragement rather than criticism, which in any case should take account of the different historical outlook in that part of the world, an argument which the

Shah himself tended to undermine by his frequent claims that Iran was already in the European league. Towards the end we were saying that the Shah's regime, whatever its shortcomings, was the best bet for achieving the kinds of objective our correspondents wanted. At no time did we openly criticise the Shah, as American officials appearing before congressional committees to defend their similar policies were wont to do. Their candour was at times quite disarming: in published proceedings one would frequently come across admissions to the effect that the Shah might be a megalomaniac but nevertheless it was in the United States' interests to support him. I remarked to a colleague in the American Embassy once that while as a democrat I applauded this, as a bureaucrat I blenched: how did they get away with it in the US Embassy in Tehran, let alone the Niavaran Palace?

'I guess,' he replied, 'we put out so much bumf that nobody has the time to read it!'

The nearest I got to such frankness was when, in the belief that we had a case to argue, and that it would do no harm to show that Foreign Office officials were more than faceless bureaucrats, I accepted an invitation to address the Cambridge University Amnesty International Group on the British Government's policy towards Iran. It was my misfortune that the policy would have been a good deal easier to defend in August 1978, when the invitation was first proffered, than it was in November, when the meeting took place and the Shah's position had declined from perilous to hopeless. My thesis was that despite his faults the Shah was worth supporting as the only unifying fact in a traditionally fragmented society, and as a better alternative than any successor in sight. The first part of the proposition evoked some merriment, my audience's view being that Iranians were united only in opposition to the Shah; but I have often wondered whether they later gave a little more credence to the second. I, at least, felt better for the encounter.

At ministerial level, consideration was given in mid-1978 to whether we should 'distance ourselves' from the Shah. But in the absence of any better alternative, the conclusion was 'warts and all'. The same question was put in the early autumn, when the decision remained that from the point of view of stability and liberalisation, the success of the Shah remained the best outcome, while reinsurance with the opposition was not an option. It was not until the end of October that a moratorium was placed on public expressions of support for the Shah, and then mainly on the grounds that they would be unhelpful to him as well as being unpopular at home. This followed a particularly robust defence of the Shah by David Owen in a television interview which was broadcast a week after he recorded it. The view that 'you don't back off when your friends are in trouble' was admirable in its way, but its timing raised official eyebrows, and seemed even more ill-judged when, during the week in question, the Shah's position had manifestly weakened. Thereafter, the official line altered perceptibly from one of support for the Shah personally to encouraging stable government under the constitution, and this virtual neutrality remained the watchword until the Shah fell a few weeks later.

As an inveterate campaigner for human rights, which were officially decreed to be a major factor for FCO departments to take into account when framing policy recommendations for individual countries, Dr Owen was going out on a limb in proclaiming his support for the Shah from the rooftops as late in the proceedings as he did. In another important respect, his boot was on the other foot, and here he had my unqualified support. At an early stage of the incipient revolution, the Iranian penchant for blaming everyone but themselves manifested itself in a virulent attack on the BBC Persian Service for allegedly encouraging the opposition. The argument was that news bulletins were being 'doctored' by anti-Shah producers or announcers in a way which not only slanted the news but sometimes positively incited trouble-makers: for example, a statement that a demonstration was expected to take place was interpreted as an instruction that it should do so. The authorities in Tehran were tacitly admitting that there was no way such information could be imparted from within the country (they were doubtless unaware at the time of Khomeini's tapes) which in a sense was something of a tribute to the 'Beeb'. But of course the complaint went further than that. Like others in the Middle East, the Iranians could not believe for a moment that the BBC was not the official voice of HMG. It followed not only that the Government could stop this nonsense if it wished, but that, since it did not do so, HMG had abandoned the Shah and was actively encouraging his enemies. Thus we got the worst of both worlds: criticised at one end for supporting the Shah and at the other for not doing so.

In these circumstances it was natural for calls to be made from some quarters for discreet intervention with the BBC. After all, they said, everybody knew that the External Services were funded by the Foreign Office, who even dictated the areas to which they should broadcast: it was a small step from that to telling them to call off the anti-Shah propaganda. To his credit, despite the embarrassment the Iranian allegations – whether true or not – were causing for our relations with Iran, David Owen ruled that the principle of the BBC's independence was paramount. This did not mean that we were not in constant, and friendly, touch with Persian Service officials; but we did not give them instructions, and it was made clear that if any complaints were to be passed on this should be done at ministerial level.

We were, of course, not convinced that the Iranian charges had any foundation in fact. Early in December 1978 I received a visit from a highly-respected Iranian academic whom I knew to be close to the Shahbanou and who had evidently come as an emissary to plead once again for a gag on the Persian Service. Our conversation was an eye-opener for me. In the first place, it was astonishing and depressing to hear the wishful thinking behind my visitor's account of the current situation in Tehran – and even more alarming to think that this was probably the sort of advice the Shah was getting from those closest to him. I was told not to get the wrong idea about the events of the preceding months; though the opposition had been vocal, it was not representative; the Shah was still supported by the silent majority, who had hitherto been afraid to speak out; but Ashura (the revered tenth day of the Shi'a holy month of Muharram) was three days away and the silent majority would assert itself. It did indeed, as already described, but on the other side.

Having got this off his chest, my informant then launched into the BBC. I explained that the Corporation was not a Government body, that the Persian Service news bulletins were not specially tailored for any political purposes, and that it was absurd to suppose that its employees were propagandists. None of this cut any ice. Those who were not familiar with the Farsi tongue (a palpable hit!) could not be expected to understand how the choice of a word here or the inflection of a syllable there could convey a wholly different meaning from that originally intended. I admitted my ignorance but still expressed my incredulity.

'Mr Lucas,' he replied gravely, 'if you were to read the Lord's Prayer (he might have meant the Magnificat!) in a certain way, you could make it sound like the Communist Manifesto'.

The Iranian who gave us most stick on this subject, and a range of others, was the able young Ambassador, Parviz Radji, who alighted on the London diplomatic scene in June 1976. A protégé of Hoveyda and a favourite of Princess Ashraf, the Shah's twin sister, the Cambridge-educated Radji got off to an inauspicious start when, the day after his arrival, his predecessor was found dead in the kitchen of his London home. Amirteymour, who was a brother of Begum Iskander Mirza (widow of the former President of Pakistan) had apparently died by his own hand. There were rumours of gambling debts. That behind him, Radji went from strength to strength. He was active in cultivating MPs, journalists and socialites. He was an excellent spokesman for his country, and so far as my department was concerned, although Radji could not help being a thorn in our sides from time to time, we welcomed the fact that the Shah's public relations were at last being conducted by the Shah's representative. At the same time, something of his British education had rubbed off on him and he was probably, as he later claimed, representing to the Shah the strength of feeling in London about the unacceptable face of the regime. It was therefore with sympathy as well as interest that I attended the occasion when, at the height of the Shah's misfortunes towards the end of 1978, Radji had the delicate task of giving his customary address at the annual dinner of the prestigious Anglo-Iranian Society, with Lord Carrington in the chair dispensing his usual combination of wit and wisdom. How would the Shah's Ambassador walk the tightrope between his official duty and his personal inclination? In fact, Radji made a masterly little speech on the theme that Iranians had known that a heavy price would have to be paid for the progress they had made – but they had not realised just how heavy it would prove to be.

This account of the Iranian revolution has so far concentrated on the political dimension. As mentioned at the beginning, however, there was also a significant religious element. Islam was not a faith familiar to many Westerners, and so far as it was known it tended to be regarded as becalmed in the doldrums of the seventh century, a view which was, perhaps, a legacy of history going back to the Crusades. With the Middle East looming larger on the Western horizon as a result of the oil price rises of the early 1970s, a campaign was launched to project a more positive image of the religion, and to make people aware of Islam's contribution to science and culture down the ages. In London, this took the form of the World of Islam Festival in 1976, which achieved considerable success in that aim. It was an unhappy irony that within three years much of the good which the Festival had done was undermined by the effect of the excesses of the Khomeini regime in Iran, so that not only did Westerners begin to associate Islam with extremism in doctrine and deed, but many Muslims themselves reacted by saying that Khomeini's theocracy no more represented Islam than the Inquisition did Christianity.

Associated with the Festival, though not a part of it, an International Islamic Conference was staged in London under the auspices of the Saudi-inspired Islamic Council of Europe, with the support of the Pakistan-led Islamic Foundation. Iran, which was prominent in the Festival (attended among others by the Shahbanou, Empress Farah Diba, whom I met at a reception hosted by the Queen Mother) played only a minor role in the conference. I went to the opening session at the Royal Albert Hall, packed for the occasion, on the afternoon of 3 April 1976. It was inaugurated by

Prince Muhammad bin Faisal of Saudi Arabia, who was followed by speakers representing most of the Muslim countries, of whom by far the most impressive was Sadiq al-Mahdi, the former – and future – Prime Minister of Sudan. He spoke of the 'Islamic awakening', ascribing it to the achievement of political independence with its consequent requirements of nation-building, together with the 'inadequacy of Westernism'. Materialism was on the retreat, and when the wind blew in this direction the sails of Islam were ready unfurled. Islam could respond to modern challenges: the question was, could the Muslims?

The answer given in the two subsequent sessions on 'contemporary Islamic movements' which I attended was hardly a resounding affirmative. The proceedings were marked by the inevitable peddling of political wares by those with their own particular grievances, but also, which was more worrying, by a distinctly anti-Christian flavour. It was noteworthy in this connection that Prince Muhammad's opening injunction not to judge Islam by the Muslims was not applied to Christianity and the Christians. Among the conference resolutions was a decision to set up two commissions to study the problems of Islamic education, and of migrant workers, in Europe: as I concluded a report I wrote on the conference, 'We have been warned!'

The fact that such a gathering had been held, and the enthusiasm it clearly aroused among some hundreds of Muslims, seemed to me worth reporting quite apart from the substance of what was said. I gave my account of it a wide circulation in the FCO and to 'Muslim' posts abroad. I do not recall that it excited any greater interest than an Under-Secretary's mild commendation of my zeal in having devoted part of my leave to the conference! However, the whole subject was soon to become a great deal more fashionable as the opposition juggernaut proceeded on its inexorable way in Tehran. Middle East Department initiated a dialogue with its posts on the 'Islamic Revival', and in mid-1978 this was elevated to the level of a formal FCO study which was eventually issued as a Research Department paper. A noteworthy feature of this exercise was that the departments dealing with the Arab world clearly attached more significance to the religious element in their countries than those with concerns farther east, so that while the Middle Eastern contribution to the study was dominant the outcome was, at least in my view, somewhat diluted.

My own approach was based on what seemed to me a striking contrast between attitudes to Islam when I first went to the Middle East in the early 1950s and those discernible in the late 1970s. Then, as described in an earlier chapter, Arab Muslims were suffering from a kind of schizophrenia. They compared the advanced Christian West with the backwardness of their own societies, and believed that the difference was due to the technological progress that the West had achieved. They therefore aimed to acquire as much of this as they could, but without importing the ideology that went with it. Where there appeared to be a conflict between the precepts of Islam and the requirements of the modern commercial world, however, many of them – particularly among the younger generation – tended to abandon the Qur'an as no longer relevant to the era of technology. The vacuum thus created was only too readily filled by alien ideologies.

Now the position was reversed. Muslims – especially the younger ones – were displaying what I have called a new self-consciousness and a new self-confidence. This had positive and negative elements. Positively, it derived from the upturn in Arab economic fortunes: Allah had blessed the faithful, and the most faithful had been the most blessed; and from the down-turn in Arab political fortunes (especially since the catalyst of the 1967 Arab/Israeli war). This produced a determination to overcome Arab and Muslim humiliations by returning to their religious roots, departure from which, and over-dependence on the West, accounted for their present plight.

The negative aspect of the 'Islamic Revival', it seemed to me, was that it represented a reaction against the Western political and cultural domination from which the Muslim world felt, understandably, that it had suffered for centuries, coupled perhaps with the feeling that economically and socially the West was no longer to be admired and envied as it had been. A Gulf Ambassador in London told me how surprised he himself had been when visiting students from his country in the United States to find that they prayed five times daily, had Qur'anic texts adorning their walls and were generally doing their utmost to hold on to their traditions in a very different environment. He had asked them, in effect, why they did not 'do as the Romans do': their reply was that they did not care for the kind of society in which they found themselves. There was a good deal of other evidence that Muslim students, having pursued their higher education in Europe or America and been exposed to the liberal influences there, were remarkably (to us) content to return to their own traditional societies and able to readapt to them. This is not to deny that many would have enjoyed the fleshpots, but even they did not want the fleshpots exported to the Muslim world. Later I came to add a proviso to this thesis: while such Muslims may not have been impressed by the permissive societies and the volatile economies of the West, they did admire our political systems – the fact that you could say what you liked about the government, and could even change it every few years without having to stage a coup.

The experts among those of us engaged in the study tended to play down the novelty of all this. They rightly pointed out that reinterpretations of Islam had been going on for centuries. To invest the current movement with the title of 'The Islamic Revival' was therefore a misleading exaggeration. Nevertheless, I believe that something new and important had occurred since the 1950s. The 'Islamic Revival' in the general sense that I have tried to describe it was – and is – a phenomenon of which we should be aware, but not afraid: it is emphatically not a 'crusade in reverse'. Alas, the same cannot be said of its extreme manifestation as part of what has been called 'Islamic Fundamentalism'. This is itself a misnomer, in that most Muslims are fundamentalists in the sense that they believe that their scriptures contain eternal truths and that their faith is more than just a religion: it prescribes everything from a code of personal conduct to a system of government. The term 'fundamentalist' conjures up a picture of a lot of grey-beards trying to turn back the clock to the seventh century. The reality is more complex. There are millions of Muslims who are devout without being fanatical: they may have rejected Western life-styles, but they do not want Khomeini-style theocracies on their doorsteps. There are many others who would describe themselves as 'progressives' rather than 'fundamentalists', and as interpreting orthodox Islam in ways appropriate to the world in which they find themselves. They include a remarkable number of young, technologically-minded and even Western-trained Muslims. There is a minority of zealots who stick rigidly to the pure milk of the doctrine, who see Western culture as poisoning their own, and who do not stop at violence as a means of furthering their cause.

It is these extremists who have given Islam a bad name and who are so often seen in the West as stereotypes of fundamentalism. It is a mistake to tar all Muslims with Khomeini's brush, just as it is a common Muslim error to regard all Westerners as implacably hostile to their religion. At the governmental level there has also often been a tendency to believe that violence can be met only with violence, and to ignore the root causes underlying the phenomenon of terrorism.

How does this analysis relate to the decline and fall of the Shah? In the first place, authoritarian regimes like that in Iran where, despite relative liberalisation, there is limited scope for the expression of political dissent, inevitably oblige opposition movements to use religion as a cloak of respectability: in the absence of the hustings, the mosque, as we have seen, becomes a legitimate platform. But in Iran there was in any case a groundswell of genuinely religious opinion outraged by the Shah's modernisation programmes and their association with Western values and life-styles. It was not only the ayatollahs who felt this way, but a generation of students influenced by a little-known figure outside (or, in certain circles, inside) Iran named Ali Shariati. He has some claim to the title of the ideologist of the revolution who, in the tradition of earlier Islamic thinkers like Muhammad Abduh in Egypt and Muhammad Iqbal in Pakistan, tried to bridge the gap between the teachings of Islam and the demands of the twentieth century, and succeeded in convincing his student followers (re-garded by the Shah as 'Islamic Marxists') that it was possible to reconcile the two. The fact that Islam generally does not distinguish between 'church' and 'state', and that Shi'a doctrine in particular takes a less than reverent view of monarchy, also contributed to the growing disenchantment with the Shah.

Considerations of this kind tended to make unmeaningful the question whether the revolution was of a political or a religious nature. It was both of these things – and more than them. In his fascinating account of the Iranian crisis as seen from Washington, *All Fall Down*[14], the White House staffer Gary Sick (would that there had been more like him in the Reagan Administration), puts the point well:

> The eagerness for change in the Iranian body politic was a manifestation of deep social, economic and historical forces. Khomeini did not invent those feelings, but he mustered them and endowed them with form and purpose. Khomeini did not cause the revolution, but it is no exaggeration to say that he single-handedly transformed an inchoate reform movement with limited objectives into a genuinely revolutionary experience with its own unique ideological content.

We ourselves underestimated the strength and the appeal of the Islamic factor until a very late stage. In this, we erred in good company, which included the Shah himself. It also included the Americans. Sick quotes an exasperated State Department official as remarking after the revolution: 'Whoever took religion seriously?'

One reason for our ignorance was the unfamiliarity of some of the relevant concepts to the Western mind. But another was the deliberate decision, taken many years before, not to try to establish contacts with the religious fraternity for fear of upsetting the Shah and undermining our 'special relationship' with him. This rubric covered a multitude of sins of omission and of commission. We were all to some extent mesmerised by the personality of the Shah, while at the same time making serious misjudgements about him. It is by no means the only example of the British penchant for regarding an oriental potentate as larger than life, and as possessing some innate, almost mystical, qualities which it is verging on the heretical to question. Oriental potentates are admittedly unaccustomed – and therefore sensitive – to criticism; yet there is an Arabic proverb to the effect that your friend is not the man who tells you what you want to hear, but the man who tells you the truth. If the British relationship with the Shah was such that home truths were out of the question then perhaps it merited closer examination than it received. Our self-denying ordinance was in any case self-defeating since, while cutting us off from important sources of information, it still did not prevent the Shah from harbouring suspicions that we were acting conspiratorially in Iran.

In addition to neglect of the religious factor and undue adulation of the Shah, a third lesson which could be drawn from our experience of the revolution was the excessive part played in our decision-making by commercial considerations of one kind and another. As I had felt in Copenhagen, a series of official committees such as Plowden, Duncan (and subsequently Berrill) had brainwashed the Diplomatic Service into believing that trade promotion was the be-all and end-all of the modern diplomat's existence. The idea took hold that since Britain could no longer influence foreign countries as she had in her heyday it was no longer necessary to know a great deal about what was going on in them. Conventional political reporting became subordinated to winning the next contract or recycling the petro-dollars. There is, of course, a need for both, but my own view is that the enterprising businessman neither wants nor expects an Embassy to do his selling for him, but looks to it for advice on political stability, market prospects, trading methods and whom to deal with. Such advice requires a more judicious mix of political and commercial work than was evident in the activities of the Tehran Embassy at the critical time, largely through no fault of its own.

A more controversial aspect of the commercial scene which calls for examination is the vexed question of 'defence sales'. These constituted a major share of British (and American) exports to Iran during the Shah's declining years. There were good reasons, and compelling arguments, for this. Iran was a principal bulwark in the Western strategic plan for the area, not least in containing the Soviet Union. Britain needed the orders and the production lines. A close defence relationship seemed the logical answer: make your ally dependent on you and do yourself a good turn in the process. Unfortunately, the logic was more than a little flawed. For one thing, far from the Shah becoming dependent on us for supplies, we were sometimes dependent on him for orders, so that the leverage could be on his side rather than ours. Secondly, the amount of sophisticated hardware sold to Iran became increasingly difficult to equate with her actual needs. Both economically and politically it represented a potential source of instability, and Iran was not the only member of the arms bazaar whose public began to wonder whether it was external enemies against whom the equipment was designed to be used; or in what circumstances and precisely against whom it would be deployed; or even why the enormous sums of money devoted to it were not being spent on purposes closer to their own needs. As a *Times* leader aptly commented some years later: ' It would be absurd if the ramparts of the Western world were to crumble under the weight of weaponry intended to defend it'.

My concern with this problem was not confined to the Iranian context. 'Regional super-powers' like Iran and Saudi Arabia – the twin pillars of Western strategy in the area – had good reason to arm themselves, albeit hardly on the scale which the Americans and the British (subject always to the views of the Israelis) were encouraging. But what of some of the smaller states in the area? They had, of course, the right of self-defence. But against whom was this likely to be exercised? If the Russians, then this seemed an improbable scenario, since subversion rather than aggression appeared the better tactic for the Kremlin; and even if the Soviet Union were to attack any of the Gulf countries, no amount of sophisticated equipment would avail them much without external assistance. If the shaikhdoms wanted arms to enable them to pursue their petty squabbles with their neighbours, was this something which the British of all people, with their historical associations in the area, should be encouraging, especially where such a policy might lead us (as in one case it virtually did) to arm a shaikhdom while one of our European partners armed its foe next door?

Considerations of this kind led me to the conclusion that our defence sales policy was not so much immoral and cynical as opposed to our longer-term practical interests. The moral issue was interesting, but a trifle academic. I remember being astonished when a high official of the Ministry of Defence Sales Directorate was interviewed on television in the late '70s. Did he not feel some qualms, he was asked, about purveying lethal equipment around the world? The extraordinarily bland reply was that when he had previously been employed in British Leyland selling lorries he had not regarded himself as being blameworthy if one of them unfortunately happened to knock down an innocent pedestrian. The fact that lorries were not designed to kill, while tanks were, was a distinction which appeared not to have occurred to this diligent arms salesman. As for cynicism, he and his colleagues were apt to argue that in any case the arms we sold were seldom used, as though this somehow justified the whole business.

It was not as if there were no legitimate justifications. Some of them have already been referred to, and most of them I deployed myself many a time. But two of them were particularly difficult to refute. One was that even if our friends demanded up-to-date weapons as status symbols (which I fear was often the case) it was not for us to play the nanny and tell them that such toys were dangerous. I was not entirely convinced that we could not have said something like this on occasions: primly anti-colonialist attitudes sat ill with neo-colonialist relationships. But the most telling argument of all was that summed up in the oft-repeated phrase, 'If we don't, someone else will'. And the someone else was not necessarily on the other side of the iron curtain. In the imperfect world in which we live, this consideration had to be the clinching factor. Yet it was not the sole answer. Even setting aside the moral issue involved in vast world expenditure on armaments when millions of the world's people are starving – and that is not entirely a clear-cut question – what bothered me (and still does) is that the arms suppliers were so intent on the quick buck that their short-term commercial gain might be bought too dearly at the cost of long-term political stability – for all the reasons cited above – which was as much in their commercial as in their wider interest. To achieve international agreement on a self-denying ordinance of this kind might seem pie-in-the-sky, though it is not unknown. But at least in our own backyard, it seemed to me, these two conflicting considerations should be weighed in the balance in specific cases, instead of the defence sales tail invariably being permitted to wag the foreign policy dog.

My final memory of these traumatic times, however, enables me to end my account of them on a lighter note. New Year's Eve 1978 found me ensconced in a garret at the top of the Foreign Office building, taking charge of the emergency unit which we had to activate to deal with the problems of evacuating British citizens from Iran, as the resident clerk had informed me at 7 o'clock that morning our Ambassador in Tehran had advised. Heavy snow, sub-zero temperatures, icy roads and the customary state of public transport in such circumstances – not to mention a holiday period – had obliged me to take a taxi to the office. I might have expected that the first and greatest problem I had to resolve was the inevitable suggestion by George Brown that he should perform his usual *deus ex machina* act by descending on Tehran to settle the crisis. My instinctive reaction was that Ministers would not welcome this intervention (which was correct, though they were curiously reluctant to tell him so themselves). I therefore stalled as best I could when George Brown made his initial telephone call. I think it must have been on this occasion – though it could equally well have been on a number of others – that he remarked somewhat petulantly, 'You're a downy bird, aren't you? – never use one word where half a word will do!'

14

'The Last Vestige of the Raj'

Arriving in Muscat in early May 1979 to take over our first Embassy, Christine and I found the omens doubly auspicious. The Omanis were still basking in the euphoria of the Royal Visit, which from their point of view had been spoiled only by some frank speaking on the part of an accompanying British Minister: he had seen fit to tell the Omani Minister of State for Foreign Affairs in no uncertain terms that if the Sultan got himself into similar difficulties to the Shah's, Qaboos should not expect us to pull his chestnuts out of the fire. Even this infelicity did not blight our relations for long, because the Omanis emitted an almost audible sigh of relief when they heard that Mrs Thatcher had won the general election in Britain. In fact, she moved into No. 10 only a few days after we took rather more temporary possession of the old Arab house which had served as both office and Residence for successive Political Agents, Consuls-General and Ambassadors for 90 years, and the site of which they had occupied for at least 120 and possibly 180.

Although one sometimes needed a vivid historical imagination to appreciate it to the full, it was an attractive building in the traditional style, with an open courtyard in the middle. More and more offices had been crammed into the ground floor as the Diplomatic Mission expanded over the years, to the detriment of the original architecture. The living accommodation and reception rooms on the upper floors appeared, however, to have been comparatively untouched by the passage of time, to the detriment of the occupants' comfort. But the saving grace was the magnificent location directly overlooking the horseshoe-shaped Muscat Bay, hard by the sixteenth-century Portuguese fort of Jalali (of evil repute in the days of the Sultan's father, who had consigned his political opponents and other miscreants to its unsavoury dungeons), while to the left the Embassy compound was adjoined by the new neo-Moghul palace of Sultan Qaboos. Although much criticised as overwhelmingly dominating the waterfront, this excrescence was not entirely without merit, and when we arrived in the small hours of a warm May morning to find it ablaze with light reflected in the waters of the bay, the scene was reminiscent of some fairy-land – or at least a pantomime set. The simile was to prove not altogether inapt. For the moment, however, the delightful ambience provided a suitable cause of good-humoured banter from my sons – ever ready, like most of their ilk, to prick the bubble of paternal pomposity – when in a frenzied attempt to respond to the local English-language weekly's demand for a quotable comment on my first impressions of Muscat, I was rash enough to say that I found this view a 'constant source of spiritual refreshment'!

There were naturally other matters to occupy my mind in the first heady weeks of being an Ambassador. Credentials had to be presented. This required a drive of fully two minutes to the palace next door, but the Omanis were meticulous about the timing, and sent a couple of officials round to the Embassy equipped with the latest walkie-talkie radios so that they could receive instructions from the palace as to precisely when His Excellency and his entourage should embark on the journey. Unfortunately, at the crucial moment these technological marvels failed to function. Could the officials please use the telephone to communicate with the palace? Alas, this apparatus too proved to be out of order, and the luckless fellows finished up by waving handkerchiefs out of the window to indicate that the cortege was on its way.

In accordance with the British tradition and the Sultan's wishes I wore my 'tropical' diplomatic uniform for the ceremony. Unlike the heavy blue cloth, gold braid and plumed hat of the winter uniform (which, owing to the heat and humidity, I donned but once during my time in Muscat) the summer whites were not at all impressive. They were crowned by a choice of headgear, either a spiked helmet which made you resemble a colonial policeman, or a peaked cap which made you look like a bus conductor. As a matter of convenience, I opted for the latter: I had seen what happened to the Ambassadorial dignity when the spiked helmet got caught on the low door of the Jaguar on alighting. The proceedings were duly televised, with the flattering result that one of my diplomatic colleagues commented in the course of my subsequent courtesy call that he had been surprised to see that the British had sent an Admiral as their new Ambassador!

Of the calls it was necessary to make on the small Diplomatic Corps resident in Muscat, none caused me greater problems than that on the Iranian Chargé, whose Ambassador had left following the revolution and was not replaced for some time. I found a bright and personable young man surrounded by pictures and posters of the Ayatollah Khomeini. Somehow the two did not seem to go together. Obviously, I could not suggest by anything I said that he was other than a zealous devotee of the regime he served. At the same time I was anxious not to give the impression that I shared his enthusiasm, if such it was. After a good deal of sparring, I finally made some lame remark to the effect that governments' relations with governments changed but people's feelings about people remained the same. His reply gave me not the slightest hint of where he stood. Meeting him later on various social occasions, I found it increasingly difficult to imagine him as a fanatical theocrat. Finally, a few weeks after our arrival, we attended a very Westernised Omani wedding at which the Iranian and his attractive wife were also present. And who but they should set the pace on the dance floor when the post-prandial jitterbugging began – in a way which the Ayatollah would most certainly not have approved!

Introductory calls on Omani ministers provided interesting contrasts in both views and life-styles. Thinking that I knew at least a little of the customs of the country, I made sure that in my first visits I did not commit the solecism of taking my leave before the coffee was served. The result was some painfully long and often desultory conversations waiting for something that never came. After several such experiences I decided to make the running at the next ministerial office, and rose to leave after about ten minutes.

My interlocutor was clearly offended, and motioned me to sit down. Eventually full honours were done with the ritual of 'halwa' (the local version of Turkish delight), coffee, rosewater and incense. But this was the exception rather than the rule, most of the ministers being more modern and businesslike than this particular grey-beard – who, in fact, was relieved of his post later the same day, so perhaps my call had more significance for him than it had for me.

As regards their views, most were predictably along official lines with the obligatory genuflections in the direction of the Sultan. At the extreme end of the spectrum was the Minister with whom I discussed Oman's robust support for Sadat's Israel policy. My own view, confided to my diary when Sadat made his historic visit to Jerusalem in November 1977, was that he was on a hiding to nothing: if he achieved nothing his Arab brothers would say, 'We told you so,' while if he achieved something within the bounds of the possible they would accuse him of betraying the cause in Egypt's own interest. Rightly or wrongly, the latter proved to be the case. But in a gesture that was more proud than prudent, Oman, together with Sudan and Somalia, stood out in support of the Camp David accords and the subsequent Egypt/Israel treaty. So, for that matter, did we, which made us duly grateful that the Omanis at least had the courage of their convictions. Whether it behoved them, suspect as they were in the Arab world for their close association with the West, to shout those convictions from the rooftops was another matter. But the Minister in question had no doubt at all that they were right to do so: that was what they thought, and therefore that is what they had to say. It was an admirable attitude in its way, a breath of candour in a cynical world. But it was also extremely naive, and uncharacteristic of the normal Arab reaction to fudge issues rather than to face them. The same propensity to 'stand up and be counted' was very nearly to get Oman into hot water in connection with the hostilities between Iraq and Iran the following year.

I was to learn that in many respects the Omanis were the most un-Arab Arabs I had encountered. Until comparatively recently they had tended to look outwards in the direction of the Indian subcontinent and the coast of East Africa rather than inwards to the Arabian Peninsula. Given their own maritime nature, the geographical barrier of mountains and desert which separated them from the heart of Arabia, and the fact that there had been precious little to look to in the rest of the peninsula, this was perhaps inevitable. But it bred a kind of isolationism, and more than a little disdain for the ignorant Bedu of the interior (stretching as far as Kuwait!) who had in Omani eyes no history to speak of. It also produced more positive qualities: a sturdy independence, a fierce pride, but an unusual degree of tolerance of foreigners, especially among the coastal people.

The majority of Omanis were Ibadhi Muslims, historically a sect which had rejected both the Sunni and the Shi‘a views on the succession to the caliphate, or leadership of Islam, after the death of the Prophet Muhammad. In faith and practice, they had been said (by the Rev. G.P. Badger, in his introduction to *The History of the Imams and Seyyids of Oman*[15]) to 'hold a position towards Islamic orthodoxy not unlike that of the Nonconformist Calvinistic bodies in this country towards the community of the established church'. Such differences were no longer apparent to the outsider, but at an earlier stage there had been a division among the Ibadhis themselves. Those of the interior ('Oman proper') tended to be conservative, eking out a precarious existence in their rugged mountains and their inaccessible valleys, and sustained by a strong spiritual faith. Those on the coast ('Muscat') were relatively moderate, their Ibadhi Muslim beliefs tempered by the practical constraints of the commercial world and by their contacts not only with external influences encountered on their travels but with folk of other races, creeds and colours settled upon their own shores, including in particular Sunni and Shi‘a Muslims. 'Religion is here of all kinds and denominations,' wrote Palgrave in the early 1860s, 'but the golden calf counts, I think, more sincere worshippers at Muscat than any other divinity soever'.[16]

Their cosmopolitan qualities certainly made the Omanis a pleasure to deal with. Nevertheless, in the last quarter of the twentieth century some of these characteristics were a luxury they could no longer afford. The Sultanate's immediate future seemed to me to demand the closest co-operation with her neighbours, while in the longer term it lay in becoming truly part of the Arab world. Accordingly, one sometimes wished that the Omani oak, solid though it appeared, could bend like the Saudi willow in the face of the prevailing wind.

This did in fact happen in the early 1980s when regional pressures encouraged the Gulf countries to set up the Gulf Co-operation Council. Growing gradually from practical habits of consultation in various fields, this organisation has been far more successful than many vaunted attempts at Arab unity proclaimed from the top with a flourish of trumpets. If the Omanis saw it in the initial stages primarily as a vehicle for defence arrangements, whereas the other Gulf states viewed it from an economic and social standpoint, as time went on the Sultanate was able to stiffen the military backbone of the GCC while having a healthy dose of political realism injected by its fellow-members. In the light of more recent events, it is amusing to recall that in 1979 Oman proposed that oil producers and consumers in the region should contribute to provide a mine-sweeping capability for the Sultan's navy. Not surprisingly at the time, this plea to 'give us the money to buy the tools and we will finish the job' fell on deaf ears.

It was a curious paradox that while the Sultanate's external postures were often exposed to the point of indecency, on the internal front the media were programmed to conceal rather than to reveal. An obsession with security partly accounted for this, but the regime's record was such that the heavy shroud of secrecy was not only unnecessary but positively harmful. It made public opinion difficult to gauge, and it invited the suspicion that there was more to hide than was necessarily the case.

During my inaugural round of calls only two ministers ventured to depart from the party line that everything in the garden was lovely, thanks to the enlightened leadership of His Majesty Sultan Qaboos, who had transformed the Sultanate in a decade. One was openly critical of the extent of corruption – in the sense of widespread abuse by Ministers and officials of their public office for their private gain – and the limits on popular participation in the decision-making process. The other suggested, without the least hint of disloyalty, that Oman had been fortunate not to have succumbed to Communist subversion. Although neither of these views was entirely unfounded, and there were also problems relating to budgetary priorities as between defence and development, and to regional distribution, Oman was far from ripe for a repetition of what had happened in Iran.

The new-look Sultanate was virtually nine years old in 1979, so that even the younger generation knew how much better things were than they had been in the locust years before Qaboos. The population was small, scattered and subservient. The Sultan himself, while lacking the charisma of a Hussain, was no mere figurehead. As a devout Muslim with a British private and military education behind him, he was well-placed to preserve what was best in the Sultanate's traditions while bringing it the benefits of modern civilisation. He accordingly avoided most of the strictures which the sterner Ibadhis of the interior had heaped upon his great-grandfather at the turn of the century.

> Although an Ibadhi like themselves, he had failed in his dispensation of justice to apply the shari'ah in strict conformity with the Ibadhi interpretation. He could not speak, read or write literary Arabic, and indeed the language in which he appeared to converse most easily was Gujerati... Faisal ibn Turki not only tolerated Hindus, Jews and Christians at Muscat, but he also permitted the importation of liquor and tobacco into the capital. He relied upon the British for his continuance in power, and he looked to India, not Arabia, for cultural inspiration.[17]

Qaboos was well aware of the need for political advance to keep pace with economic and social progress. He often used to say that the trick was in the timing: if you introduced democratic processes too early, you encouraged people to run before they could walk; if you left it too late, you found yourself forced to make concessions, each of which was regarded as a sign of weakness, so that you lost control of the game. He regarded the Shah as having made the latter mistake. Between 1979 and 1981 he gradually introduced a greater non-governmental share in decision-making, culminating in the establishment of a Consultative Council for the State. Without going so far as an elective system, this at least broadened the base of the administration, made Ministers more accountable to the public and provided a two-way channel between government and the governed. A decade later, in response to the prevailing climate at the time of the Gulf War, he was to take the process further forward with his 'majlis ash-shura'.

As far as Britain was concerned, the relationship with Oman could certainly be described as 'special'. Historical links and current ties made diplomatic access unusually easy, and we were generally on the same wavelength. The 6000 or so British expatriates working in business, government or the armed forces returned the welcome they received by a genuine affection for the country and the people. Yet one had to be careful not to be beguiled by the charms of Oman and the Omanis into ignoring the possible pitfalls. The Sultanate was no less (and no more) stable than any of its Gulf neighbours, but the British commitment to it was such that if anything were to go wrong our exposure could have more serious consequences than elsewhere. While the British involvement was greater than ever before, so was the Sultanate's independence. We were therefore in some danger of finding ourselves in the same position of 'responsibility without power' which had bedevilled us in the rest of the Gulf prior to 'withdrawal' in 1971.

Many were the foreign diplomats and journalists who came to congratulate me on presiding over 'the last vestige of the Raj'. I could understand how they obtained this impression. The British presence, though for the most part discreet, was sometimes too obtrusive for comfort: even FCO mandarins who came out on visits expressed themselves as disturbed by aspects of it. But it was a far cry from 1887, when the American Deputy Consul reported (doubtless with more than a tinge of envy) that 'the Sultan is completely in the hands of the British representative here, and generally does as he is told by that official'[18]. I found myself trying to convince the foreigners that Sultan Qaboos was very much his own man, and my London-based colleagues that 'Omanisation' could not be rushed – and that meanwhile, although the British presence helped us commercially and in other ways, it did not always give us a commensurate influence.

This was about to be eroded to some extent by a new United States interest in the Sultanate. Following their disastrous experience in Vietnam of direct intervention against what they regarded as the inexorable expansion of world Communism, the Americans had adopted a fresh approach to their global responsibilities. They now set about building up strong regional powers as their proxies. In the Middle East the chosen instruments of their 'twin pillar' policy were Iran and Saudi Arabia. But the collapse of the Shah early in 1979 had knocked away the major prop of this strategy, while that event, coming on top of the Camp David process, had weakened the other by exposing it to radical Arab criticism of its fruitless association with the United States. With the Soviet invasion of Afghanistan at the end of 1979 providing additional impetus, and President Carter enunciating the doctrine in his 1980 State of the Union message that, 'Any attempt by any outside force to gain control of the Persian Gulf will be repelled by any means necessary including military force,' Washington's credibility demanded a fresh approach. This took the form of creating a Rapid Deployment Force which would be able at short notice to act as a fire brigade in the event of trouble, for example in the Gulf, emanating either from the Soviet Union or now from revolutionary Iran. This strategy depended, however, on facilities, if not bases, being made available for the pre-positioning of equipment and stores and the construction of the necessary infrastructure for use in an emergency by American aircraft, ships and troops.

In principle, the granting of such facilities was anathema to the majority of Gulf countries, for whom it would represent a considerable political liability in Arab terms. In practice, most of the local Governments were not averse to having the Americans 'over the horizon', but somehow expected them to be able to bail them out at the drop of a hat in the event of trouble. The Omanis took a predictably more robust and realistic view, and agreed to open negotiations for an 'access agreement' by which the United

States would obtain facilities at Masirah and other places, under certain conditions. Apart from financial provisions, the most important of these were that activation of the facilities should be allowed only after mutual consultation and for purposes of which the host country approved. The negotiations took many months to conclude, and were not helped by the occurrence, shortly after they began, of the abortive hostage rescue attempt by the Americans in Iran in April 1980. To say the least, this alerted the Omanis to the kind of problem to which the proposed access agreement might expose them. However, it proved only a minor hiccup, thanks in part to some timely British advice, for which the Embassy received a gratifying bouquet from Washington.

Although this was rather more than our role at the time deserved, it was true that my US colleague and I remained close both literally and metaphorically. The US Embassy occupied a site just behind our own, renting an old Omani house overlooking ours. One of its features was that, being built into the neighbouring hillside, it boasted an upstairs bathroom of which one wall was solid original rock. The Americans were fond of telling the story of a visiting Congressman who, repairing to the facilities after dining well but not too wisely, emerged with the astonished enquiry, 'Say, Mr Ambassador, how the hell d'ya get that huge stone into the bathroom?'

When we gave a farewell dinner to Marshall Wiley I took the opportunity to quip that it had always been a comfort to know that the Americans in Muscat were exactly where they should be – right behind us. Wiley responded in kind by commenting that it had been no less a pleasure for him to look down on us! More seriously, the British Government view of the new US dimension in Oman was that although it would undoubtedly make some inroads on our previously privileged position in the Sultanate and sharpen the commercial rivalry (not least in the cut-throat competition for arms sales) these considerations paled beside the community of interests which we shared in the area generally. There were now things which the Americans could do in and for Oman which we could no longer do, and there were still things we could do which they could not. Provided we kept in close consultation with the Omanis and with each other, and observed a reasonable degree of give and take, there was no reason why the American presence should not supplement rather than supplant that of the British.

Needless to say, it was not quite as simple as this. Efforts we and the Americans made to engage the Omanis in trilateral talks about the military and other aspects of our joint involvement in the Sultanate came to naught, perhaps because the Omanis feared that a triangular framework would enable unwelcome pressures to be brought in other directions. Moreover, both Wiley and I had our servicemen to contend with. He understood how important it was for them to maintain a low profile if the Omanis were not to be embarrassed internationally by the American presence; but he was constantly frustrated by Washington's inability to keep anything quiet or to keep quiet about anything, as well as by the high-key behaviour of the American forces involved in implementing the access agreement or participating in military exercises. This in turn upset the British element in the Sultan's armed forces, whose habitual discretion was found wanting when it came to concealing their obvious distaste for the American incursion into what they regarded as their 'patch'. This situation often called for a good deal of diplomacy.

A Persian poet once wrote: 'Muscat gives to the panting sinner a living anticipation of his future destiny'. One summer night the thermometer on our upstairs verandah registered 90° while its companion hygrometer was recording over 100° of humidity: the combination was devastating. We were surrounded by rocks which absorbed the heat in the day-time and exuded it at night, like some natural storage heaters. But somehow we kept better health in the wet heat than in the dry heat of Kaduna (and later Damascus); and anyway the provision of air-conditioning in Muscat was not ungenerous, and what there was increased and improved during our incumbency. We also benefited – as did our staff and numerous visitors – from a large swimming pool which some worthy predecessor had installed in the garden at the back of the Embassy.

After the initial excitements of settling in to the house and the job, I found that the ensuing summer months were a period of comparative official inactivity. We used them to undertake one or two 'industrial visits' in the capital area – to the desalination plant, the flour mill, the Danish-run Oman Dairies, and the satellite station. Later we were shown round the oil installations at Fahud in the interior of northern Oman. This had been part of the area which first excited the interest of the oil companies back in the 1950s. But after drilling a dry well there the Iraq Petroleum Company consortium had abandoned the concession. It was subsequently taken up by Shell, who soon struck lucky no more than 400 yards away, and this was the beginning of Oman's oil era. We could still see the original well which stands as a monument to the hazards of the exploration process.

Apart from anything else, these visits provided for children out for the holidays interesting diversions from the routine of days spent at the oil company beach, or weekend launch trips along the coast to the local beauty spots. The favourite was Bandar Jissah, which had been the centre of a *cause célèbre* in Anglo-Omani relations in 1898: Oman's 'Fashoda incident'.

The Sultan of the day, the Gujerati-speaking Faisal, wearying of the tiresome British complaints about his trade in slaves and arms, turned to the French, who were more relaxed about such things. He agreed to let them establish a coaling-station at Bandar Jissah. This was too much for the British, one object of whose presence in Muscat had for long been to frustrate French designs on the region. The Sultan was forced to rescind his agreement with the French on pain of having his Muscat palace blown to smithereens.

For fishing or swimming trips down the coast we became dependent on the generosity of others after the inevitable FCO inspectors, visiting us within weeks of our arrival and having thoroughly enjoyed the amenity of the aged Embassy launch, abolished it as an unjustifiable luxury: it seemed that although Muscat might lack some of the facilities which to the ordinary man compensate for the difficult climate, it was paradise compared with another post where the inspectors called – Mogadishu. I could not seriously quarrel with this, nor with the decision over the launch (shades of Aden ten years before!) especially when a Royal Navy officer from the nearby Oman navy base, whom we had invited to inspect the craft, immediately recognised it as one he had condemned in Singapore 15 years earlier.

Both this first summer and later we joined in a number of excursions arranged by the Oman Historical Society, mostly within the vicinity of the capital area, but sometimes farther afield. The great thing about these was that among the members of the society there were knowledgeable and interested Omanis, as well as expatriates who were familiar with the country, so that one could go well off the beaten track, and obtain some unusual insights in more senses than one. On our own account, though we did not subscribe to the local zeal for camping (personally, while I was prepared to rough it in the daytime, I preferred my creature comforts at night), we explored a good deal of the Sultanate. The two-hour drive to the old interior capital of Nizwa, with its fascinating suq abounding in Omani silver and its ancient round fort adjoining a modern mosque, became a familiar trek. Farther west, towards the United Arab Emirates, was the favourite mountain village of Misfa, nestling in the rocky hillside and the steps of its stone streets worn smooth with the tread of countless generations. In the plain below, Hamra al-Abriyyin, with its mud houses, its date-gardens and its life-giving 'falaj' (water channel) running through, and in places under, the buildings, was the archetype of an Omani country town. There was Bahla, whose market was frequently the venue of sheep and goat auctions; and Jabrin, where an Italian/French team was restoring a particularly attractive old castle. A feature of most of these visits was the genuine invitations one received into the homes of the villagers, an Arab tradition which further west is now honoured more in the breach than the observance.

To the north, we visited the forts redolent with history at Nakhl, Barka, Rostaq and Sohar along the Batinah coast, leading eventually to the rugged and almost inaccessible Musandam Peninsula overlooking the Straits of Hormuz, shortly to become a household name with the outbreak of the Gulf War and the establishment of the Royal Navy's Armilla patrol. My naval and Air Attaché kindly arranged for me to spend a night aboard one of the ships, to which I proceeded by helicopter. Less kindly, perhaps, the appointment was made for Trafalgar Night, thus ensuring that I, not he, was invited to propose the immortal memory. At least the fare on this occasion was not bully beef; but I could not resist pointing out the incongruity of serving Beef Wellington, however good, by way of celebrating the great victory of Nelson. I also got my own back on my Attaché colleague by complaining about the incredible volume of signal traffic which passed through the Embassy between the patrol and the Ministry of Defence, and which was especially galling to an Ambassador who was rationed by the Foreign Office to about two telegrams a week, not exceeding ten words apiece. (Honesty compels me to admit that he later evened the score when I seized on a massively long message giving details of the menus on some VIP flight from London to Sydney. 'All very mouth-watering,' I observed sourly, 'but what on earth does it have to do with us?'

'Perhaps, Sir, you have overlooked the fact that Muscat has to provide the victualling for one leg of the journey?')

To the south, Oman was another country. The little island of Masirah, now no longer an RAF station but an Oman Air Force training centre, with covetous American eyes being cast in its direction, was still home to the BBC's British Eastern Relay Station. It was still a pretty God-forsaken spot, where the major amusements were sand-yachting, turtle-watching and 'wadi-bashing'. But, as often happens with Britons in such places, it was a remarkably happy community, no doubt helped by the fact that the normal tour of duty was six months (or twelve if accompanied).

The southern province of Dhofar, scene of the recent civil war, was quite unlike northern Oman, to which it became connected shortly before we left by a 600-mile road between Nizwa and Salalah (thus prompting the apt comment on Oman TV that the project would 'go a long way' to uniting the two parts of the country). The palm-fringed seashore and the black mammies in the suqs of Salalah gave a more East African than Arab appearance to the capital. A few miles inland the 'jebel' rose sharply from the plain, the ridge at the top marking the monsoon line, so that at certain times of year you could see from the air the stark contrast of green on one side and brown on the other.

The authorities, rightly proud of having defeated the ten-year insurrection apart from about 40 rebels still holed up in the hills, were keen to show the development which peace was bringing to the area: schools, clinics and houses, grouped in Government centres for security and ease of administration, were replacing the crude hovels in which the wild Dhofari tribesman had lived for generations. On our first visit, a zealous British officer of the Royal Oman Police drove us to the top of the jebel to admire the new police station there. We arrived to find some kind of *contretemps* in progress between the arm of the law and a group of tribesmen, naked to the waist, partly daubed in blue dye and their hair in long oily locks – a fearsome-looking crew. A badly-wounded cow was slumped in the back of a pick-up truck, bleeding profusely from a shattered limb. The animal had evidently been one of a number run into the night before by some daredevil young driver. The argument was about the compensation which the Dhofaris could claim, and a regular bazaar haggle was under way. Our police officer explained that the price had risen sharply when the tribesmen had discovered the identity of the culprit, the son of an Omani Minister. A bargain was finally struck, but it availed the wretched animal little. It was beyond human help except to put it out of its misery, and its throat was duly cut before our very eyes.

The most interesting of our visits in the south was to the Kuria Muria Islands off the coast not far from Salalah. The islands comprise five peaks of a submerged mountain range and consist largely of gravel shores leading to low barren granite hills. Only the largest of them, Hallaniya, eight miles long and 22 square miles in area, is inhabited. It had enough water to support small herds of goats. The other islands have no vegetation and are populated only by sea-birds.

By a curious quirk of history it was these creatures which were responsible for 113 years of nominal British sovereignty. For when a passing British merchant captain in early Victorian times spotted deposits of guano and reported this back to London, he was instructed to open negotiations with the then Sultan, with a view to purchasing the islands, ostensibly as a suitable stopping-place for the Royal Navy. The somewhat romantic upshot of the negotiations was that the Sultan, declaring that if Queen Victoria wanted any part of his dominions she had only to ask, presented the islands to her in perpetuity. An embarrassed Foreign Secretary, Lord Clarendon, returned the compliment with true British modesty by sending Sultan Sa'id a silver snuff box. In due course the Kuria Murias became a joint responsibility of the British authorities in Aden and the Gulf, though the precise division of labour between them appears to have been rather confused – not least to the headman on Hallaniya in the early 1960s. He demanded to know of the visiting Governor of Aden and the Political Resident in the Persian Gulf whether they had the authority of the Sultan to set foot on the islands. Eventually, to the displeasure of the newly-independent Government in Aden, the Kuria Murias were handed back to Oman in 1967. History does not record what became of the snuff box.

By the mid-1970s the population of Hallaniya had dwindled to fewer than 100. They lived exceedingly primitively, and the island was extremely difficult of access. Sultan Qaboos felt that it would be in their best interests to move lock, stock and barrel to the mainland. This view was strengthened by an epidemic resulting from malnutrition which reduced the number of womenfolk to two. But the inhabitants declined to leave. Qaboos accordingly decreed that the distaff side should be reinforced, by subsidisation – provided that the ladies came from Oman. The islands then came under the wing of the Civil Aid Department in Salalah, under whose auspices and in the comfort of whose 'Skyvan' Christine and I visited Hallaniya in March 1980. The population then numbered 77: 50 men, but still only half a dozen women, and a score of children. Instead of the previous stone huts, the islanders were living in modern, if simple, concrete houses. They had their school (with an Egyptian teacher), their mosque and their clinic, converted from the original mosque when it was discovered that, despite the advice of a holy man on its siting, it was not facing in the prescribed direction of Mecca. The clinic was run by a resident orderly, supplemented by a flying doctor service from the mainland. A fish freezing plant was in operation. Apart from fish, practically everything (as well as wives) had to be imported. But improvements had been carried out to the water supply, and regular communication, supplies and building materials were maintained by the Skyvan service from Salalah. Life remained hard, but in some ways seemed almost idyllic: certainly the islanders themselves still had no wish to be resettled.

After six months in the post, I returned to London for a Middle East Heads of Mission conference. Somebody in the FCO with a sense of humour cast me for the role of opening speaker in the debate on arms exports, with the redoubtable (but always very friendly) Ron Ellis, Head of Defence Sales, in the opposite corner. I deployed the kinds of argument which have appeared in these pages. Ellis, paradoxically disarming, countered with the familiar line that a great proportion of the sales which his department promoted was 'non-lethal' and that anyway much of what did not fall into that category was never used. Needless to say, despite these disingenuous observations, he won the debate, if not the argument. On return to Muscat, however, I was pleased to receive a letter from another lone voice, who said that he had been glad to find that at least one Ambassador had spoken realistically on this issue. My gratification was only slightly modified when I came to the end of the letter and found that its signatory was the Head of the FCO Arms Control and Disarmament Department!

As it happened, this trip to London had somewhat harrowing associations. My mother, who had been unwell for weeks and had recently suffered a fall, died peacefully while I was at home: it was at least a fortunate coincidence that I had been able to see her a week before. A less happy one was that the wife of my Defence Attaché in Muscat died on the same day: she had flown home only six weeks earlier suffering from what appeared to be a minor stroke but turned out to be massive cancer. The day before returning to Muscat I attended her funeral at Eltham in the morning and my mother's at Southampton in the afternoon. To add to the cup of sorrow I saw outside the church the husband of our old family nanny. My mother had kept in touch with her over the years and she had been ill for some time. He was weeping copiously, which seemed to be a singular tribute to my mother – until he told me that his wife had died that very morning.

The Soviet invasion of Afghanistan, the Iranian revolution and the Iran/Iraq War combined to make Oman very much the centre of attention, if not the eye of the storm, during this period. One consequence was that we had a constant stream of visitors: brasshats, politicians and senior officials. They usually contrived to come in the winter months, when the climate was very pleasant, and the majority stayed with us in the Residence, so that we got to know some of them quite well. By and large it was not a particularly encouraging experience. I recall especially one Cabinet Minister who delivered over the privacy of our dinner table a stirring defence of the Civil Service but when asked by a service colleague why he did not say such things in public replied lamely that if he were to do so he would be the laughing-stock of his constituents.

Most of these visitors came to proclaim British support for the Sultanate without unduly emphasising the commercial element of our interest: the Omanis were understandably sensitive to any suggestion that we were 'only here for the beer'. The dilemma became particularly acute with Mrs Thatcher's visit in April 1981. This was the first visit ever to Oman by a British Prime Minister in office, and naturally one of the highspots of my mission. Unfortunately it later became associated with a controversy over the award of a lucrative contract for the Sultan Qaboos University (about which I was pursued by the British press in Damascus nearly three years later). The Prime Minister was alleged to have promoted the interests of a firm with which her son was connected. She claimed that although the matter of the contract had been discussed, she had only 'batted for Britain'. Though no Thatcher fan myself, I maintained (and still do) that during the 36 hours she spent in Oman I never saw or heard her put a foot wrong in this respect. That is not to say that the sudden appearance on the scene of Mark Thatcher himself (totally unexpected, even by his mother) by courtesy of certain highly-placed friends of his in Oman, was not a potential embarrassment – as Whitehall was duly warned.

Those 36 hours were typically action-packed, with the Embassy staff called upon to perform a range of duties from official briefing to making arrangements for the care of the Prime Ministerial coiffure. The party arrived in Muscat late one evening, when one of my first tasks was to convey a last-minute request by my fellow Heads of Diplomatic Missions to add to the next morning's already crowded programme a meeting to pay their respects to Mrs Thatcher. The entourage predictably demurred, but left it to me to pursue the matter with the Prime Minister. She not only raised no objection, but carried out the engagement with great charm and to the evident delight of my colleagues. This was followed by a coffee reception at the Residence for senior British businessmen and all Embassy staff before we set off for the airport for the VC10 flight to Salalah, where immediately on arrival the Prime Minister had a one and a half hour audience with the Sultan. To say that there was a meeting of minds would be a mild understatement: the 'Soviet threat' was taken for granted. Christine and I joined in a private lunch with the Thatchers in the sumptuous suite placed at their disposal by Qaboos in the new guest palace, which the Prime Minister and her party were in fact christening and in which our own relatively modest apartments were more luxurious than anything we had ever known.

Then we were off on an exhausting afternoon round, visiting the English Language Teaching Institute, opening the Salalah English-speaking school, and sight-seeing in the jebel (slaughtered cows well out of sight on this occasion!). Returning to Salalah we found some irate British television crews complaining that the PM was too late to catch the evening light and that they had consequently been put to the inconvenience of moving their equipment indoors for the interview – as though the entire purpose of the visit was to accommodate the TV cameras! The day ended on a somewhat formal and quiet note with the Sultan's official banquet, but with Mrs Thatcher showing no signs of flagging.

At 7 o'clock the following morning we were off on a helicopter trip to the Omani border post at Sarfait. This was a spectacular fortification perched high on a cliff with a sheer drop down to the Indian Ocean to the south, and the People's Democratic Republic of Yemen to the west. Unfortunately, on this particular occasion, visibility was practically nil because of a thick fog, but Mrs Thatcher and her party duly made a tour of inspection and chatted with the Omani and British troops in this remote outpost. Writing in *The Times* the next day, Robert Fisk, who was among the accompanying hordes of pressmen, commented that although the frontier area had been shrouded in mist, the Prime Minister had experienced no difficulty in discerning the Communist enemy on the other side. Then there was a quiet lunch with the Sultan out at his summer residence in the gardens at Mamurah, a final press conference and the visitors took off in their VC10 from Salalah while we returned by the Oman Royal Flight to Muscat. It had been an exhilarating and highly successful visit, thanks largely to Mrs Thatcher's amazing energy.

One unexpected bonus was the Prime Ministerial U-turn on our aid programme to Oman. This amounted to a modest £350,000 a year, devoted mainly to technical co-operation and training programmes which were admirably run by our British Council colleagues and were making a real contribution to enabling Oman to stand on its own feet. Indeed in the long run this kind of help was likely to prove even more valuable than our military assistance, provided, in both cases, that the pair of crutches we were supplying did not make the Omanis more, rather than less, dependent on us. The cold economic winds blowing through the corridors of power in Whitehall had, however, recently decreed that the aid programme worldwide should suffer an overall cut. Oman was an obvious priority candidate: oil production and prices (uninhibited by membership of OPEC, to which the Sultanate had shrewdly chosen not to belong, while enjoying the benefits of the union's activities) were on the increase, and although the sentence of lingering death which had been pronounced on our aid programme was an irritant in our relations with the Omanis, I had not felt able to argue strongly against it. Mrs Thatcher, however, immediately perceived the political implications and at once pronounced a reprieve. This was a welcome development, whatever light it may have shed on the processes of government.

In addition to ministerial contacts, supplemented by rather fewer in the opposite direction, we were also favoured by a number of royal visits or transits. The most significant was that of the Duke of Gloucester, who came to represent the Queen at the tenth National Day celebrations (the anniversary of Sultan Qaboos' accession) in November 1980. HRH was accompanied by his equerry Simon Bland, whom we had last known as Assistant Military Adviser in Karachi. They arrived by a commercial flight which was an hour late. It failed to appear at all for the royal departure four days after, whereupon the Sultan stepped nobly into the breach by placing his personal jet at the party's disposal for the return flight to Britain. Gratified as I was by this generous gesture, I could not help thinking that it was regrettably symbolic of the changed fortunes of our respective countries.

In between these alarums, however, the Duke packed in a number of excursions. These included an inland helicopter tour of various forts (the first of which I had to identify for the Chief of Proctocol!) concluding with a lunch by the Wali of Nizwa which was painfully slow, and as we were already behind the clock in a full schedule I had to indulge in some not so gentle nudging; and a visit to Tim Severin's reproduction of an ancient Omani dhow, the *Sohar*, which we had seen under construction at Sur and which was now about to embark on its epic voyage to Canton. The more formal programme embraced the range of customary National Day festivities: a military parade, as ever unashamedly British in its inspiration but imperfectly Omani in its execution; a garden party Buckingham Palace-style; a students' display which could only be described as Omani-style; and two private engagements with the Sultan. One of these was an audience at the Muscat Palace, memorable only for Simon Bland's largely unsuccessful juggling with the set of uniformed model soldiers down the ages which was the Duke's gift for Qaboos; and the other a delightfully relaxed dinner *al fresco* at one of the out-of-town royal establishments, to which the Sultan had invited his cousin Sayyid Fahd (a leading contender for the succession, if any, and the Duke's royal escort throughout his visit) with his rarely-seen French wife, and the (British) service commanders with their ladies. The elegant atmosphere, the Mozart in the background and above all the excellent rapport which HRH established with HM made this a memorable last evening of the visit. But also a late one: when the party broke up at 12.30am I was contemplating without enthusiasm the hour-long drive back to Muscat, and the prospect of being up at 5.30 for the Duke's departure, when to our joy and relief the ever-thoughtful Qaboos provided a helicopter which landed us on the pad just beside the Embassy.

Two months after the Thatcher visit I received the unexpected and unwelcome news that I was to be transferred early in 1982 to Damascus, once again to try to fill the ample shoes of Patrick Wright. Our farewells at the end of the year proved more than usually hectic. First of all, I had launched at the end of October the proposal that the Sultan should be invited on a return State Visit to Britain, and was keen that the public announcement of this should be made before my departure. By the end of November, Buckingham Palace was also in a hurry for the Sultan's formal reply to the Queen's invitation, for its own reasons. It proved impossible to bring forward my own farewell audience in order to kill these two birds with one stone, so I flew down to Salalah specially for the purpose. After the by now familiar lunch-time wait of two hours, I was ushered into the presence for what I expected to be a five-minute encounter from which I would emerge with the coveted reply. To my surprise, we had the longest (one and a half hours) and the most interesting conversation I ever had with the Sultan, but without so much as a word about my object in coming! When I ventured to raise the matter shortly before taking my leave, Qaboos said he would hand over his answer the following week, when I was due to accompany Douglas Hurd and have my own farewell audience. (What the Sultan thought I had come for on this occasion I never discovered, but the conversation was a distinct bonus).

Douglas Hurd's visit was the second complicating factor in our departure. As Minister of State in the FCO he had come quite often, once accompanying the Prime Minister but otherwise on his own. One particular visit stands out in my memory, when we had to go out into the desert to see Qaboos, who was engaged in one of his meet-the-people tours. He explained the purpose of these in alarmingly ambiguous terms: 'I hear the complaints of my subjects, give the necessary orders to my ministers and officials, and then make sure that they are executed'.

The Sultan received us in a simple tent, sitting Arab-style on a rug and his haunches, a posture which after only a few minutes Douglas Hurd and I found it impossible to emulate. As it happened, we were followed on that occasion by the UN Secretary General, Kurt Waldheim, who must have experienced even greater difficulty. Whether or not it was the discomfort or the international situation at the time, I remember him as a particularly gloomy individual when he joined us afterwards in another tent for a very late lunch.

This last visit of Hurd's actually coincided with our final days in the Embassy – we took off, leaving him and his Private Secretary in sole possession. But before that, we had flown down to Salalah once more, where Christine called on the Sultan's mother, a lady of humble origins but considerable influence, as was often the case in those parts; I had a very perfunctory audience, but consoled myself with the thought of the previous week's, and came away clutching the precious piece of paper. The announcement of the State Visit was duly made before we left Muscat. It took place the following March: too late for me, as the Queen's visit to Oman had been too early!

We returned from Salalah to face a full evening in which Christine had to go alone to our Indian colleague's farewell dinner for us while I accompanied Douglas Hurd to a private dinner with his Omani opposite number, a charming and able man named Qais Zawawi. I liked to think that, after a slow start, I had eventually established a good relationship with him. (He later became Deputy Prime Minister but sadly died in a road accident in 1995). I went on to the Indians after this, and found myself eating a second dinner as well as having to respond to an inordinately long and flowery valedictory oration.

The farewell speech I treasured most was that given by the acting Dean of the Diplomatic Corps when I was accorded the customary honour of the Corps' presentation. In Muscat, this took the form of a local silver 'khanjar' (curved dagger) – all the more acceptable in the light of the many contributions one had made for previously departing colleagues. The acting Dean was one of the Gulf Ambassadors, who had taken the trouble to circulate beforehand a copy of his speech in translation. This described me as 'an equal to, active and cooperated man', which had had 'the affect (sic) to set up bridges of love, friendship and good relation between us, that we will always remember'. The spirit of this encomium was evidently not shared by those who had decreed that we should take the road to Damascus.

15

The Road to Damascus

If someone in the FCO had decided that after grazing in the lush pastures of Oman for two and a half years it was time we learned what the real world was like, the transfer to Syria could hardly have been a better choice. Instead of living in a prestigious location with a view offering 'spiritual refreshment', we found ourselves installed in a modest suburban villa commanding a prospect of the neighbours' washing lines across the street. We were now the poor relations of the French and the Americans, both of whom lived in some splendour. Yet most of our diplomatic colleagues, who lived in impressive apartments with spacious reception rooms, would gladly have exchanged them for our limited entertainment facilities but our detached and comfortable family home, with its vine-covered patio overlooking a colourful garden and its small plunge-pool (which it became the bane of my life to maintain).

The bad news was that our villa happened to be along the street from a block of flats occupied by the family of the President's brother. As with similar sites in other parts of the city, this meant that a road barrier was erected right outside our house and we – and even senior Syrians visiting us – had to run the gauntlet of the security guards every time we left or returned home.

Another hazard was a defective boiler which caused us endless problems, as it had our predecessors, on one occasion prompting a telegram to London warning ambiguously (and vainly, as it happened) that if it was not replaced before the Ambassador's return from leave the Administration Officer feared that there might be an explosion.

We also had difficulties with the small domestic staff. One was that unless there were living-in facilities, which the villa did not enjoy, working hours in Damascus ceased after lunch. Dinner parties required overtime, and if there were casual evening callers it was Her Majesty's Ambassador who answered the doorbell. Another was that, although we employed a maximum of four servants at any time, the number of permutations and combinations among them as regards Muslims/Christians, Syrians/Palestinians and men/women were endless, so that an almost permanent state of unarmed conflict existed.

Without labouring the point, which was not unique to Damascus though most acute there in our own experience, we both found that having finally reached somewhere near the top of the tree our involvement in the most mundane tasks necessary to maintain a base from which to operate as a diplomatic team was infinitely greater than it had been lower down the ladder – and very different from the public image of the diplomatic life as one of untrammelled ease and luxury.

At the work level, too, Damascus presented some sharp contrasts with Muscat. Our introduction to Syrian politics took place before we even arrived there. Due to the vagaries of other airlines rather than any feeling of loyalty to Syrianair we flew to Damascus by the latter. When we were within about two hours of our destination, the captain announced that there was a problem about permission to overfly Turkey and we would have to land at Istanbul to clear the matter up. This seemed an unlikely story. It seemed even more unlikely when, as we landed, fire-engines and other emergency vehicles could be seen racing towards the aircraft, while instructions came over the loudspeakers that passengers should disembark with all possible speed. When we did so, we saw that we were on the other side of the airport from the normal terminal, and we were promptly shepherded into a ramshackle building, luggage and persons subjected to a rigorous search, and the flight resumed after a delay of six hours. It eventually transpired that shortly after taking off from the transit stop at Munich the captain had received a radio message to the effect that there was a bomb on board. Fortunately, there was not, but no risks could be taken, so the aircraft had to be combed for any tell-tale signs. We learned later that the Muslim Brotherhood, who had been responsible for a number of recent terrorist incidents against the Ba'thist regime in Syria, had announced that Syrianair was a legitimate target of their operations. British officials were prudently banned from flying this way thereafter.

Meanwhile, the delay at Istanbul meant that instead of reaching Damascus at a reasonable hour of the evening we arrived in the small hours of the following morning, by which time the official greeting committee had understandably dwindled away, leaving only my Head of Chancery and my Administration Officer to do the honours. Perhaps this was in its own way as symbolic as our arrival in Muscat two-and-a-half years earlier, to find ourselves in fairyland. The bomb scare was certainly followed within two weeks by a major internal upheaval in Syria, when the Brotherhood instigated an uprising in the central city and religious hotbed of Hama. For about three weeks in February/March 1982 parts of the town were in the hands of elements opposed to the regime. Although this was not the first such demonstration of dissatisfaction with President Hafiz al Asad that the country had experienced in recent years, it was undoubtedly the most concentrated, the most violent and the most serious. The Government ordered a bombardment of the old quarter of the town, and destroyed nearly a third of it. The figures of casualties were hotly disputed: the only official figure given to me was 1200; the Brotherhood claimed 30,000; the truth must have been between the two, possibly about 10,000. Syrian reactions varied. As many as condemned the regime for its ruthless repression of the insurrection blamed the Brotherhood for needlessly provoking it. There is reason to believe that they did so because a series of security raids had uncovered a number of arms caches, and the 'rebels' felt that they had to strike before it was too late. They accordingly murdered a number of party members and security officials, thus unleashing the strong arm of the law.

Whatever the rights and wrongs of the situation, and whatever long-term resentments the Government's reaction might have created, the net result was to cow the opposition into submission for the next three or four years, except that the Minister of Information having rashly come out with a prediction to this effect while Hama was still in a state of unrest, his own Ministry in Damascus was subjected to a car-bomb attack. This happened to be half a mile along the Mezze autostrada from our house, which was not a particularly auspicious start to our occupation. I had a first-hand account of the incident later the same day from Michael Frenchman, a journalist who had been waiting in the Minister's outer office when the bomb went off. It appeared that the car had been intended to be driven into the underground car-park beneath the building, but it hit an outside wall on the way, thus considerably reducing the damage and the casualty list which the original plan would have involved.

The Syrians were remarkably successful in keeping the news of the Hama episode out of the world headlines. The number of dead and the physical damage done were almost certainly greater than those incurred later in the year in the Sabra and Chatila camps in Beirut, where the massacre of Palestinians by Lebanese Christians rightly aroused the horror of the outside world. Moreover, the Hama killings were of Syrians by Syrians, which arguably made them worse than those in Beirut. Nevertheless, when I went to present my credentials to President Asad on 11 February, it was well enough known in Damascus what was going on 125 miles up the road. To judge from the President's demeanour, however, one could not have guessed that anything untoward was happening. He looked like everybody's favourite uncle, and conversed easily with no apparent sign of strain. The same could not be said of the new British Ambassador. I had asked to be allowed to present my letters soon after arrival in order to be fully operative by the time of a ministerial visit which was to take place in mid-February. To my surprise, this request was granted with almost alarming alacrity: I was telephoned late the previous evening to be told that the next morning I should make my initial call on the Foreign Minister, to be followed immediately by the credentials ceremony – a most unusual procedure. Though duly grateful, I found this something of a nightmare, not least because the Arabic translation of my speech was thrust into my hand just as I was leaving for the

Presidential palace and I was obliged to read it virtually impromptu. Nevertheless it was impossible to fault the Syrians for their courtesy on this occasion.

Syria was still smarting from the Israeli annexation of Golan in December 1981 and reeling from the effects of the Hama affair when a potentially far worse disaster struck. Using the shooting of the Israeli Ambassador in London as a pretext, and claiming that their object was to secure 'peace for Galilee', the Israelis invaded Lebanon on June 6 and attacked the PLO there. It soon became clear that their war aims ranged far beyond destroying the PLO as a military force (which in any case presented no fundamental threat to the Israeli state, and had not even fired rockets into Galilee for the previous 12 months). The PLO had, however, become relatively 'respectable' in recent times, and its growing political credibility posed a much greater threat to the Israelis. It was to eliminate this danger, I believe, that they embarked on the invasion of Lebanon; and then they decided that while they were about it they might as well kill two birds with one stone by turning Lebanon itself into a client state. The ruthless way they went about it impelled even President Reagan to telephone Mr Begin to protest against the indiscriminate bombardment of Beirut. But in the end they failed to achieve their major objectives by military means, and although the PLO was expelled from the country and became fragmented this proved to be a short-lived success. Israel's plan for Lebanon also went awry. As two Israeli writers, Ze'ev Schiff and Ehud Ya'ari, summed up the enterprise in their book *Israel's Lebanon War*[19]: 'Born of the ambition of one wilful, reckless man Israel's 1982 invasion of Lebanon was anchored in delusion, propelled by deceit and bound to end in calamity'.

Ariel Sharon's ambition nevertheless posed an awkward dilemma for President Asad. As the self-proclaimed champion of the Palestine cause, and indeed the 'throbbing heart of Arabdom' itself, with forces which had been in Lebanon since 1976 ostensibly to keep the peace in that troubled land, Syria could not afford politically to stand aside and let the Israelis get at the Palestinians, as the Israelis explicitly sought. At the same time Asad, who is nothing if not a realist, knew perfectly well that an all-out confrontation with the Israelis could only result in the defeat of his forces, perhaps the occupation of his capital and possibly even the downfall of his regime. In these circumstances, Asad walked the tight-rope with characteristic skill. He engaged in open hostilities for the inside of a week before agreeing to a cease-fire on 11 June, while regular troops of the so-called Arab Deterrent Force remained in West Beirut fighting side-by-side with the Palestinians until the eventual evacuation in September. The resulting balance-sheet was a fairly even one. Syria retained some credibility as the only Arab country to match words with deeds, however inadequately. Public opinion, while not swallowing the more exaggerated claims made for the heroic exploits of the armed forces, had some reason to be proud of what they had achieved – and even more reason to be pleased that they had not ventured more and lost all. The Syrian performance, though criticised by other Arabs who had done far less, put the regime in a somewhat better position to extract further Danegeld from them. Finally, Damascus held on to some bargaining counters, mainly in the shape of its residual military presence in Lebanon, for the attempt to salvage something of its political position in whatever Lebanon was going to emerge from the trauma of the invasion.

Against these benefits had to be set serious disadvantages. The Syrians sustained a severe strategic defeat and grievous losses of men and material. Their air force took a particularly heavy beating, losing in all about 85 aircraft and many pilots, who were more difficult to replace. Above all they had lost their predominant influence in Lebanese politics. But Asad set about repairing the damage with the shrewdness of a card-player with a poor hand which was strengthened by the aces dealt him by his opponents. His military losses were made good by the Soviet Union, who supplied Syria with new and more sophisticated equipment. The political trump cards were provided largely by the United States. Despite two unusually unanimous Security Council resolutions in June calling for immediate and unconditional Israeli withdrawal from Lebanon, the Israelis, with the support of the Americans and the acquiescence of the rest of the international community, declined to comply unless the Syrians also withdrew. They then set about trying to achieve by diplomatic means what they had failed to obtain by force of arms. Under American auspices they negotiated with the Maronite Christian-dominated Government in Beirut the famous agreement of 17 May 1983, under which the Israelis undertook to withdraw – but only on certain conditions which would have taken Lebanon out of the Arab ranks and which required Syria to withdraw simultaneously.

The ace which Asad used to such good effect lurked in that second provision (which was in fact not part of the agreement itself but rather an 'understanding' between the Israelis and the Americans). Damascus was not formally consulted during the negotiations leading to the agreement, but was presented with a *fait accompli*. Dubbing it 'Camp Shultz' as an echo of the Camp David accords which had removed Egypt from the Arab front line, the Syrians predictably (at any rate, to observers of these events sitting in Damascus) rejected the Jerusalem/Washington manoeuvre. Moreover, they refused to accept that their presence in Lebanon was on a par with that of the Israeli forces: historically the relationship between Syria and Lebanon was *sui generis*, and Syrian troops were in Lebanon by invitation. Asad therefore decided to sit it out, accepting that this meant no voluntary withdrawal by the Israelis but confident that in course of time life would be made so uncomfortable for their occupying troops in southern Lebanon that domestic political opinion in Israel would demand that the boys be brought back home. This is precisely what happened: not only to the Israelis but also to the Multi-National Force (American, British, French and Italian), which had originally been brought in to keep the peace following the assassination of President-elect Bashir Gemayel and the massacre of Palestinians in Sabra and Chatila in September 1982, but had increasingly got itself into the position of propping up the Maronite regime. Reacting to the crude pressure of murderous terrorist attacks on the American and French contingents, the Multi-National Force 'redeployed' in the early spring of 1983; the Lebanese Government resigned and was replaced by an administration more amenable to Syria; and the Lebanese army went up in a puff of smoke. Syria and her Lebanese protégés were left in possession of the field in West Beirut, and on 29 February President Amin Gemayel (brother of Bashir) made his pilgrimage to Canossa for talks with Asad which resulted on 5 March in the formal abrogation of the 17 May 1983 agreement. At this juncture most roads led to Damascus, even if, unlike Gemayel, few underwent conversion on the way.

Despite these setbacks to western policy in Lebanon, neither Washington nor London could bring themselves to accept Syrian aims there. These were seen to embrace at best partition, with Syrian annexation of parts of the neighbouring territory; or at worst the fulfilment of 'Greater Syria', meaning the wholesale incorporation of Lebanon and eventually other lands to the south. Neither scenario seemed to me accurate. Partition could be effected only on confessional lines, which would have had serious repercussions for Syria's own minority problems: there were comparatively recent historical precedents for autonomous states for the Alawites in the north west and the Druze in the south, neither of which would Asad have found palatable. 'Greater Syria' was more of a pipe-dream than a policy option: Asad had enough indigestible items on his plate without wanting to choke on Lebanon's as well.

Syrian policy in Lebanon may have been tactically inconsistent but strategically it was based on classic balance of power principles, playing one side off against the other in order to maintain Syrian influence in an area vital to its interests and closely linked by both history and geography. Prejudice aside, this need not have conflicted with the overall Western objective of promoting peace and stability.

In the related Arab-Israel dispute, Asad was seen as the intractable hard-liner who frustrated every attempt to reach a peaceful solution. He argued that painful experience had shown that it was useless to sit round a table with the Israelis and their sponsors unless and until one could negotiate from a position of approximately equal strength. Otherwise the inevitable result was a partial (in both senses of the word) settlement of the dispute instead of the just, durable and comprehensive solution desired by all right-minded people. Negotiations must therefore be delayed until the Arabs achieved 'strategic balance' with Israel, which meant not only military parity but also political, economic and technological equality. If this took 200 years, so had the expulsion of the Crusaders.

This idealistic approach showed little sympathy for the plight of the Palestinians under Israeli occupation, nor appreciation of the moderate Arab standpoint, which was that Israel was creating so many new facts on the ground in Gaza, the West Bank, Jerusalem, southern Lebanon and Golan that by the time 'strategic balance' was achieved (if it ever was) there would be nothing left to negotiate about. But in their somewhat puny and one-sided efforts to bring about Arab-Israeli peace at this time, the Americans were severely handicapped by the fact that their credibility in the region was somewhere below zero. Washington had reneged on its promises to call a halt to Israeli settlements on the West Bank. It was generally believed to have at least connived in the Israeli invasion of Lebanon. It had not only failed subsequently to deliver on the Israeli withdrawal in accordance with its own undertakings and with the unanimous resolutions of the Security Council but had suffered the humiliation of having its policy in Lebanon reduced to tatters by the Syrians.

If Palestine and Lebanon were not sufficient cause for Syria to be at odds with the West, a third area of disagreement was the Iran/Iraq War of 1980-88, in which Asad had come down firmly on the side of the revolutionary regime in Tehran. How was it that Syria, as 'the throbbing heart of Arabdom', came to be allied with a non-Arab country at war with an Arab brother? How was it that Syria, which was bent on suppressing religious extremism within its own borders, found itself in bed with the epitome of religious extremism in the Middle East? When such questions were put to Syrian officials, they invariably denied that Arabism and Islam were relevant to their relations with Iran. It was simply that Saddam Hussain had betrayed the anti-Zionist cause by diverting attention and resources from the struggle against the Zionist entity by waging his absurd war against Iran. Tehran, on the other hand, was irrevocably committed to the cause, as was Damascus, so they were natural allies.

This disingenuous line ignored the fact that Tehran's devotion to the cause was less than whole-hearted, as the Irangate revelations of the US/Israel/Iran arms link-up were to demonstrate. Although the Damascus-Tehran axis had many facets, economic and religious overtones among them, the main reason for it was summed up in the old Arabic proverb that 'the enemy of my enemy is my friend'. Rivalry between Damascus and Baghdad had existed since the Umayyads lost their leadership of the Islamic community to the Abbasids in the eighth century AD. More recently it had been exacerbated by the split in the Ba'th Party in 1966, when a kind of Moscow/Peking syndrome manifested itself, with both the Damascus and Baghdad factions claiming to uphold the pure milk of the doctrine. These differences had been reinforced by what appeared to be a mutual and obsessional hatred between Hafiz al Asad and Saddam Hussain. Perhaps they had too much in common, though subsequently the comparison between the way Asad got what he wanted in Lebanon and Saddam failed to get what he wanted in Kuwait left no doubt who was the shrewder.

Nevertheless the Iran alliance must have caused Asad some anxious moments in 1982/3. At the height of the Israeli invasion of Lebanon, he had allowed Iranian zealots to cross into Lebanon via Damascus. *En route* some of them could be seen around the Shi'a shrine of Sayyida Zainab (the Prophet's eldest daughter) on the southern outskirts of the capital. Others invaded the Damascus hotels demanding the closure of bars and cabarets. Taken to see the glories of the Umayyad Mosque they were said to have complained that they had not come to visit the historic sites of Damascus but were on their way to liberate Jerusalem. More seriously, these would-be liberators harboured the militant Hizbullah who turned against Amal, the moderate Lebanese Shi'a. At one time there was a possibility that the secular regime in Damascus would be squeezed between Islamic republics in Beirut and Baghdad.

Syria's relations with the two super-powers were another source of misunderstanding. Damascus often tried to portray the Soviet Union as an eternal friend and the United States as an implacable foe. The reality was different. In the Soviet case, while it was true that Syria was almost wholly dependent for her military equipment on the Russians, had signed a treaty of friendship and co-operation with Moscow in 1980 and received much project aid from the Eastern Bloc (notably the Soviet-built Euphrates Dam which proved something of a disappointment), Syrians generally felt no affinity with the communist world. Nor was Asad a puppet of the Kremlin. Damascus and Moscow differed on a number of issues, especially on Asad's activist policies in Lebanon and his proprietorial attitude to Arafat and the PLO. One Soviet Ambassador in Damascus had been heard to complain that 'The Syrians take everything from the Soviet Union – except advice'. In other words, the Russian patron had no more control over its Syrian clients than the American over its Israeli equivalent.

Indeed the marriage of convenience between Moscow and Damascus stemmed to a considerable extent from the latter relationship. In the underlying Middle East issue one super-power was seen as ranged irrevocably on the side of Public Enemy Number One so there was no alternative but to reinsure with the other: it was American policy that had driven the Syrians literally and metaphorically into the arms of the Russians. Yet the partnership was an uneasy one. Neither side was quite sure how far the commitment of the other could be taken for granted, and when Soviet support for Syria during the Israeli invasion of Lebanon fell far short of expectations, the writing was on the wall.

As for the United States, Damascus had every reason to distrust American policy in the Middle East, from its part in the creation of the State of Israel and its undeviating support for it ever since, through American efforts in the 1950s to enlist Arab states in regional defence arrangements aimed at the Soviet Union, to what Syrians saw as Washington's complicity in the removal of Egypt, and attempts to remove Lebanon, from the Arab front line. Nevertheless, the Syrians recognised that if the Arab-Israeli impasse were ever to be resolved, it would be through American rather than Russian influence. They only rarely blocked channels of communication with Washington, and at the higher echelons Asad established considerable rapport with Americans such as

Kissinger and Carter. Practical contacts between the US Embassy in Damascus and the Syrian Foreign Ministry seemed to me closer and more frequent than those of the Soviet Embassy.

Unfortunately, the Reagan Administration saw Syria through a pink looking-glass. The politics of the Middle East generally were viewed back to front and 'reds' seen under every bed. The Arab-Israeli problem, which in the Washington context was an issue not of foreign policy but of domestic politics, became in the Middle East context not a regional but an East/West confrontation. Like a perverse self-fulfilling prophecy, American attitudes seemed designed to bring about the very outcome they were trying to avoid. Syria was not a Soviet satellite, and only the kind of policy being pursued by Washington in the early 1980s could have made her one. At a time when the troubles in Lebanon were at their worst, a visiting British Minister asked his Syrian counterpart who in his view was the best friend of the Soviet Union in the Middle East. Without hesitation the Syrian replied, 'Ronald Reagan'.

United States diplomats on the spot tended to share this general assessment. But I believe they felt that nobody back at the ranch wanted to hear. The Washington establishment was obsessed by 'the evil empire'. My own feeling was that if they could bring themselves to be more even-handed on the main issue of Middle East politics they would find a ready response from Damascus, and to some extent this was borne out by subsequent events.

Our own relations with the Syrians during my time could best be described as correct rather than cordial. British responsibility for Palestine outweighed our role in liberating Syria from the French. Except as a member of the European Community (in which the Syrians, like other Arabs, seemed to repose more faith than it could sustain) we were no longer seen as a particularly effective force in Middle Eastern affairs.

Curiously enough, the topic on which I was able to get a better hearing than on any regional subject was the Falklands. World-wide, we mounted a more intensive lobbying-campaign on this issue than on any other I could recall in my career. We did not in the end persuade the Syrians (who had their own reasons for looking at the conflict from a Latin American standpoint) but we could not complain that, in the Foreign Ministry if not in the press, they did not listen to us.

My first encounter on the matter was with the redoubtable Abdul Halim Khaddam, the diminutive but dynamic Foreign Minister of some 12 years' standing at that time. He had the reputation of being forceful to the point of rudeness, and of possessing a waspish wit in debate, and I had in fact seen previous records of his encounters with British Ministers in which both sides engaged in a verbal punch-up rather than a diplomatic exchange. In my experience, however, Khaddam was never less than courteous, though his tongue was as sharp as his mind and he was formidably well-informed. His favourite diversion appeared to be to lecture us on the iniquities of the Europeans in general and the British in particular from the Crusades onwards. I never had the nerve to point out to him – though on one occasion I deflated one of his acolytes with the observation – that the great Syrian hero of the Crusades, Salahuddin, was not only of Kurdish origin but hailed from the town of Tikrit on the Tigris which was the home of Saddam Hussain and his clan.

Early in April 1982 I had instructions to inform Khaddam that Lord Carrington regretted that he would be unable to pay his official visit to Damascus, arranged for the following week, for the very good reason that he had resigned over the Argentine invasion. Replete with the FCO guidance with which we had been flooded, I took the opportunity of rehearsing the British view, making the point that underlying it was the principle of self-determination which I knew was dear to Syrian hearts.

Khaddam listened patiently to my recital, and then said with a twinkle in his eye: 'We do, of course, applaud Mrs Thatcher for upholding the principle in the Falklands. But we are a little puzzled that she should go to the lengths of sending an Armada... 8000 miles... for the sake of 1500 islanders, when she does not care about applying it to 4 million people just down the road from here.'

'The Prime Minister is clearly on record,' I rejoined, 'as

supporting self-determination for the Palestinians. But our direct responsibilities in the two cases are quite different.'

Slightly mollified, Khaddam decided to have a little tease. 'How,' he asked, 'do these islanders earn their living?'

'They are largely engaged in sheep-farming, Your Excellency,' I replied.

'Really?' he mused. 'That's very interesting... And how many sheep are there?' The guidance had nothing to offer at this point, and I was caught in the slips.

My Argentine colleague at the time of the Falklands invasion was a delightful elderly man who was much respected throughout the Corps. We maintained discreet personal relations even after our official connection was severed. Then he was taken ill at his own dinner-table, and sadly died – according to some mischievous tongues, of a heart broken by British perfidy. We decided to adopt a more 'correct' attitude towards his successor, a less agreeable character, but this was not always easy. On one occasion I found myself seated next to him at the World Day of Peace liturgy in the Church of St John Damascene (attended also by Senator Jesse Jackson, who had come to Damascus to secure the release of an American pilot shot down by the Syrians over Lebanon). Appropriate though this may have been in a sense, we were grateful to our Cypriot colleague who arrived a couple of minutes later and tactfully inserted himself between us.

Not long afterwards, at the time of Mrs Thatcher's post-war visit to the Falklands, I attended a reception at the Brazilian Embassy. On my way out I could not help passing the Argentinian. He immediately buttonholed me:

'I wish to thank you, Excellency,' he leered, 'for your Prime Minister's visit to my country'.

Despite the lack of substance in our relations with the Syrians, and the unfortunate cancellation of the Carrington visit, the number and level of ministerial visits exchanged between London and Damascus were unusually high during my tenure. On the Syrian side two ministers went to Britain, and the Speaker of the People's Assembly, Mahmud Zu'bi (later Prime Minister), paid a particularly successful visit in November 1982. Once again a

British Prime Minister responded to last-minute importunings for a meeting.

Alas the goodwill thus generated was soon dissipated. A high-powered Arab delegation was going to London shortly afterwards in connection with the Arab-Israeli situation. HMG refused to accept a member of the PLO as part of it. As there was by then no ban on lower level contacts with the PLO – we had many meetings with its representatives in Damascus – I was instructed to put a compromise proposal to Faruq Qadoumi, the PLO 'Foreign Minister'. He gave me the shortest possible shrift in the nicest possible way, and it was not until the following spring that an acceptable delegation, led by King Hussein and including Abdul Halim Khaddam, as well as an 'unobjectionable' Palestinian, was received in London.

I often thought it a pity that the pragmatic British could not bring themselves to admit at that time that, for all his obvious shortcomings, Chairman Arafat had effectively chosen the path of peace, even though he could not be prevailed upon till several years later to say so publicly. By shunning him as we (and still more blatantly, the Americans) did we ensured that by the time he achieved political respectability his negotiating position with the Israelis was hopelessly weak.

In the inward direction, our major visitors were two Foreign and Commonwealth Secretaries, Francis Pym in October 1982 and Geoffrey Howe in January 1984. The first remains in my mind as a classic example of the hazards of diplomatic entertaining. It fell to us to offer at home, where our modest table could seat no more than 20 guests, the return hospitality for Khaddam's dinner in honour of Pym, given at the familiar venue of the Orient Club in Damascus. Syrian protocol required the advance submission of a guest-list. This would have been a courtesy anyway, since Khaddam was to be the guest of honour. But it was compulsory in Damascus, where the obsession with 'security' embraced the need to keep a close watch on contacts between Syrian nationals and foreign diplomats.

Three days before the dinner I was summoned to the Foreign Ministry to be told that we could not invite ladies, since Mr Pym would be unaccompanied. I argued vainly in favour of the fair sex. We then set about unscrambling the party as arranged, and turning it into a stag affair. I produced a fresh list. The day before the party the Chief of Protocol himself sent for me and said that this would not do either. He proceeded to cross out the names of five of the ten Syrians to be invited. I saw at once that they were all non-officials. I protested that when our Ministers went abroad they liked to meet as wide as possible a cross-section of the host country's society: they did not wish to sit down to dinner with precisely the same people whom they had been meeting in their offices all day. The Chief of Protocol would not demur: 'We will tell them they cannot come,' he said (for it was understood that informal invitations would already have been sent out).

On the evening of the twice-reorganised party, I happened to be hovering near the front door as the guests arrived. The first thing that happened was that a Syrian Minister turned up – with his wife! Some nimble footwork was required, resulting in the lady's discreet disappearance (and, next morning, my calling on the Minister to eat humble pie: he was absolutely charming about the whole thing, and we became good friends with both him and his unfortunate wife). The next hiccup was that one of the proscribed Syrians from outside the charmed circle of officialdom appeared on the threshold. I consulted the Chief of Protocol urgently: should I throw him out, or risk Khaddam walking out? Grudgingly, he agreed that we should find the unwitting gatecrasher a place at the table, which meant that I was obliged to ask one of my Embassy colleagues to emulate the example of the Minister's wife.

The Syrians could be sticklers for protocol in a way of which Marcus Cheke, the repository of all wisdom on the subject when I first joined the Service, would have approved. One of my predecessors in Damascus suffered the embarrassment of having a Syrian guest turn his plate over and walk out of the house when he considered that he had been seated at table in a place not consonant with his status. We ourselves are now inclined to adopt a more relaxed attitude. There is a story – possibly apocryphal – about an Ambassador who used to take the trouble to put a table plan in the hall so that guests might see on arrival who their dinner partners were to be and thus avoid exhausting their conversations over the pre-prandial drinks.

On one occasion, a formidable dowager, having inspected the *placement*, accosted him and complained that as the senior lady present she must insist on being seated on the Ambassador's right. Not wishing to make a scene, the envoy agreed, and asked his wife to give the necessary instructions. When the party assembled in the dining-room, the dowager, all smiles now that she had got her own way, said to her host, 'I hope, Your Excellency, that you did not take my concern amiss. It is so important, don't you think, to be correct about these things?'

'My dear lady,' replied the Ambassador, 'please do not give it another thought. My own philosophy on the subject is that those who mind don't matter and those who matter don't mind'.

The Howe visit involved different kinds of trauma. It was planned at short notice as an addendum to visits elsewhere, and an audience of a convalescent President Asad was virtually made a precondition. This made it difficult to sell, and meant that the protracted negotiations were concluded only at the eleventh hour. I actually woke on the morning of Sir Geoffrey's arrival knowing that the Syrians had had no time to arrange a detailed programme. Fortunately, they were past masters at the art of improvisation, and the visit of less than 24 hours (though it seemed much longer!) went off very smoothly. Not for the first time, I was struck by the fact that a few hours' ministerial exposure to an Embassy's problems was worth months of routine reporting. I have to add that on this occasion the general reaction was that though there was something in what the Syrians said, the way they said it did not endear them to their interlocutors. But at least Sir Geoffrey Howe was perhaps the only British Minister in my experience who got the measure of the wily Khaddam.

Asad's illness in the winter of 1983/84 created the greatest degree of internal tension since the Hama episode of spring 1982. The Syrian public relations machine made its customary hash of the event. Not content with telling a lie, it told a bad one – namely, that the President had undergone an emergency operation for appendicitis. The Syrian leader is a man of many parts, but not that many: his one appendix was reliably reported to have been removed over 20 years earlier! Intimations of his mortality provoked a jockeying for position among contenders for the succession. This resolved itself into what some observers described as a 'power struggle' between the President's younger brother Rif'at and the military hierarchy opposed to him - on personal rather than political grounds. The rivalry between these two factions, both largely from the ruling Alawite minority group, degenerated into the armed forces under their respective commands confronting each other on the streets of Damascus and elsewhere for a period of some weeks. The show of force was not directed against the President himself. Nevertheless it produced an ugly situation over which he was unable to assert his authority during his illness and which was potentially – and in at least one instance in Latakia, centre of the Alawite area in the north west, actually – violent.

The audience which we had secured for Geoffrey Howe in January was the first to be granted to a foreign visitor since the onset of Asad's indisposition. It lasted for 90 minutes, of which Asad spoke for approximately 89. Further signs of recovery followed. In March, Asad reshuffled his pack, as one result of which Rif'at and Khaddam became two of three vice-presidents. But he did not finally reassert his authority in full until the end of May, and then by the characteristic touch of sending the principal protagonists in the 'power struggle' on a mission to Moscow under the leadership of his brother, who subsequently spent a lengthy period of exile in France and Switzerland.

With so little to go on apart from the official party line our knowledge of the internal Syrian scene was even more scanty than that of the external, on which there were other sources of information. I tried to draw up a balance sheet of opposition to, and support for, the regime. Religious opinion, which embraced a far broader section of the population than the vocal and extremist Muslim Brotherhood, regarded it as 'too sectarian and too secular'.

70% of Syrians were Muslims, and 90% of all Muslims were Sunnis, and they resented the domination of the Alawite minority.

This sect, hailing originally from the mountainous region behind Latakia, formed no more than about 10% of the population but had risen to power partly because it was a closely-knit and cohesive force compared with the far more numerous but disparate Sunni ruling group which it supplanted in 1963; and partly because it was able, for a variety of historical reasons, to infiltrate and eventually to control the seats of power in the Ba'th Party, the Armed Forces and the Intelligence Services. Politically, the Party had the advantage of a defined ideology, expressed in the slogan 'Unity, freedom and socialism', though these principles have increasingly come to be superseded by the instinct to survive. From the religious standpoint, the Alawites are something of an unknown quantity, being organised on rather Masonic lines, and although they have links with Shi'a Islam both their doctrine and their practice appear to have certain Christian overtones. For all these reasons many Muslims consider them heretical, if indeed as Muslims at all.

Secular opposition to the regime embraced other, often overlapping, groups. The former ruling class – landowners, rich merchants and the like – objected to being 'ruled by the servants', as they sometimes put it. The commercial community chafed under the straitjacket imposed by an East European-style of economic management, with some 75% of the economy in the public sector, and the natural trading instincts of the Syrians, as they saw it, stifled also by the structural problems arising from a chronic foreign exchange shortage and a crippling burden of defence expenditure. Finally, an increasing number of Syrians of all classes felt that stability was being bought at too great a price in terms of restrictions on personal freedom and of what they regarded as the unacceptable degree of corruption and arrogance in the predominant military circles.

But there was another side to the picture. Religious opposition to the secular nature of the regime was tempered by the generally more relaxed attitude to Islam of even devout Syrian Muslims. Geographical proximity and historical exposure to the Christian

West had not exactly bred a tendency to take their religion more lightly than their co-religionists further east, but had encouraged them to regard it as a private rather than a public matter. The residual Christian minorities in Syria, amounting to some 12-14% of the population, positively preferred secular to Sunni rule, for obvious reasons.

Many Syrians, especially those living in the countryside, had benefited materially from the regime's early economic and social reforms. The position of women in particular was more advanced than in other parts of the Arab world: some held important public office (though one of them to whom I made some complimentary remark on these lines at a party countered by assuring me that it was all very different when she got home!). Numerous Syrians had 'come in from the cold' or established other kinds of vested interest in the regime's continuance. The population was notably young (about half under the age of 18) so that there was a growing majority of those who had known nothing but Ba'thist Syria. Lastly, there were those even among the regime's natural opponents who grudgingly admitted that a strong hand was needed and who would draw favourable comparisons between present stability and past innumerable coups, and between Syrian order and Lebanese anarchy.

The Christian community in Damascus represented every conceivable denomination. Obscure doctrinal divisions long lost in the mists of time had become enshrined in the various Churches: Orthodox and Catholic of the Greek, Syrian and Armenian persuasions. There were Maronites, and more recent Protestant accretions like the born-again Southern Baptists whose unfamiliar Sunday morning worship we attended at the American School except during the rare visits of an Anglican Chaplain from Beirut. Each confession clung to its identity and its own liturgy. Many were presided over by beatific Beatitudes: Patriarchs whose outward appearance belied their reduced circumstances but who nevertheless wielded some authority and were always a great pleasure to visit. To attend the religious and family festivals of the different churches was an education not only in the past but also the present, for despite the changes wrought by the Ba'thists, deep down it was religion which directly or indirectly made people 'tick', whether they were Christian or Muslim.

Whatever professional and domestic problems Syria may have posed, it had one saving grace. The country was a tourist paradise – without tourists. Its antiquities range from third millennium remains through Graeco-Roman ruins to Crusader castles and Ottoman palaces. Its landscape varies from arid desert to fertile plain and lush mountain. Its climate can be harsh – I experienced most variations from blinding sandstorm in the Euphrates Valley to impassable snowdrift on the main road from Damascus to Aleppo – but much of it is Mediterranean-style.

Damascus itself must be one of the most pleasant of all the Arab capitals, and perhaps the most Arab, although mingling biblical with its Islamic and Ottoman associations. When I was at MECAS I learned of a charming legend according to which the Holy Prophet, having crossed the desert from Arabia, came upon the heart-easing sight of Damascus but refused to proceed into the city because it was written that man should enter Paradise only once. There is a southern suburb of Damascus called Qadam (meaning 'foot') where a mosque contains a piece of rock bearing what purports to be Muhammad's footprint at the point of no entry. I found it one day. Though a less than inspiring sight, it provided a useful talking point when I was calling on the Grand Mufti of Syria and had run out of conversation. The old man agreed that it was a charming tale, only to add that it was, of course, quite untrue. The Prophet had never got any nearer Damascus than Bosra, not far from the present Jordanian frontier, where he had had a famous encounter with a Christian monk named Bahira.

We explored more rewarding parts of the city with the Friends of Damascus, an unofficial body whose leading lights were Syrians from the Department of Antiquities. They had access to places not normally open to the public, and we made many delightful expeditions on foot with them. Other happy times were spent visiting friends in the Ghouta, the ring of orchards surrounding (or, more accurately, being increasingly absorbed by) the capital, or in the prosperous hill resorts of Bloudan and Zebadani close to the Lebanese border. A short drive northward from Damascus would take us to the Orthodox convent of Sednaya with its painting of the Virgin attributed to St Luke, and the Aramaic-speaking village of Malloula, where the Catholic monks of Saint Sergius would dispense a glass of home-made wine while playing a tape-recording of the Lord's Prayer in Aramaic.

To reach the touristic attractions in central Syria required a rather tedious drive up the main highway towards Aleppo. This became familiar to us on weekend trips. On the way to Roman Apamea, which became a favourite spot, we enjoyed picnics by the creaking water-wheels on the Orontes at Hama, mercifully untouched by the events of February 1982; and at Shaizar, where the river was overlooked by the ruins of an impressive old fortress. Driving through the nearby Ghab plain in springtime, surrounded by a multi-coloured carpet of wild flowers stretching in every direction, was an experience not to be forgotten.

Palmyra was an obligatory item on the agenda of all our visitors, but we never tired of it. Northward-looking Aleppo presented an entirely different atmosphere from its great rival Damascus, and was endowed more splendidly with its magnificent citadel and miles of covered suqs – not to mention the romantic but somewhat Spartan hospitality of the celebrated Baron Hotel. Within easy reach was the beautiful Basilica of St Simeon Stylites, though little remained of the 50-foot pillar on which he spent anything from 27 to 42 years, depending on which guidebook you read.

Krak des Chevaliers was another frequent objective, though not necessarily our favourite Crusader castle. We gave the palm to the more rugged Salahuddin, memorable not least for the needle of rock which once supported the drawbridge.

Beyond Palmyra to the east was the Euphrates Valley. I made three lengthy journeys there. On the first occasion we went with my Defence Attaché and his wife in their Range Rover, spending a night *en route* at a paper-mill camp at Deir-az-Zor and driving down to within spitting distance of the Iraqi frontier. We took in some remarkable sights and sites. The Arab fort of Rahba stood high above the fertile plain, with spectacular views across the broad green strip to the river. Dura Europos, a fortified city on its southern bank and founded by the Macedonians in the fourth century BC, shimmered in the heat of a May morning. At Mari, excavations were unearthing traces of a civilisation which had existed about 3000 BC. On the way back we diverted from the main road to see the remote and much more modern (third century AD) city of Halabiye set in a triangular shape on the steep slope above the river; and the ruined desert town of Risafe enclosed within a vast rectangular wall. Its long and complex history encapsulated many of the influences which contributed to the heterogeneous nature of modern Syria, going back to the days when the land was a crossroads for armies or caravans moving north/south and east/west, and the battleground in the struggle for supremacy between the civilisations centred on the valleys of the Nile and the Tigris/Euphrates.

Unfortunately the photographs I took on this odyssey were ruined. I therefore retraced our steps subsequently on my own, at the wheel of our little Suzuki, doing a weekend round trip of over 1000 miles in high summer and taking almost the same pictures. These came out excellently, but were purloined from our car a year later in a traumatic robbery which we suffered in Rome. After another twelve months I tried again. The water-pump was still chugging away on the other side of the Euphrates from Dura Europos – and I can hear it now. The river flowing through Deir-az-Zor was a fine sight at sunrise and sunset, when the cafes on its bank were thronged with holiday-makers celebrating the 'Id al Fitr' marking the end of Ramadan. Unfortunately I ran into the aforementioned sandstorm, which prevented me from negotiating the perilous track to Halabiye. But the storm relented for a while over Risafe, and so far as all my photos were concerned it was a case of third time lucky.

To the south of Damascus, less well-worn paths led to the basalt moonscape of the Hauran and the black stone buildings of the picturesque sites in this stronghold of the Druze. We liked this area particularly because it was possible to get there and back in a day from Damascus. Shahba housed a wonderful collection of mosaics.

The temple of Zeus in the hilltop village of Qanawat provided another of our frequent picnic venues. The Roman theatre at Bosra was as fine as any we have seen, and the surrounding town worth hours of exploring.

Many of the trips we made to these far-flung parts of Syria were combined with official visits to provincial centres. For the most part they were professionally unrewarding, since one could just as well have sat in Damascus writing reports on what the Regional Governors and other dignitaries would have to say. But my visit to Suwayda in the Jebel Druze was a throwback to the Trucial States of the 1950s. I spent a night with the jolly Greek Orthodox bishop, a frequent visitor to Damascus who looked like the original Father Christmas but was alleged to have more sinister leanings. Next day I called on the Druze leader, Abdullah Pasha al Atrash. I had expected a cosy chat *à deux* in his office. Instead, I was received outside by a gathering of some 40 Druze in traditional costume, and ushered into a 'majlis' (assembly room) where a flowery address of welcome was delivered. It was as though the British were still the 'protectors' of the Druze (as had to some extent been the case in the nineteenth century). Great Britain was adjured not to turn her back on old friendship – and, by the way, would I please convey their greetings to Her Majesty The Queen when I next saw her? (Alas, I never had the opportunity.) I fear that my impromptu reply in Arabic to this wholly unexpected display of enthusiasm did not altogether rise to the level of the occasion.

So far as cross-border operations were concerned, we exchanged visits more than once with our opposite numbers in Jordan, Alan and Marta Urwick. They preferred the antiquity (and antiques!) of Damascus to the modernity of Amman, while we rediscovered the delights of Jerash and Petra (for the intrepid traveller now almost too comfortable and easy of access). Incursions into Lebanon were limited by the wartime conditions there to odd shopping trips to Chtaura and Zahle, across the embattled Bekka Valley from the Syrian frontier. But a few weeks prior to leaving Damascus we made a nostalgic pilgrimage back to where it had all begun in 1952. Accompanied by an obligatory escort of British RMPs, who met us at the border, we drove down to Beirut, through country which had once been a model of natural beauty but was now a monument to human folly: not a single village had remained untouched by bombardment by friend and foe alike. Nevertheless, if our colleagues there were living more dangerously than we were in Damascus, they were also living a great deal better! The Lebanese mercantile genius seemed to have survived almost unscathed by a decade of civil war, though their traditional optimism and resilience were showing signs of wilting under the pressure.

Now the time came when I had to balance the fascination of travelling in the region and of studying its politics against the professional and domestic frustrations of remaining in Damascus. For, by an unhappy irony, the very day after the trauma and the triumph of the Howe visit in January 1984, I learned that my future options were narrowing effectively to seeing out my time there or retiring three years early. After some weeks of agonising, I chose the latter. It was not that Syria lacked interest, but as a diplomat one observed, analysed and reported without ever being able to influence, let alone persuade. And as a British diplomat one was increasingly exposed to what I called the post-Berrill syndrome.

The Berrill Review of Overseas Representation of the mid-1970s had not outraged me as much as it had some of my colleagues: many of its recommendations designed to bring the Diplomatic Service into line with the more rigorous requirements of the world in which it operated commanded respect. But it ruined its case by exaggeration and by adopting the perverse doctrine that because Britain was not the power she had been the need for diplomacy on the scale we practised it was no longer necessary. The truth was precisely the contrary, especially as regards the invaluable contribution being made to our overseas interests and reputation by the British Council and the BBC External Services. The 'Establishment' accordingly had little difficulty in torpedoing the report. The subsequent advent of the Thatcher Government unfortunately replaced the formula: 'Less power, therefore less diplomacy' with the equally unattractive proposition: 'More diplomacy, but fewer resources'. To the practical problems of relentless penny-pinching was added the morale issue. The Civil Service generally, and the Diplomatic Service in particular, no longer appeared to enjoy the esteem of their political masters, an impression which was reinforced for me when I learned on return home that there was neither a 'farewell audience' nor a formal leave-taking of the Secretary of State for 'Ambassadors of your grade' (this despite the fact that some years earlier a single 'senior grade' had been established, ostensibly to increase flexibility in the system: evidently, though Ambassadors were now all equal, some were more equal than others!).

These pinpricks notwithstanding, I felt regret neither at having spent a lifetime in the Service nor, in all the circumstances, at having decided to leave it when I did (especially when my successor in Damascus had to pack his bags in a hurry on the rupture of relations with Syria two years later!). The Diplomatic Service is a body of remarkably dedicated men and women – the latter including especially those often unsung and always unpaid heroines, the wives. One might sometimes have wondered whether what it is called upon to do these days requires quite so many people of intellectual as distinct from broader human qualities as it boasts; but one never felt anything but pride in belonging to it.

16

Indian Summer

Retirement at 57 had the compensation that I was still young enough to embark on something new. Or not so new: early in 1985 I was fortunate enough to secure an appointment as one of two Assistant Secretaries-General of the Arab-British Chamber of Commerce. This prestigious body was celebrating its tenth anniversary. It was active in promoting Arab-British trade in a number of ways. Those which came under my supervision included the Business Information and Membership Services Department, the Printing Section, the Library and the Computer Unit. At one extreme I found myself plunged into the deep end of the revolution in information technology. I recall with some amazement having, as a complete novice, persuaded the Finance Committee to update the computer system and the printing machinery, as well as to invest in a new-fangled device called a fax, which was not then the commonplace item it has since become in every office, not to mention many homes. At the other extreme I was able to gain further experience of public speaking at in-house seminars or 'workshops' held at provincial Chambers of Commerce country-wide.

My work with the Chamber involved me in several trips abroad. In March 1985 I flew to Athens to attend an Arab-Hellenic Congress on Economic Co-operation. This was opened by Prime Minister Andreas Papandreou in a speech which reminded me of a conversation with my Greek colleague in Damascus when I had pulled his leg about the way in which his political masters made his job so much easier than mine by telling the Arabs exactly what they wanted to hear.

'You must remember,' he replied gravely, 'that we Greeks are more oriental than occidental'.

I continued to Cairo, to join the Chamber's Secretary-General for a visit to the Yemens. The contrast between the two was instructive. On arrival at San'a our Arab hosts were nowhere to be seen, and the day was saved by the timely appearance of Her Majesty's Ambassador, David Tatham, my erstwhile No. 2 in Middle East Department. It took some time for the local Chamber of Commerce to grind itself into action and produce a programme, which was largely of a touristic nature. On arrival in Aden, however, we were not only met by the local chamber but given a printed programme which was followed to the letter and was commendably businesslike. I could only ascribe this to a happy combination of British bureaucratic tradition and Marxist regimentation.

The message which the Aden chamber wished to convey was that they had by now forgiven the British their colonial sins but that there had been precious little response. Evidence of this was the fact that the airport extension project was being carried out by a French firm, we were put up in a luxury French hotel at the Khormaksar roundabout, and taken to lunch at a Bulgarian hostelry overlooking the old Gold Mohur Beach Club. As we sat drinking German beer I asked our Adeni bear-leader what the British were now doing here.

'Drinking the beer,' he answered laconically.

Happily, the current incumbent of the British Residence at Lawn House (another of my former Middle East Department colleagues, Peter Williams) was able to give my Chamber mentor a rather better impression of British commercial activity and the Embassy's role in it.

This was something of a nostalgia trip for me. Only ten months later, in January 1986, Aden exploded in yet another bout of internecine strife. The Royal Yacht *Britannia* happened to be in the area at the time and was able to evacuate many expatriates, including various Embassy staffs, among them the Chinese. Some time afterwards I heard the then British Ambassador giving an account of the episode to The Royal Society for Asian Affairs. A sinologist in the audience said that he would be interested to know what sort of Chinese they were.

'Very grateful Chinese,' returned the Ambassador.

Early in 1987, I found myself in a snowbound Dublin for the launching of the Arab-Irish Chamber of Commerce. At a reception, I was buttonholed by a couple of lady journalists in search of snippets for their gossip columns. By way of explaining why I was inclined to be cagey with the press I related the story of my experience in Nigeria when I was alleged to have 'had no comment to make on the brutal disgusting and inhuman treatment handed out to a Nigerian diplomat in London'. As reported in the *Irish Press* the scene became Damascus and the occasion an assault on a British citizen!

In June, a warm and welcoming Geneva was the venue for a conference on the Arab trade boycott of Israel which brought me into contact with a number of Syrian acquaintances, still very friendly despite yet another break in diplomatic relations the previous October. This was the result of what seemed to me Mrs Thatcher's over-reaction to the 'Hindawi affair', in which a Syrian hand had been detected behind a plot to place a bomb on board an El Al aircraft at Heathrow.

When my three years with the Chamber were up, I found fresh woods and pastures new in the shape of joining a select team of diplomatic dinosaurs in the Foreign and Commonwealth Office who reviewed official papers coming up for release to the Public Record Office. By a strange coincidence, the very first file that came my way concerned Saudi Arabia in 1958, and contained my own prediction of imminent revolution there. The rules did not permit me to suppress this. Indeed the whole thrust of the operation, which found a ready echo with me, was to release as much as possible to the public domain, and this movement has since gathered pace under the 'open government initiative'.

The work was often tedious, but relieved by the occasional nugget among the dross. Among the most bizarre was some ancient correspondence with a colonial hopeful who had written to enquire whether a family heirloom constituted entitlement to a pension. The item in question was a scarf knitted by Queen Victoria, and sent in recognition of services rendered during the Boer War. The optimist appeared to regard this as hardly less distinguished than a VC. He was rapidly disillusioned, though the official reply let him down lightly by acknowledging the value of the services: 'credit but no cash,' as one of my colleagues remarked.

Perhaps the most amusing file entry came at the end of a lengthy exchange of bureaucratic minuting on an issue which had arisen in our post-Suez relations with Egypt. At the time in question we had a mini-Mission in Cairo headed by Colin Crowe, whose primary task was to process the claims of those whose property had been sequestrated following the 1956 débâcle. We were keen to get this upgraded to a full Embassy, while the Egyptians were more interested in obtaining British financial aid. The arguments went to and fro on the files, until the neat summing-up by the Permanent Under-Secretary, Sir Derick Hoyer-Millar, who minuted: 'What we need is a quid pro Crowe'.

I also liked the report on social conditions in a South American country in which the writer recorded that: 'The Anglican clergyman in… told me that a sharp increase in the size of his congregation was due not to an appreciation of the eloquence of his sermons but to an astonishing run of success enjoyed by his hymn numbers in the "Chica" (national lottery)'.

'Things that might have been better expressed' may be the appropriate category for the account of a visit to the Gulf in 1952 by a Treasury official who was accompanying a Foreign Office delegation on a delicate mission to advise the newly oil-rich Rulers how best to spend their sudden wealth. It was, he admitted, a difficult task in one particular case when everything had to be translated into Arabic and even then the shaikh did not appear to understand the point. However, added the Treasury man, 'I did not think the Ruler as backward as some of my colleagues'.

When I first joined the reviewers, our office was situated close to Waterloo Station. My journey there frequently involved crossing the 'bull-ring', a haunt of the homeless which was sometimes known as 'cardboard city'. It was a pitiful sight, yet one hesitated to respond to pleas for 'change' for fear that it would soon be spent in the nearest pub – or worse. Nevertheless some kind of positive reaction was called for, and mine took the form of volunteering to help the charity Crisis with its shelters over subsequent Christmas periods.

This experience proved quite an eye-opener. The majority of the Crisis 'guests' were not lay-abouts so much as psychotics who had fallen on hard times for reasons they could often not explain to themselves let alone anyone else, but once on the slippery slope could not pick themselves up. Many should have been in mental hospitals, but the official policy of reducing these in favour of something optimistically called 'care in the community' was clearly not working. The people who ran Crisis combined compassion and common sense to an admirable degree. There was no mawkish sentimentality about the operation. Volunteers, of all ages and from all walks of life, and called upon to do the most menial of tasks, were given clear and down-to-earth guidelines about how to handle the sensitive situations which inevitably arose from time to time (for example, with attempts to smuggle liquor into the shelters, which was strictly against the rules). One way and another this was human nature at its worst and its best.

My part-time activity with the FCO continued for seven years until I reached my second retirement age of 68. Although it provided a useful way of keeping in touch with 'the Office', the glimpse it gave me of the new diplomacy made me thankful not to be fully part of it any longer. 'Management' may have been little more than a buzz-word replacing the old 'administration' but other new concepts had more insidious connotations. 'Market testing' was based on the notion that business practice was necessarily always better than bureaucratic. 'Cost-effectiveness' embraced the idea that everything in the diplomatic field could and should be neatly quantified. 'Efficiency scrutinies' and outside 'consultancies' told us not only what we should be doing but what we were doing.

Whether all this saved more than it cost was an open question. The attempt to live up to the precepts of the brave new world may have made the Service to some extent 'leaner and meaner'. But the FCO had for many years had its own in-built mechanism for ensuring good housekeeping. The 'new look' involved a great deal of navel-gazing at the expense of getting on with the job itself. Too little consideration seemed to be given at the political level to the conflict between cutting costs and reducing staff on the one hand and, on the other, the increasing demands being made on the Service by the post-cold war world, ranging from the opening of new posts to the expectations of growing numbers of British tourists abroad.

Parallel with these developments was a pernicious change in the nature of diplomacy itself. This was 'diplomacy by television'. Acting with motives which no doubt included sincerity but also sensationalism, the cameras would focus upon the horrors of Somalia before moving rapidly on to those of Rwanda or Bosnia. Public indignation was aroused, and politicians reacted with their characteristic knee-jerk response, which was that they must be seen to be doing something. In some cases masterly inactivity might have been a more appropriate response. In any case, by the time action was in hand the focus had more often than not shifted elsewhere. Underlying all this was the continuing failure of sections of British public opinion to accept that our role in the world had changed beyond recognition since 1945. The failure was particularly evident in the debate about 'Europe'.

The media invasion of diplomacy has had another unwelcome effect. Delicate negotiations are made immeasurably more difficult when even before the participants have got round the table they are subjected to speculative grilling about the outcome, and the moment they have concluded their business they are expected to give detailed comment on their deliberations. The media obsession with instant news and aggressive interviewing has become a farce.

On the other hand 'open covenants openly arrived at' are a worthwhile ideal to aim at. Investigative journalism may employ some reprehensible methods (hounding and trapping those suspected of wrong-doing, in a way which is not permitted of the forces of law and order) but without it much skulduggery would remain undetected. The Scott enquiry into arms for Iraq posed acutely the dilemma that government cannot always be completely frank but should avoid being positively misleading. Beneath the displays of righteous indignation on both sides of the political divide was revealed a blurring of this issue, compounded by some extraordinary intellectual gymnastics by clever men in authority, and attitudes towards Parliament which sat ill with professions in other contexts of concern for its sovereignty. We have yet to find a middle way between obsessive secrecy and harmful indiscretion.

The enquiry also disinterred the hoary old arguments about the ethics of arms sales. Jobs, exports and profits had clearly been accorded priority over the nature, and possible hostility, of the arms customers. One point which was not made, to my knowledge, is the dubious logic of selling defence equipment before war breaks out (a result to which the sales must at least have contributed), imposing an embargo when the weaponry starts being used, and resuming sales as soon as the fighting is over. But logic does not have a notable place in this debate. To add to the remark of the arms salesman in the 1970s that he felt no more compunction about selling tanks for use in warfare than he had had about selling trucks which might be involved in traffic accidents, I heard a spokesman in similar vein claiming during the Scott aftermath that it made sense to supply arms rather than let others do so because this meant that you knew how the things worked when they were used against you.

In addition to my staple diet as a 'reviewer', I embarked upon a fresh bout of lecturing and writing on Middle Eastern topics. These activities culminated in a three-year stint (a result of answering an advertisement in *The Economist*) at the Cambridge Centre of International Studies. The Fellowship in the International Politics of the Middle East was funded by British Aerospace, which was not without its irony in my case. It involved dealing with postgraduate students from all over the world undertaking a year's course for an M. Phil in International Relations. My concern was principally with those whose theses I supervised, because they covered Middle Eastern topics. By a curious quirk of fate one of these turned out to be the great-grandson of the Ruler of Bahrain whose path I had crossed in the mid-1950s.

The preparation of lectures and organisation of seminars concentrated the mind wonderfully on the experience of the previous 40 years, added to which was the inestimable value of more recent contacts in various Middle Eastern circles in London. My own thoughts revolved mainly around the three major regional developments during the first half of the 1990s: the collapse of the Soviet Union and of international communism; the Gulf War and its aftermath; and the Arab-Israeli 'peace process'.

I had long been struck by the view of an historian of the old 'Eastern Question' that 'The lasting hostility between Britain and Russia was based on a quite unreal fear of each other's supposed aggressive intentions'[20].

It seemed to me that this judgement could well have been applied *mutatis mutandis* to the Cold War between the United States and the Soviet Union from 1945 to 1990. Certainly in the Middle East super-power rivalry had involved exaggerated mutual fears. Alliances and patron/client relationships were established, often failing because they did not address the real concerns of the regional members. Regional problems were seen through the prism of global conflict, and the resulting distortion led to serious policy errors on both sides. Nevertheless, the 'stability' engendered by the Cold War might be difficult to sustain, especially as the demonology of the 'Soviet Threat' was now being replaced by that of 'Islamic fundamentalism', with Tehran cast for the bogeyman role previously played by Moscow.

The exaggeration, generalisation and stereotyping to which this phenomenon has given rise have been referred to in chapter 13. They have their mirror image, of course, in many Muslim perceptions of the Christian West. Much is being done at the intellectual level to correct the misunderstandings on both sides and to search for the common ground between them. So far as Islam is concerned, it simply is not the monolithic, militant monster so often portrayed in the Western media. It varies widely from one area to another, depending largely on historical circumstances. If there is a legitimate generalisation to be made it is perhaps that, in a confused world, Muslims are still faced with an identity problem.

Nor is it easy to see how Iran, where revolutionary fervour has lost its first fine careless rapture and both the economy and the administration are in considerable disarray, is capable of orchestrating all extremist activities from Bahrain to Beirut, as some alarmists would have us believe. This is not to say that the Iranians, like the Russians before them, do not exploit situations in the region which arise for more localised reasons. Nor does it mean that the problems posed by the extreme manifestations of Islam – and other religions – do not have to be addressed. In the Middle East context at least, terrorism has its roots in political, economic and social conditions. The world's statesmen concern themselves with treating the symptoms rather than curing the disease. Some of them persist in believing that violence can be met only by violence; or produce impressive catalogues of administrative, intelligence and other measures to deal with the issue. These may be a necessary, but are not a sufficient, part of the solution.

The immediate aftermath of the Soviet collapse saw a new and welcome co-operation in the context of the second major development which interested me. This was the Gulf War of 1990/91. I found myself for the first time in many years agreeing with American policy, both in going to war against Saddam and in ending it when they did. The result was no doubt a mess, and it was not long before the wiseacres were saying that Desert Storm had been useless, or the campaign should have been extended as far as Baghdad, or both at once. The arguments have been fully rehearsed, but my belief is that if Saddam had been allowed to get away with one jot or tittle of his aggression against Kuwait it would have been the thin end of the wedge. Given his obsessive ambition to inherit for Iraq the mantle of Arab leadership which Sadat abandoned for Egypt by making peace with Israel in 1979, within a measurable time this tyrant would have harnessed the emotional upsurge of Arab feeling to dominate the entire region.

What is disappointing about the Gulf War is the trail of broken promises that it left behind. Many pious utterances were made during the crisis. Things would never be allowed to be the same again. We would not permit the build-up of arms which could ignite such a conflagration, let alone be used against our own forces. Regimes like the Kuwaiti would have to liberalise themselves if they were to avoid internal strife and deserve external support. The great gap between the haves and the have-nots in the Arab world would have to be bridged by a more equitable distribution of oil wealth.

None of these changes has in fact occurred. Gulf arms consumers drew the conclusion from the events of 1990/91 not that their vast expenditure on sophisticated military hardware had availed them nothing when it came to the point, but rather that they must spend even more, as well as turning increasingly to the Western powers for their defence, which hitherto had been regarded as the kiss of death. The Western politico-strategic complexes have predictably done nothing to dissuade Arab governments from such thinking, while the latter have been prepared to place massive orders for defence equipment as an insurance premium to keep foreign troops on their soil. How representative these governments are of feeling at the grass-roots is another matter.

Lip-service, and in some cases a little more, has been paid to the need for democratisation of the traditional regimes. This need not – and should not – mean a sudden infusion of Westminster-style party politics in places where this would be alien to local traditions. Events in Algeria since elections were annulled in 1991/92 have understandably given pause to advocates of extending democratic rights to extremists who believe that sovereignty does not reside in the people but comes from God. They might well use the democratic ladder to achieve office, only to kick it away afterwards.

Nevertheless, Arab regimes ignore at their peril the demand which has been growing for years now among the increasingly large proportion of their populations who are young and well-educated for a degree of 'participation' in the governmental process, and the right to have a say in how the country is run. King Hussain has shown how meeting such political awareness half-way can work, despite the risks. Early in 1996, the Palestinians and even the Algerians themselves seemed to be making some effort to follow the democratic path (while Bahrain and Saudi Arabia were moving in the opposite direction). It is probably the only way to defuse the situation in which otherwise the expression of political dissent can only take a religious, and often a violent, form.

If there was a positive outcome of the Gulf War, it was to contribute to breaking the log-jam in the Arab-Israeli dispute. Until the Israeli invasion of Lebanon in 1982, I had been able to maintain a similar level of objectivity to that enunciated by Sir Ronald Storrs when he was Military Governor of Jerusalem after Allenby's occupation in 1917.

> Two hours of Arab grievances drive me into the Synagogue, while after an intensive course of Zionist propaganda I am prepared to embrace Islam.[21]

Subsequent events made such a dispassionate approach increasingly difficult. The mould had, however, been broken by the 'intifada' or uprising in the occupied territories which had begun in December 1987. This had lost the Israelis the moral high ground and introduced a new and more moderate strand into the Palestinian leadership. Now Saddam's aggression led to some agonising reappraisals in the Arab world. Outside, although Saddam's tactical manoeuvre to link the invasion of Kuwait with the occupation of Palestine was dismissed by Western Governments, the comparison between their rapid reaction to his aggression and their continuing toleration of Israeli occupation was too odious to be ignored. The charge of 'double standards' put pressure on the Americans in particular to renew earlier efforts to promote a solution. The resulting 'peace process' is the third major development referred to above.

It began with the revival of the old idea of an international conference, even if this was largely an umbrella under which bilateral talks took place. When the Madrid Conference of October 1991 and the contacts which it engendered ran predictably into the sand, they were superseded by the Oslo accords of 1993 and the subsequent famous handshake on the White House lawn in September of that year. In both cases it was extraordinary how, in a triumph of hope over experience, the experts greeted these events with such euphoria. Admittedly, friends of the Arabs who had long fretted at Abba Eban's jibe that they 'never missed an opportunity to miss an opportunity' could take comfort from Arafat's belated recognition that half a loaf was better than no bread. The trouble was that the half loaf now on offer was no more than a few crumbs of comfort, with a vague suggestion of jam tomorrow. Gaza, to change the metaphor, was merely a poisoned chalice.

The result has been a vicious circle. Israelis, whose prime consideration is security, have demanded that Arafat control Palestinian extremists, which they themselves were never able to do. His limited success in doing the Israelis' dirty work for them undermines Israeli support for the peace process. Whereas Israel, having decided that Arafat was their best bet, should be strengthening his hand by providing tangible evidence of the advantages of the process, precisely the opposite is happening. Economic conditions are if anything worse than before, Israeli troops and settlements remain on the West Bank, while longer-term Palestinian aspirations recede further and further into the background.

It is the Israelis, as the party in possession, who have to cut this Gordian knot. By a typical Middle Eastern irony, it looked as if it had taken the assassination of Yitzhak Rabin in November 1995 to concentrate minds on all sides. This at least helped to hasten the Palestinian elections of January 1996 (18 months behind the original timetable) which, among other things, exposed the limitations of extremist appeal. But Rabin's death, and Peres's uncharacteristic launching of 'Operation Grapes of Wrath' in Lebanon (shades of 'Peace for Galilee' in 1982), also brought forward Israeli elections to May 1996. In the light of Netanyahu's victory at the polls it is difficult to share even the 'cautious optimism' which holds that, for all the evident pitfalls, the peace process has gained a momentum which makes it irreversible.

To my mind, what always made the Middle East so fascinating was the way in which the religious, political and economic factors at work in the region interacted upon each other to produce such an intricate pattern. In particular, emotions about the perceived betrayal and humiliation over Palestine reinforced – and were themselves reinforced by – the Arab and Muslim tendency to turn away from the West. Policy-makers have not always perceived the connections.

In recent years, however, I have been able to turn away from this scene and to go some way towards fulfilling my ambitions farther east. Thanks to a son in the Hong Kong Shanghai Bank, we have visited Hong Kong itself three times, Malaysia (briefly) and Indonesia (for three weeks in 1994).

Hong Kong, on first acquaintance, seemed like a claustrophobic concrete jungle. On later and more leisurely visits we have been seduced, like many others, by its sheer vibrance as well as fascinated by the Far Eastern culture and life-style, so much more frenetic than the comparatively languid pace of our Arab deserts.

In Malaysia in the spring of 1987, we saw something of Penang and the Cameron Highlands, and had a day in Kuala Lumpur. There was something attractive, if atypical, about the 'old colonial' atmosphere of Georgetown. Its dingy shopping areas, its pedlars and pedallers, were reminiscent of Karachi; its administrative and commercial buildings more akin to Kaduna. The Eastern and Oriental Hotel in particular had a whiff of Somerset Maugham, its walls adorned by dinner-dance programmes of long ago and copies of old government gazettes announcing that Mr and Mrs Jones had 'returned from Home and resumed their duties in the Secretariat'. Mosques and temples, and the curious amalgam of words like 'imigresen', 'ekspot', 'motosikel', were more familiar. Smart-looking children in their neat and clean blue uniforms were a signpost to the future. So, perhaps, was Dr Mahathir's narrow re-election by the UMNO Congress, an event covered by editorials which recalled the florid style of Pakistani English-language newspapers.

If this brief exposure to Malaysia was an appetiser for the attractions of South East Asia, a more substantial meal was provided by Indonesia seven years later. I had always wanted to round off my 'Muslim' experience by seeing something of Islam in the country which boasts the largest Muslim population in the world. In fact, it is a far more relaxed brand of the faith than that of the Arab world: closer in this respect to northern Nigeria than to the Gulf. This is partly due to the cultural mix, in which Islam was leavened to some extent by Hinduism, Buddhism and Christianity. The first two have also bequeathed to posterity a wealth of remarkable monuments. True, Indonesia's politics are another matter, and her human rights record leaves a good deal to be desired. But considering the ethnic diversity, together with the facts that the population numbers 190 million spread over 300 inhabited islands (out of a total of over 1300), and that the distance from one end of the country to the other is the same as that between London and Tehran, the wonder is that it has been kept together at all, let alone made such a going concern.

In any case we were not there as diplomats but as tourists. The debate on 'Asian values' and 'tigerism' concerned us less than the lush and beautifully terraced countryside, the variety of natural resources and the 'get-up-and-go' character of the people, all of which contrasted favourably with much of our experience elsewhere. Indelible memories crowd in: an enchanting afternoon at a school in Bandung watching children perform a programme of traditional music and dance – and ourselves learning by numbers how to play a kind of reed instrument called an 'anklung'; the magnificence of the Buddhist stupa at Borobudur, the largest in the world, with its bell-shaped cupolas housing sculpted figures of the Gautama; a moonlight performance of the Ramayana Ballet against the spectacular backdrop of the Hindu temple complex at Prambanan; standing in the midday sun at the Kraton Palace in Yogyakarta oblivious to the heat as we watched the exquisitely graceful movements of the young dancers, all fingers and toes; and two contrasting memories of Bali: a kind of harvest festival ceremony at a Hindu holy place at Gunung Kawi, where slender girls wrapped in colourful saris swayed up the hillside carrying on their heads veritable pillars of fruit, flowers and other offerings to be blessed by a priest and placed in shrines nearby; and, finally, sipping cocktails as we saw the sun sinking slowly into the sea beyond the snake temple at Tanah Lot, its darkening outline etched against a gold and crimson sky.

Later the same year, we visited Copenhagen for the first time since leaving Denmark nearly 20 years before. The occasion was an unusual one, to say the least: the hundredth birthday party of Ingrid Tvermøs, the *grande dame* of a family with whom we had kept in touch during the intervening years. Four generations (all female!) were represented at the celebration in the family home at Søllerød Slot, just outside Copenhagen. The dinner for 100 guests was in the best tradition of 'hyggelig' (cosy) Danish hospitality and the old lady made a splendid speech so far as the remnants of my Danish enabled me to judge – together with the frequent recourse to the English expression 'happy landings'!

Apart from the pleasure of renewing old acquaintances, we also revisited some of our old haunts. This was a less heartening experience. Our suburb of Gentofte, and especially its beautiful lake, was comparatively unspoiled. But the centre of Copenhagen had deteriorated. The areas of the walking street – Strøget – debouching into the grand square of Kongens Nytorv looked seedy and run-down. Nearby, the picturesque facade of the French Embassy was crumbling and short of paint, while the old British Residence in Bredgade had been turned into offices. The Chancery complex in Kastelsvej was surrounded by ugly hoardings covered in graffiti, and visitors were discouraged by a formidable array of security works. The days seemed long ago when Bredgade echoed to the sound of music from the Embassy ballroom or the Hotel d'Angleterre in Kongens Nytorv to the bark of George Brown inveighing against the iniquities of Peter Shore.

Now my Indian summer is turning into autumn, with the accent on mellow fruitfulness more than mists. The younger generations afford us constant reminders of spring and summer. Our own sons – two in the literary world in addition to the one in banking – are fortunate in having reasonably secure employment. But the contemporary rat race is such that they seem to have to live to work rather than, as I did, work to live. It is just as well that the young are more adaptable and resilient.

Their own children will live in a world very different from ours, or even theirs. The opportunities will be greater: so will the pitfalls.

On the whole, the world we have known seems preferable – but doubtless the older generation has invariably felt that way.

Meanwhile, cute grandchildren regularly replenish my stock of 'the things children say'.

Georgina (aged 4): 'Mummy. I've already got a little brother, so this time I want a sister, please'.

Mummy: 'Well, Georgina, these things do not always happen to order, I'm afraid, so you'd better get used to the idea of another brother'.

Georgina (after a pause for thought): 'Mummy, if it turns out to be a boy, couldn't we just CALL it a girl?'

Nicholas (aged 6, on the arrival of a third sister): 'Daddy, you know I still want a little brother?'

Daddy: 'Yes, but you do understand that one can't choose'.

Nicholas: 'Of course, but couldn't we go on having babies until there is one?'

Daddy: 'Well, that might be a bit difficult. Apart from anything else, I'm not sure I could afford any more'.

Nicholas: 'Don't be silly Daddy – you don't just go out and buy them'.

Life itself proceeds at a growing pace which is rather reminiscent of one of those old gramophone needles. Starting slowly on the outer rim of the records it seemed gradually to gather speed as the circumference of the track decreased, until it rushed to its headlong conclusion. So the annual cycle seems to get shorter and shorter as the seasons come around with increasing rapidity. Fortunate is the man in whose personal life at least the gramophone plays ever sweeter music.

Notes on the text

1 (page ix) Curzon, quoted in *High Noon of Empire*, Michael Edwardes, Eyre & Spottiswoode, 1965; *Orientations*, Sir Ronald Storrs, Nicholson & Watson, 1945

2 (page 10) *Palestine Mission*, Richard Crossman, Hamish Hamilton, 1946

3 (page 24) *Syria and Lebanon*, A.H. Hourani, Royal Institute of International Affairs, 1945

4 (page 44) *Sultan in Oman*, James Morris, Faber & Faber, 1957

5 (page 45) *The End of Empire in the Middle East*, Glen Balfour-Paul, Cambridge University Press, 1991

6 (page 60) *Asia and Western Dominance*, K.M. Pannikar, George Allen & Unwin, 1953

7 (page 84) *Lords of the Golden Horn*, Noel Barber, Macmillan, 1973

8 (page 94) *Shades of Amber*, Sir Kennedy Trevaskis, Hutchinson, 1968

9 (page 106) *Orientations*, Sir Ronald Storrs, Nicholson & Watson, 1945

10 (page 122) *The Scandinavians*, Donald Connery, Eyre and Spottiswoode, 1966

11 (page 138) *The New Totalitarians*, Roland Huntford, Allen Lane, 1972

12 (page 145) *A History of Christianity*, Paul Johnson, Weidenfeld & Nicolson, 1976

13 (page 168) *The Old Regime and the French Revolution*, Alexis de Tocqueville, quoted in *The Pride and the Fall*, Sir Anthony Parsons, Jonathan Cape, 1984

14 (page 181) *All Fall Down*, Gary Sick, I.B. Tauris, 1985

15 (page 190) *The History of the Imams and Seyyids of Oman*, G.P. Badger, Darf Publishers, 1986

16 (page 190) *Narrative of a Year's Journey Through Central and Eastern Arabia*, 1862-3, W.G. Palgrave, London 1866

17 (page 192) *Tribes, Politics and Religion in Oman*, J.B. Kelly, in *The Arabian Peninsula: Society and Politics*, D. Hopwood (editor), George Allen & Unwin, 1972

18 (page 193) *Britain and the Persian Gulf 1894-1914*, Briton Cooper Busch, University of California Press, 1967

19 (page 214) *Israel's Lebanon War*, Ze'ev Schiff and Ehud Ya'ari, George Allen & Unwin, 1985

20 (page 243) *Britain and the Eastern Question*, G.D. Hudson, University of London Press, 1971

21 (page 246) *Orientations*, Sir Ronald Storrs, Nicholson & Watson, 1945

Bibliography

Personal and official records

On 25 November 1946, the day I first set foot outside the United Kingdom (as a raw subaltern in the Royal Artillery), I began to keep a diary. I have done so daily ever since, so that this particular record reaches its fiftieth anniversary this year.

At first the diary was a very full one. To it were committed not only activities but reactions to them. In time it began to take me over: I not only wrote for the diary but almost lived for it. In 1950 it therefore became a more truncated version, with the insidious introspection cut out. From 1985 it was further reduced – though the shortest entries are still able to conjure up clear visions from the past.

In writing the book I have drawn heavily on the diary. It has been supplemented by refreshing the memory from such official records as are available and have been 'released'.

Published Documents

In the Middle East particularly, history and religion provided invaluable clues to current affairs. This is one reason why the Research Department and its present day equivalents have always been an essential part of the Foreign and Commonwealth Office. The collective memory of the Service has suffered from a number of factors. The fewer officials there are, the more they are obliged to concentrate on the here and now. This tendency has been reinforced by the increasing emphasis being placed on immediate commercial interests. Officials working in political departments and subject to frequent transfer have had to rely on the research cadres for background information. There is even a danger that pressure of work on those at the coal face may bring the researchers more into the policy field, with detrimental effects on their historical role.

The titles below have been chosen from the library I have accumulated over the years. They include some of the books which I found most useful in preparing myself for different assignments. But most are of more recent date, since my earlier diplomatic postings were in places about which comparatively little had been written until the advent of oil made them a growth industry. Nigeria provided a welcome change from this point of view. The 1980s and 1990s have seen an outpouring of literature on the Middle East and Islam, which it has been hard to keep up with for purposes of lecturing or reviewing. The bibliography is therefore both selective and subjective.

Middle East – general

Antonius, George, *The Arab Awakening – The Story of the Arab National Movement*, Hamish Hamilton, 1938

Balfour-Paul, Glen, *The End of Empire in the Middle East – Britain's relinquishment of power in her last three Arab dependencies*, Cambridge University Press, 1991

Bromley, Simon, *Rethinking Middle East Politics – State Formation and Development*, Polity Press, 1994

Butt, Gerald, *A Rock and a Hard Place – Origins of Arab-Western Conflict in the Middle East*, Harper Collins, 1994

Efrat, Moshe and Bercovitch, Jacob (eds.), *Superpowers and Client States in the Middle East – The Imbalance of Influence*, Routledge, 1991

Field, Michael, *Inside the Arab World*, John Murray, 1994

Fromkin, David, *A Peace to End All Peace – Creating the Modern Middle East 1914-1922*, Andre Deutsch, 1989

Hourani, Albert, *A History of the Arab Peoples*, Faber & Faber, 1991

Mansfield, Peter, *A History of the Middle East*, Viking, 1991

Monroe, Elizabeth, *Britain's Moment in the Middle East, 1914-1956*, Chatto & Windus, 1967

Lewis, Bernard, *The Middle East – 2000 years of History from the Rise of Christianity to the Present Day*, Weidenfeld & Nicolson, 1995

Storrs, Sir Ronald, *Orientations*, Nicholson & Watson (Definitive Edition), 1945

Taylor, Alan R., *The Super-Powers and the Middle East*, Syracuse University Press, 1991

Yorke, Valerie, *Domestic Politics and Regional Security: Jordan, Syria and Israel – The End of an Era?*, Gower/International Institute for Strategic Studies, 1988

The Middle East – A Handbook, Facts on File, 1988

Islam

Ahmed, Akbar S., *Postmodernism and Islam: Predicament and Promise*, Routledge, 1992

Ahmed, Akbar S., *From Samarkand to Stornoway: Living Islam*, BBC, 1993

Armstrong, Karen, *Muhammad: A Western Attempt to Understand Islam*, Victor Gollancz, 1991

Bannerman, Patrick, *Islam in Perspective – A Guide to Islamic Society, Politics and Law*, Routledge/Royal Institute of International Affairs, 1988

Cantwell Smith, Wilfred, *Islam in Modern History*, Princeton University Press, 1957

Esposito, John L., *The Islamic Threat – Myth or Reality?* Oxford University Press, 1992

Fuller, Graham E. and Lesser, Ian O., *A Sense of Siege – The Geopolitics of Islam and the West*, Westview Press, 1995

Halliday, Fred, *Islam and the Myth of Confrontation – Religion and Politics in the Middle East*, I.B. Tauris, 1996

Leach, Hugh, *Introducing Islam*, unpublished, 1987

Lewis, Bernard, *The Origins of Isma'ilism*, Heffer, Cambridge, 1940

Lewis, Bernard, *Islam in History – Ideas, Men and Events in the Middle East*, Alcove Press, 1973

Mortimer, Edward, *Faith and Power – The Politics of Islam*, Faber & Faber, 1992

Roy, Olivier, *The Failure of Political Islam*, I.B. Tauris, 1994

Arabia and the Gulf (except Oman)

Bidwell, Robin, *The Two Yemens*, Longman/Westview, 1983

Burrows, Bernard, *Footnotes in the Sand – the Gulf in Transition 1953-1958*, Michael Russell, 1990

Busch, Briton Cooper, *Britain and the Persian Gulf 1894-1914*, University of California Press, 1967

Graham, Helga, *Arabian Time Machine – Self-Portrait of an Oil State* [Qatar], Heinemann, 1978

Halliday, Fred, *Arabia Without Sultans*, Penguin, 1974

Hawley, Donald, *The Trucial States*, George Allen & Unwin, 1970

Holden, David, *Farewell to Arabia*, Faber & Faber, 1966

Hopwood, Derek (ed.), *The Arabian Peninsula: Society and Politics*, George Allen & Unwin, 1972

Ingrams, Harold, *Arabia and the Isles*, John Murray, 1966

Ledger, David, *Shifting Sands – The British in South Arabia*, Peninsular Publishing, 1983

Little, Tom, *South Arabia – Arena of Conflict*, Pall Mall Press, 1968

Kelly, J.B., *Arabia, the Gulf and the West – a Critical View of the Arabs and Their Oil Policy*, Weidenfeld & Nicolson, 1980

Peterson, J.E., *Yemen – The Search for a Modern State*, Croom Helm, 1986

Thesiger, Wilfred, *Arabian Sands*, Longmans, 1959

Trevaskis, Sir Kennedy, *Shades of Amber – A South Arabian Episode*, Hutchinson, 1968

Wilson, Sir Arnold, *The Persian Gulf*, George Allen & Unwin, 1928

Zahlan, Rosemarie Said, *The Making of the Modern Gulf States*, Unwin Hyman, 1989

Oman

Bhacker, M. Reda, *Trade and Empire in Muscat and Zanzibar – Roots of British Domination*, Routledge, 1992

Hawley, Donald, *Oman and its Renaissance*, Stacey International, 1977

Ibn-Razik, Salil, *History of the Imams and Seyyids of Oman from A.D 661 to 1856*, translated and edited by Rev. G.P. Badger, first published 1871, reprinted by Darf Publishers, 1986

Landen, R.G., *Oman Since 1856 – Disruptive Modernisation in a Traditional Arab Society*, Princeton University Press, 1967

Maurizi, Vincenzo (Shaik Mansur), *History of Seyd Said*, first published 1819, reprinted by Oleander Press, 1984

Morris, James, *Sultan in Oman*, Faber & Faber, 1957

Peterson, J.E., *Oman in the Twentieth Century*, Croom Helm, 1978

Risso, Patricia, *Oman and Muscat – An Early Modern History*, Croom Helm, 1986

Sirhan Ibn Sirhan and others, *Annals of Oman*, first published 1874, reprinted by Oleander Press, 1984

Skeet, Ian, *Muscat and Oman – The End of an Era*, Faber & Faber, 1974

Skeet, Ian, *Oman, Politics and Development*, Macmillan, 1992

Wilkinson, John C., *The Imamate Tradition of Oman*, Cambridge University Press, 1987

Iran and Iraq

Bakhash, Shaul, *The Reign of the Ayatollahs: Iran and the Islamic Revolution*, I.B. Tauris, 1985

Ehteshami, Anoushiravan and Nonneman, Gerd, *War and Peace in the Gulf – Domestic Politics and Regional Relations into the 1990s*, Ithaca, 1991

Fischer, Michael M. J., *Iran: From Religious Dispute to Revolution*, Harvard University Press, 1980

Freedman, Lawrence and Karsh, Efraim, *The Gulf Conflict 1990-1991 – Diplomacy and War in the New World Order*, Faber & Faber, 1993

Graham, Robert, *Iran – The Illusion of Power*, Croom Helm, 1978

Halliday, Fred, *Iran – Dictatorship and Development*, Penguin, 1979

Heikal, Mohamed, *The Return of the Ayatollah: The Iranian Revolution from Mossadeq to Khomeini*, Andre Deutsch, 1981

Khadduri, Majid, *Independent Iraq – A Study in Iraqi Politics Since 1932*, OUP/RIIA, 1951

Longrigg, S.H., *Iraq 1900-1950*, OUP/RIIA, 1953

Parsons, Sir Anthony, *The Pride and the Fall: Iran 1974-1979*, Jonathan Cape, 1984

Radji, Parviz C., *In the Service of the Peacock Throne – The Diaries of the Shah's Last Ambassador in London*, Hamish Hamilton, 1983

Sick, Gary, *All Fall Down: America's Fateful Encounter with Iran*, I.B. Tauris, 1985

Thesiger, Wilfred, *The Marsh Arabs*, Longman, 1964

Libya

First, Ruth, *Libya, The Elusive Revolution*, Penguin, 1974

Keith, Agnes Newton, *Children of Allah – Between the Sea and the Sahara*, Michael Joseph, 1965

Khadduri, Majid, *Modern Libya, A Study in Political Development*, John Hopkins Press, 1963

Palestine and Israel

Chomsky, Noam, *The Fateful Triangle – The United States, Israel and the Palestinians*, Pluto Press, 1983

McDowall, David, *Palestine and Israel – The Uprising and Beyond*, I.B. Tauris, 1989

O'Brien, Conor Cruise, *The Seige: The Saga of Israel and Zionism*, Weidenfeld & Nicolson, 1986

Palestine Royal Commission (Peel) Report, Cmd. 5479, HMSO, 1937

Parkes, James, *A History of Palestine, From 135AD to Modern Times*, Gollancz, 1949

Shipler, David, *Arab and Jew – Wounded Spirits in a Promised Land*, Bloomsbury, 1987

Shlaim, Avi, *Collusion Across the Jordan – King Abdullah, the Zionist Movement and the Partition of Palestine*, OUP, 1988

Smith, David, *Prisoners of God – The Modern-Day Conflict of Arab and Jew*, Quartet Books, 1987

Stein, Leonard, *The Balfour Declaration*, Vallentine, Mitchell, 1961

Sykes, Christopher, *Cross Roads to Israel – Palestine from Balfour to Bevin*, Collins, 1965

Syria and Lebanon

Abd-Allah, Umar F., *The Islamic Struggle in Syria*, Mizan Press, 1983

Betts, Robert Brenton, *The Druze*, Yale University Press, 1989

Bliss, Frederick Jones, *The Religions of Modern Syria and Palestine*, Scribner, 1912

Dawisha, Adeed I., *Syria and the Lebanese Crisis*, Macmillan, 1980

Drysdale, Alasdair and Hinnesbusch, Raymond, *Syria and the Middle East Peace Process*, Council on Foreign Relations, 1991

Fisk, Robert, *Pity the Nation – Lebanon at War*, Andre Deutsch, 1990

Gaunson, A.B., *The Anglo-French Clash in Lebanon and Syria, 1940-45*, Macmillan, 1987

Gilmour, David, *Lebanon – The Fractured Country*, Martin Robertson, 1983

Friedman, Thomas, *From Beirut to Jerusalem*, Collins, 1990

Hopwood, Derek, *Syria 1945-1986, Politics and Society*, Unwin Hyman, 1988

Hourani, Albert, *Syria and Lebanon, A Political Essay*, RIIA, 1945

Karsh, Efraim, *The Soviet Union and Syria – The Asad Years*, Routledge/RIIA, 1988

Khoury, Philip S., *Syria and the French Mandate – The Politics of Arab Nationalism 1920-1945*, I.B. Tauris, 1987

Longrigg, S.H., *Syria and Lebanon Under French Mandate*, OUP/RIIA, 1948

Ma'oz, Moshe, *Syria and Israel – From War to Peace-making*, OUP, 1995

Petran, Tabitha, *Syria, A Modern History*, Ernest Benn, 1972

Pipes, Daniel, *Greater Syria – The History of an Ambition*, OUP, 1990

Roberts, David, *The Ba'th and the Creation of Modern Syria*, Croom Helm, 1987

Seale, Patrick, *The Struggle for Syria – A Study of Post-War Arab Politics 1954-1958*, OUP, 1965, reprinted by I.B. Tauris, 1986

Seale, Patrick, *Asad – The Struggle for the Middle East*, I.B. Tauris, 1988

Schiff, Ze'ev and Ya'ari, Ehud, *Israel's Lebanon War*, George Allen & Unwin, 1985

Springett, Bernard H., *Secret Sects of Syria and the Lebanon*, George Allen & Unwin, 1922

Nigeria

Beetham, T.A., *Christianity and the New Africa*, Pall Mall Press, 1967

Bovill, E.W., *The Golden Trade of the Moors*, OUP, 1958/68

Bovill, E .W., *The Niger Explored*, OUP, 1968

Crowder, Michael, *The Story of Nigeria*, Faber, 1962/66

De St Jorre, John, *The Nigerian Civil War*, Hodder & Stoughton, 1972

Johnston, H.A.S., *The Fulani Empire of Sokoto*, OUP, 1967

Heussler, Robert, *The British in Northern Nigeria*, OUP, 1968

Hogben, S.G. and Kirk-Greene, A.H.M., *The Emirates of Northern Nigeria – A Preliminary Survey of their Historical Traditions*, OUP, 1966

Nadel, S.F., *Nupe Religion – Traditional Beliefs and the Influence of Islam in a West African Chiefdom*, Routledge & Kegan Paul, 1954

Nicolson, I.F., *The Administration of Nigeria, 1900 to 1960 – Men, Methods and Myths*, Clarendon Press, 1969

Schwartz, Walter, *Nigeria*, Pall Mall Press, 1968

Sharwood-Smith, Sir Bryan, *But Always as Friends – Northern Nigeria and the Cameroons 1921-1957*, George Allen & Unwin, 1969

Trimingham, J. Spencer, *Islam in West Africa*, OUP, 1959

Trimingham, J. Spencer, *The Influence of Islam upon Africa*, Longman, 1968

Pakistan and Asia

Binder, Leonard, *Religion and Politics in Pakistan*, University of California Press, 1991

Binsayeed, Khalid, *Pakistan, the Formative Phase*, Pakistan Publishing House, Karachi, 1960

Callard, Keith, *Pakistan, A Political Study*, George Allen & Unwin, 1957

Pannikar, K.M., *Asia and Western Dominance: A Survey of the Vasco da Gama Epoch of Asian History – 1498-1945*, George Allen & Unwin, 1953

Scandinavia and Denmark

Connery, Donald, *The Scandinavians*, Eyre & Spottiswoode, 1966

Huntford, Roland, *The New Totalitarians* [Sweden], Allen Lane, 1972

Jones, W. Glyn, *Denmark*, Ernest Benn, 1970

Lauring, Palle, *A History of The Kingdom of Denmark*, Høst and Søn, Copenhagen, 1960

Oakley, Stewart, *The Story of Denmark*, Faber & Faber, 1972

Index